BASIL BUNTING ON POETRY

Basil Bunting on Poetry

EDITED BY PETER MAKIN

THE JOHNS HOPKINS UNIVERSITY PRESS   *Baltimore and London*

Lectures by Basil Bunting © 1999 The Estate of Basil Bunting
© 1999 The Johns Hopkins University Press
All rights reserved. Published 1999
Printed in the United States of America on acid-free paper
9 8 7 6 5 4 3 2 1

The Johns Hopkins University Press
2715 North Charles Street
Baltimore, Maryland 21218-4363
www.press.jhu.edu

A catalog record for this book is available from the British Library.

LIBRARY OF CONGRESS CATALOGING-IN-PUBLICATION DATA
Bunting, Basil.
    Basil Bunting on poetry / edited by Peter Makin.
        p.   cm.
    Lectures originally delivered between 1968 and 1974.
    Includes bibliographical references (p.   ) and index.
    ISBN 0-8018-6166-7 (alk. paper)
1. English poetry—History and criticism.   2. American poetry—
History and criticism.   3. English language—Versification.   4. Poetics.
I. Makin, Peter.   II. Title.
PR503.B86   1999
821.009—dc21   99-15161
                                                           CIP

Pages 233–34 are an extension of the copyright page.

The editing of this book is dedicated
  to or for,
  by, with, or from
  Correa.

"What is the use of talking, and there is no end of talking,
There is no end of things in the heart."

S.I.C. †15 December 1997

Contents

Illustrations

Acknowledgments

Without Peter Quartermain this edition would not have been thought of, for I should not have known of the Newcastle lecture manuscripts that Bunting had entrusted to him. Since the day he sent me copies, he has been as generous, cross-checking readings and drawing up bibliographical descriptions of the materials. Richard Caddel has given all he could from the beginning in logistical and scholarly support. At the Bunting Archive at Durham University, whose begetter he is, I found the taped lectures recorded by Kelsey Thornton that complement the Quartermain manuscripts. John Halliday, as executor of the Bunting estate, was in at the beginning and supported the project throughout. Beth Rainey, librarian in charge at the Bunting Archive, delivered with speed materials of so idiosyncratic a nature that less organized minds would have lost track of them.

Mary de Rachewiltz's selflessness with anyone who would want to be called a disciple of Pound is known, and I have benefited from it. My brother, John, with infinite patience provided infinite bytes of data, besides discovering who "Keeling" was. Hugh Kenner, sage and example, thrust tapes of Bunting's interviews and Wordsworth readings into my hands unasked. Masatake Dantsuji, learned phonologist, helped in my studies of rhythm and solved practical word-processing problems. I owe thanks to Diana Collecott, director (with Richard Caddel) at the Bunting Archive, for help with H.D.; to Anthony Flowers for information about Bunting's early musical contacts; to Andrew Crozier for a preview of his work on Bunting's relations with Kaplan, and for correcting my earlier error about the authorship of the essay "Paper." My revered teacher Bill Scobie shed light on premediaeval iconography. Ruth Darton, music librarian at the University of London Library, led me to valuable facts. The verger at Hexham Abbey spent hours with me making sure of "King Aelfwald's tomb," then adamantly refused to give his name.

There are few learned friends whom I have not badgered for expertise, or mere general wisdom, for this book: as Giuseppe Picca, on a train to Venice, for Dantescan prosody; Mark Treharne for rectification on Malherbe; Charles Vernon, one of the few Westerners (I suppose) who will ever be entrusted with charge of a Chinese course at a Japanese university, for tone patterns in Chinese verse. Noboru Tanaka, whose faltering disciple I am in fields of granite, helped me to see relations between form and matter, without which, as Bunting would have agreed, art is not.

Introduction

Organisation of some sort has got to be there or music fails to function.
There's a repetitiveness which distinguishes music from noise, to that extent
order is necessary; but there can be a great deal of what most people would
regard at first sight as disorder.

—Bunting, 1974–75

These lectures are the fruit of a poet's brief career in late life as a university lecturer, and of his much longer effort, dating almost from the time he first consciously drew breath, to understand the main medium of verse. They take prosody—"the total articulation of the sound of a poem," Pound had called it—to be the center of the art of poetry, and they follow its development in English verse from Chaucer to Zukofsky.

The main argument can be sketched quickly. Bunting assumes that art is shape, not content. There is no excuse, of course, for decoration: it simply spoils shape. In this art, in the English language, rhythm is the most essential shapable: and if the poet has the rhythm right, he probably needs nothing else to give main form to his poem. The noticeable patterning of phonemes (the sounds of consonants and vowels) will be as unnecessary as brilliant eye-catching metaphors and will be to that extent a distraction. If the poet puts it in, it is most often a self-indulgence. In the English poetic tradition, Spenser fell for this fatal lure, and lured Shakespeare, Marlowe, Milton, Keats, Swinburne, and a whole lot of "moderns" after him, so that even a Pound found it hard to get the sugary mess off his fingers: Zukofsky, Bunting says, was one of the few who managed the true Campion limpidity.

But rhythm, the whole key to English verse, Bunting says, has to be made by English means. Languages vary in their constitutions; what has force in one may have little in another; stress is the key to English, though not to French. Unfortunately, "the tradition" has imported the French concern with syllable count; coupled with a foolish rigidity in ideas about sequencing stresses, this has given birth to the bastard form called the "iambic pentameter." This grotesque has only heightened the English propensity for fluff, for decoration (as above): for the pentameter is too long and invites glittering nothings to fill it out. Hence the magnificent sonnets of Shakespeare and the preposterous "violence" (as Bunting called it) of some of the writing in *Othello* and *Macbeth*. The cure is, first, a return to the essential for English, which is the play of strong stresses, irrespective of overall syllable count (and this was always exploited by the better writers of so-called iambics); second, an ear for music, for music is the true parent of poetry. The flexibility and intricacy of song as a frame for words taught Wyatt and Campion to bring forth words equally varied and alive in their cadences. Twentieth-century poets, even though not writing for song, should learn from song a similar "suppleness" of rhythm.

Bunting's views are likely to be both underrated and overrated, for false reasons, which it is worthwhile taking some time to set aside. Poets (it will be said) of course *do* the things that Bunting is talking about here: they are the ones who make rhythms. As a poet, Bunting should therefore have privileged insights. But (it will also be said) poets may do these things by the seat of their pants; do they necessarily know how they do them? Bunting was not a professional prosodist or a linguist; nor was he a close student of literary history.[1]

A look, first at Bunting's approach to his own writing and then at the relation of his views on rhythm to those of the prosodic tradition, will resolve some of these doubts.

BUNTING IN THE TWENTIETH CENTURY

Bunting was a self-conscious artist; he could be called, though he would have hated the epithet, a literary poet. *Beowulf* and "The Fight at Finnsburg" give a series of phrases and cadences to his *Briggflatts* and to the earlier *Spoils*.[2] So when in *The Spoils* we come upon this war scene:

> Rosyth guns sang. Sang tide through cable
> for Glasgow burning:
>   "Bright west,
>   Pale east . . ."

we are almost certainly in presence of another illusion of dawn, from the Finnsburg fragment, where the warrior shouts:

". . . gables burn!"
Hnaef then shouted, —battle-young king,—
"This is not day that dawns from the east, nor yet does a
    dragon fly here . . ."

Bombed Glasgow—seen from a ship in the Firth of Forth, in the early years of the war—was indeed "burning in the west beyond the hills when the dawn came," as Bunting explained.[3] But that phenomenon may have stuck in his mind because of the Finnsburg fragment: so much did literary skeletons draw his experience to them. Again, in Corbière there is a passage about mendicants—"Ces propriétaires de plaies"—at a peasant festival:[4]

En aboyant, un rachitique
Secoue un moignon désossé,
Coudoyant un épileptique

.   .   .   .

Là, ce tronc d'homme où croît l'ulcère,

.   .   .   .

Cet autre pare le cautère
De son petit enfant malsain:
—L'enfant se doit à son vieux-père . . .
—Et le chancre est un gagne-pain!

which ultimately gave rise to a more powerful passage in Bunting's *Briggflatts:*

. . . on gladly to hills
briar and bramble vest
where beggars advertise
rash, chancre, fistula,
to hug glib shoulders, mingle herpetic
limbs with stumps and cosset the mad.

This was obviously not something just encountered; it must have been waiting in Bunting's mind for the right place: for it is entirely absorbed into the semantic logic of his poem. The source, as far as the reader is concerned, has become accidental. That is the nature of Bunting's literariness. But it depends on a life's reading.

Bunting was never not "thinking poetry": the vivid relating together of things as lived, plus the emotive pulses of them as manifestable in words. But the sense and the movement of the words had to come out of snatched hours in libraries (for he had always to be thinking where the next meal might come from): ranging over Catullus, Lucretius, and delectable lines in Horace — *sive per Syrtes iter aestuosas*[5] — to be remembered and quoted to his "ancient friend" Zukofsky on a wartime journey through the Libyan desert.

Bunting was not a naïve poet: he knew the practice of his predecessors with a certain intensity. He was also reasonably well equipped with the systematizing faculties, if skill in navigational trigonometry is any proof, or skill as a diplomat in analyzing geopolitical intricacies. That is, he was a conscious man and a self-conscious poet.

On the other hand, there were limits to his literary professionalism, and he set these deliberately. He avoided the kind of career (as reviewer, or as editor) in which he would have become a professional knower of books, like an Auden or an Eliot: the obvious career for a writer with no private income. He decided early that a poet who knew only books would be a recycler, however cleverly disguised: Corbière would stay Corbière, uncolored by Bunting.

So by program he was naïve, at least to the extent that his learning by intention stayed patchy and fallible. Better stay ignorant in certain ways. Don't bother with commentaries! Beware the pedants! — was his constant advice to verse readers. Yet Warren Vernon on the *Paradiso* was illuminating. . . .

And there it is, on the shelves with the remains of Pound's library at Brunnenburg Castle: Bunting's copy of the *Divine Comedy,* dated "Newburn, 1925," rebound and interleaved with blank pages for Bunting's minute and devoted commentary on meanings and allegories, his chief source being Vernon.[6]

It is an ambiguous position, and easily mocked: the Hemingwayan man of action and poet *à ses heures,* with the *Divine Comedy* and Omar Khayyam (in Persian) in his pocket throughout his wartime journeys. And it looks perfectly contradictory. You must take a professional interest in the technicalities, this view seems to hold, but never in what the specialists say, or even in the kind of way in which they say it.

Yet I should say it is required by, and requires, the real advance of modernist poetry, between about 1910 and 1930, over (with certain exceptions) all the English-language poetry of the nineteenth century. Compared with it, the Blakean and Coleridgean revolutions are a surface, and whatever modern poets have thought they were writing about a side issue. It acknowledges that words are things operating in systems that need to be understood by the poet; but it also says that there is a point beyond which they cannot be understood. And this must apply to any would-be understander of verbal artefacts, whether writer or prosodist.

Bunting was "liberated into poetry" mainly by the example of Ezra Pound: in particular at the moment when Nina Hamnett, the painter, handed him the *Homage to Sextus Propertius* in the year of its publication, 1919.[7] The relation (and the tensions) with Pound never died, and a look at them will help us to see what exactly this Modernist position consists of.

The generation of 1912 (Pound, H.D., William Carlos Williams) talked always of *craft,* and the term imposed certain requirements. It required the fullest knowledge of everything relevant: where *relevant* in turn meant "contributing to the present whole: the poem." In relation to the demands of this master, nothing could justify either lack or superfluity in any expertise (musical, linguistic, factual).

Since this "whole" could not be named (it was certainly not the poem's message), the conception may be set aside as just another post-Coleridgean mysticism of the indefinably coherent. This would be a mistake. A poem, directly or indirectly, creates an emotivity of an exact shade. Too much knowledge, hence elaboration, in one area—diffusing the attention other areas require—will sabotage this as effectively as any switch in semantic density caused by the poet's mere ignorance. And so the modernist conception turns out to impose labors very concrete and pragmatical.

The three-decades-long three-way correspondence between Pound, Bunting, and Pound's other disciple, Zukofsky, shows how. Bunting responds in detail to Zukofsky's comments on the draft of his *Spoils* (1951). Yes, he says, there is a problem in some patches with the level of detail: "What's gained by providing the tinker with a slide rule (degree of explicitness) is lost by dissipating the reader's attention—Marinism."[8] No, there is no problem with the specialized register (or is it the level of semantic differentiation?) of the word *hogg.* An American countryman will know it as well as Northumbrian: it's only a "provincial" New Yorker like Zukofsky himself who won't. And "*Scut* is the correct term."[9]

"Get a dictionary/and learn the meaning of words"—the prescription of the master craftsman, Ford Madox Ford, as recorded at Rapallo the year before Bunting and Pound met Zukofsky there.[10]

Bunting and Zukofsky came to the scene late. Bunting first went to find Pound—in Paris—in 1924; Zukofsky sought contact with the great man in 1927, by submitting to Pound's magazine *Exile* a longish "Poem Beginning 'The.'" By that time, these main Modernist principles had not only been made explicit in manifestoes but had also been functioning as writing and editing methods. Bunting and Zukofsky each underwrote them, but each brought a pre-Poundian formation that set off a divergence, with long consequences.

The idea of the writing as "whole," where no part or element (factual, rhetorical, musical) must distract or diffuse, and each part and element must be variously, and proportionately, contributive: this applies as much to a political (or a seducing) speech as to a musical shape such as a rondo or a symphony, and a fortiori to the possible marriage of these, which is an ode, a sonnet, a poetical "prelude," or some poetic form as yet unpredicted. All the Poundian gang propounded this. But it assumes further that there are no special matters in verse. It is never sufficient to state some message that current fashion happens to vibrate to. A poem is not a lecture, and its value is not made by the level of its truth to reality.

Very conscious that a poem was not a lecture, Bunting and Zukofsky both looked for a model of wholeness that was not tainted by denotation (which brought hurrying in its train these problems of Truth and Significance). Music was this model. Both poets seem to have brought to their encounter with Pound a predisposition to be concerned first with the musical element of poetry. They picked up on all that Pound had said on the subject: that rhythm must not be of the metronome, that the future lay in quantitative metrics, and (at least in Zukofsky's case) that the key lay in the Dantescan union of love and song. And they concluded, in the words of Zukofsky's *"A"* 6, "The melody! the rest is accessory": the poet must concern himself above all with the sound of the words.

I do not think Pound had ever seen the question in quite this light. He thought craftsmanship with sound indispensable, but probably (as in his old "centaur" metaphor) in the role of the emotion carrier for the central "revelation." With all his New England moral inheritance, there is no doubt he thought that the value of poetry was ultimately its ability to bring necessary understanding to the reader, hence to save, in one way or another, civilization, or at least *il salvabile*.

Before World War II, Bunting seems to have gone along with the Poundian view, which he would state at times very naïvely.[11] But by the end of the war there had occurred a great change, in his explicit opinions at least.[12] These changed opinions give the rationale of a good deal of what Bunting says in the present lectures. Yet the older view persists, governing both Bunting's individual criticisms of others and the way he wrote his own verse.

In the present lectures, as very frequently in the interviews he gave in his late years, Bunting sets forth the principle that "it doesn't matter a damn" what the poet says.[13] Considerations of sincerity or truth to reality should have no force whatsoever in evaluating verse: indeed, the reader need not even trouble himself with understanding what is being said.

Bunting put this point in some telling forms. In the mid-seventies he told an interviewer that poetry would be good or bad whether it rendered the impulse precisely (as Pound had required) or not: "If it was the content that mattered to us then let us say you are a good Scots Presbyterian; you would find Dante's poem horrifying, a really wicked performance." And since the value of a poem cannot lie in the supposed validity of what it says, it must lie in the form: "All the arts are concerned only with form in the end, and whatever you may use them for temporally it is only by form that they will live."[14]

But in Bunting's mind, this point identifies itself with another: the point that the unique characteristic of poetry is sound shaping, that is, the music of words. He took care to qualify this by saying that *unique* did not mean "only"; but to the extent that one was discussing the art or relative merit of any piece of poetry, this was the one characteristic that needed to be talked about.

And this is why Bunting gives himself the program he undertakes in the present lectures. When he sets out here to chart the sound-handling of English poetry, he is talking, in his view, not about some minor specialist concern but about poetry in its one essential: the form, *which is the form of its sound.* And there comes always, with pitiless rigor, the corollary: neither writer nor reader need concern himself or herself one jot with the poem's meaning. It need not have any.

He explicitly justified this from Pater, as we shall see in these lectures.[15] But what Pater had said was that all the arts strove to eliminate the distinction between matter and form; that music was the only art in which this "perfect identification" was possible; and that therefore all the other arts must aspire to the condition of music. He had also said that all art was forever trying "to get rid of its responsibilities to its subject or material": thus the best poems were those in which "form and matter, in their union or identity, present one single effect to the 'imaginative reason.' "[16]

This does not mean that the matter should cease to have effect; only in music can that happen. And somehow the matter is to attain "union or identity" with the sound (and the poem's other features). Presumably it can do this only by being formally analogous with it, and with them. It cannot be formally analogous with the sound (or, for the reader, have form at all) unless the reader understands it.

Because Pater's ideal of form was in a sound art (music); and because poetry's one unique feature was its sound patternings; Bunting seems to have concluded that the other elements of poems (the plot, for example) could not be given form, or that if they could, it was insignificant.

Yet he could not be consistent about this. He explained the abstract form of his *Briggflatts* as most like a mountain range, with climbs, descents, peaks. These were, he said, peaks of *emotive level.* No doubt, challenged, he could have claimed that the differences of emotive level were created by the word-music alone. But it's clear that, like the other movements, the second movement has two peaks, and that the second one in this case is higher (which reflects the general design Bunting intended), and that this results in good part from what Bunting has put into the various parts of the *plot:* an effort he himself described at the time: "Oh yes, I've taken care to make Bloodaxe as telling as I can . . . but in fact he is driven only by his own nature. Pasiphae has something more monstrous and more terrifying to submit to, of her own volition, but in the universe-busting mission that someone has to face — a few in each generation." He would certainly have conceded that if he had failed to present Pasiphae's congress with the bull with more intensity than Bloodaxe's death, the shape of that movement would to that extent have failed: and the overall form of the poem with it. Hence his great and triumphant labor with the concrete denotation of the hooves and bloody sand, recorded in extensive correspondence with the same fellow poet.[17] If some part of the plot had failed to "affect," as plot, in the intended way, the arrangement of the matter would have failed, its form would have been weakened, and this form would have failed of the required union with the sound form. So he labored to make sure no part would so fail.

This is the basic inconsistency in Bunting's theory of the insignificance of meaning: that it has very little to do with his own practice. He himself would have scorned to write a poem whose content, and the arrangement of it, did not in some way ring true as experience. (This is one reason his book of poems is so short.) Others, he frequently complains, lacked this rigor. What was wrong with Spenser's great work? That "he so stubbornly attempted themes which were not his; the whole design of the Faerie Queene is false so that it lives only in the incidentals."[18] (Evidently the successful arrangement of matter, at this level, depends on one's deep belief in it.) The problem with Eliot's *Four Quartets*? They contained too much pastiche.[19] Now pastiche is something, precisely, that you *can* concoct out of a dictionary—and something that cannot be detected merely by comparison with a dictionary. It consists of queasy relations of words, not with other words, but with a connecting thread of experience that they seem to imply. Bunting knew very well that the moment a reader detected pastiche, the effect of the passage on him would change, and therefore also its effect as part of the overall form.[20]

"Get a dictionary / and learn the meaning of words": Bunting knew this was not enough, and that his friend Zukofsky was making too much of his verse out of the contents of the *Century Dictionary*. That is why he himself had set out, from the beginning, to be a Ralegh, a man of action who *also wrote*.[21] Only that sort of knowledge—derived from action—would be a solid enough basis. And so we find he constantly berates poets for narrownesses of content: see the remarks in the present lectures on the English Augustans; on Crabbe; on H.D., who was never in danger of lacking a "supple enough measure" but who "could not think of anything much to do with it": her Greeks lacked life.[22]

If Bunting had put into practice his late doctrine that meanings didn't matter, that all a poet had to do was to make pleasing sound-objects, he would have been somewhat alone in modern poetry.[23] In fact he is aligned with much, if not most, that has been valuable in the works of Creeley as well as Zukofsky, MacDiarmid and David Jones as well as Pound. His poetic is a great deal less isolated than it might seem.

I began with the question: When Bunting, in the lectures that follow, gives a critique of English prosodic practice, is he speaking as a Poet Who Knows—without knowing how; or as a linguist, who is aware of the reasons in the language why one option works and another does not? I have given a part-answer: Bunting and his fellow Modernists required conscious knowledge of the elements that go into a poem: of the sound systems of words as much as of any "matter" they may carry, because an imbalance in the one would skew the emotive direction of the whole, just as much as an imbalance in the other. (One's words referred to the world: defective knowledge of that part of the world would create defective effect.) That was the common aesthetic they started from. Sketching it, I have uncovered a peculiar twist to it, and perhaps a weakness, that Bunting shared with Zukofsky.

If we look at Bunting's relations first with contemporaries and younger poets and then with the critical academy, it will define his aesthetic further and perhaps show in it a relative strength. And I think it will complete the answer to my opening question.

BUNTING AND OTHER POST-POUNDIANS

Bunting wrote to George Oppen in 1973: "I think I was trying to say to you that WCW's clinical training, of the eyes, of the precise reporting of what's seen, has somehow to be incorporated into the practise of the more complex poets before we get where we all set out to go." [24] Examined in the light of Bunting's other remarks, this prescription turns out to be: Fenollosa plus Bunting's own doctrine of objectivity.

Ernest Fenollosa's famous theory of verse had said: Set things against things, as the Chinese written character does, and they will interact, and that interaction will be your meaning. This at least was Bunting's interpretation of Fenollosa, and it is set out very cogently in the penultimate lecture of the present collection. Such a method allows the poet, Bunting says, great concision: he can dispense with explanations; he can leave gaps. Thus Fenollosa underlies Bunting's remarks when he explains his own method of elision in meaning-structure:

> I know it is naughty. It outrages both Ezra and Louis, and must
> have given TSE the horrors when I leave gaps in the grammar
> or omit a few chapters of narrative. They all do it themselves,
> though. . . . For me, I see Beethoven hopping along without bridge
> passages in his last quartets, and Monteverdi not even putting in a
> cadence when the matter changes suddenly, and nobody except the
> layers down of the Rules of Harmony etc ever even notices.[25]

This sort of thing is what Bunting means by "the practise of the more complex poets" in our century. His own *Briggflatts* has some seventeen heroes in twelve distinct plots, with no bridge passages. The gaps create meanings.

But to Bunting, Fenollosa's ideas imposed another demand: "things," to put together. This is why he wrote to Oppen of William Carlos Williams's medical training.[26] Williams saw things, accurately, and got them,

accurately reflected, into his poems; and such seeings were the indispensable bricks of the "ideogramic method" Fenollosa propounded. Bunting
made this into part of his own personal interpretation of Objectivism.
He accepted, of course, the view in Zukofsky's Objectivist manifestoes
that the poem, as resulting, must be "an object." But Objectivism—as
Bunting understood it—also held that the writer should communicate
by the "unexplained," impersonal, *objective* showing of things. This was
part of Bunting's understanding of the shared aims of the group,[27] and
he rebuked Zukofsky for not cleaving to it: for submerging it in the other
aspect, elaborated into a futile metaphysic. He even developed it into
an interpretation of Eliot's "objective correlative": by the presenting of
concrete data shalt thou communicate thy emotion, and by no other
method, for in fact no other method works.[28]

That Fenollosa is a main basis of Pound's writing seems obvious, and
the working out of it in the *Cantos* has been sufficiently described.[29]
Pound knew that it was more or less meaningless to say, for example, that
the Presbyterian bankers of New York were the opposite of Hanno the
Carthaginian; or that (as D. H. Lawrence would have formulated it in his
slacker moments) the one belonged to the realm of Death, or Negation,
and the other to Life, or some such. Instead, Pound put these blocks of
perception in Canto XI, and left them to speak to each other. They also
echoed in some way the bankers of Canto XII, who in turn had been
juxtaposed with another sort of Hanno called Baldy Bacon (who was half
a banker himself) . . .

So far, so good; the weaknesses of Pound's writing entered, Bunting
makes clear, when he failed to cleave to the two basic requirements of
the doctrine of the ideogram. Pound (like Spenser) insisted on writing of
things of which he knew not, such as leopards and Bacchic wildness; and
when he got to the *Pisan Cantos,* he let his management of the juxtaposi-
tion of blocks of experience go slack, and meandered.[30] As for Zukofsky,
he had sharp enough eyes, but wilfully imposed drastic limits on his experience—as Pound had complained in the '30s, even at the moment
when Zukofsky was taking the most daring steps he was ever to take outside his small Brooklyn world,[31] and as Bunting complains here below.
Zukofsky also insisted on forcing what he knew through tight grids of
arbitrary, often mathematical, pattern making.[32] And he tried to plan
and structure a long poem, not on "things fully known" interacting in
the manner of components of ideograms but on things—hopefully so
interacting—sequenced for him partly by the mere lapse of time. That is,

his *"A"* is partly structured as a diary.[33] All these are specific complaints Bunting made against the poets he thought of as, respectively, his greatest immediate forebear and his greatest contemporary. Each amounts to a failure of the "sharp eyes plus ideogram" method, as we may call it.

It is well known that Fenollosa also underlies a good deal of the postwar effort in American poetry. In 1938 Pound, in the *Guide to Kulchur* (dedicated to Bunting and Zukofsky), had justified the "ideogramic method" as a way round the truncations and false appearances of knowledge imposed by scholastic thought habits. The age of Aquinas had taught us to explain experience by sorting bits of it into categories such as Negation, Love. This was the starting point of all the processes that we know as Reason: first assign phenomena to categories and then demonstrate what cannot function in the same way as something else because it belongs to a different category on that, or on a higher, level. The problem with this is that categories leak. The phenomena put into any category, examined closely, turn out to exist on more than one plane: even the term *plane* implies too geometrical a neatness. Charles Olson picked up on this insight in a big way, but his manifestoes show a line of development that marks out another Buntingian divergence from his forebears and juniors.

Bunting's remarks about Olson may seem strangely reductive,[34] considering how much in Olson's ideas goes along with ideas Bunting (with his friends Zukofsky and Irving Kaplan) had been enunciating back in the thirties: partly out of Fenollosa, partly from Whorf and Sapir and perhaps Jakobson.[35] But the main push in Olson's discourse, by both example and content, is toward metaphysics: a mode of thought for which Bunting entertained the most wholehearted loathing.[36]

If you argue from Riemann and Heisenberg and the history of science to "the nature of our age" and then further to the way present-day poets ought to write, you are claiming an understanding of the relation between science's facts and those of poetry that, Bunting would have said, will naturally express itself in terms like these: "the overall 'space' of *Moby-Dick* . . . and those of which it is made up, have the qualities of projective space."[37] And if we had the kind of knowledge that such abstractions posit, there would certainly be no need for poetry: whose merit is that it sticks to what it knows. Those are in fact the terms of a metaphysic: a metaphysic of the Self and the Other, which is Olson's real concern.

Olson's discourses inveigh against Hellenic abstraction, and they call on pieces of particular technical knowledge as part of their stance and demonstration. Olson talks very technically about prosody in particular (which of course is Bunting's main concern): not only about "breath" but also about the syllable, the line, and even quantity. Examined, these discussions turn out to be mere gestures at technicality. Olson says nothing about line, syllable, or quantity that betrays real observation of them;[38] the terms are in fact further components of his metaphysic of Self and Other. They perform as subsections of his "breath," an essentially spiritual entity whereby he hopes to inform the surrounding Other with his Self.

Given this attitude to fact, it is also not surprising that Olson should have developed his metaphysic in a direction that collides head on with Bunting's idea of good poetic practice. The poem's composition must be treated, Olson said, as the interaction of objects in a field, none of whose elements can exist without possible modification by the others. (So far, Bunting would have agreed entirely.) But not only must all the elements of the poem interact; they must all be discovered by the act of writing as that occurs, since the act of writing, necessarily, changes the field of "what is" as it proceeds.

The young who visited Bunting and read his pronouncements in the seventies were greatly influenced by the Olsonian doctrine that the writing of a poem must be an act of discovery. In Bunting's responses they would run flat against what seemed to them mere dogged antiquarianism: talk of sounds, and craft, and planning. Bunting would offer unbelievable analogies: "You don't take a block and start making a woodcut without some notion of what you're going to put on that woodcut, even if it's only that you mean to leave this corner blank and fill up the other corner with something." [39] How can a poet *plan* his poem, without cramping the interaction of its field as it develops? How can he usefully study blank verse, or the meter of *Beowulf*, when "form is never more than an extension of content" (Creeley, as quoted by Olson)? If Wyatt's sounds were good, they were good in his poems because appropriate to those poems' occasions. To study them as preparation for one's own writings would necessarily be to risk bringing in "preconceptions from outside the poem" (in Olson's treacherously double-barreled phrase).[40]

I do not think Bunting ever confronted these ideas directly, but I surmise that his unspoken answers might have been somewhat as follows. He remarks with a craftsman's pride that the tenor bull whose brag opens *Briggflatts* had been in his notebook ten years before he found a use for it.[41] Anyone who reads Bunting's prose will discover peculiarly personal images (black basaltic pebbles-as-testicles, for example, or an earth "shaved" of vegetation) that go back much farther than that, and of whose continuity in him Bunting himself was very possibly unaware. Neither the one kind of continuity, stored in the notebook, nor the other, recurring unawares, need be a falsification of the writer's present inner knowledge—though it may be: and it is the basic equipment of the honest writer that he know when, as he brews up his writing, he is stewing up some image or idea beyond what it really means to his present conception, which must relate to his own deeper self. As a poet can learn from his own past, so he can learn from the pasts of other writers: their articulations of matter, their techniques that worked, for particular purposes, and that failed. There is at least that much continuity within and between us.

Metaphysics and subjectivity: I surmise that it was these drifts that made Bunting write to George Oppen in 1973: "Yet I admit that I feel far surer of Hugh McDiarmid, with all his parade of learning, and even David Jones, whose footnotes are an encyclopedia of odd knowledge, than I do of anybody left over since Ezra's death (bar LZ, whose stubbornness is a virtue outweighing some things I dont like)." [42] Certainly it was not MacDiarmid's or Jones's use of Fenollosan electric gaps that could have made Bunting admire them. In its main semantic structure, David Jones's *In Parenthesis* is more like a novel than it is like the "ideogramic" *Cantos*, *"A,"* or *Briggflatts*. As for MacDiarmid, nothing could be more rationally explicit. He gets no concision from parataxis. In a typical MacDiarmid poem, the central metaphor is constructed with such laborious explicitness that, by the time the capstone is put on, the reader has lost patience with it. But this does not make the main block of knowledge, almost always sharply observed, any the less necessitated by its own coherence.

If these are Bunting's reasons, they put Fenollosan interactions distinctly second to objectivity: the effective presenting of things as objectively existent. [43] And that is probably a true description of how Bunting felt. Category-words were not only useless but falsifying; main-emotion-naming words named nothing that the reader could lay hold of. What method, then, ultimately, but Ford Madox Ford's? "Ford at his best names *things* and lets them evoke the emotion without mentioning it." [44] They cannot do that unless they are first seen, by the writer, steadily enough for him to make them live in the mind of the reader. Again, "Poetry with too many [adjectives] loses its energy *and its touch with the world we feel and see.* [45] In sum, a writer can do nothing at all, by Fenollosa's route or any other, unless he first, as Pound put it, "shows us his world."

But a writer who writes anything longer than a five-line lyric must plan, if the final result is to have any shape; and you can plan only with what you (in some sense) understand. So Bunting had written in 1934: "A writer has to know, he dare not leave it to chance: that is, the language, those aspects grammar as taught cant cope with. A lucky line finder tacks ten misses to his hit or waits ten years for another, it takes knowledge amounting to character to subordinate ready-made inspirations from the unconscious to what is constructed by acquired skill to produce an effect gauged and willed in advance." [46] Yet for prosody in particular, this still begs the enormous question, what can one in fact "know"?

At this point we have to consider what versification is: in what way it occurs in composition and, hence, what part of it can or cannot belong to the domain of the planning consciousness.

BUNTING IN THE ACADEMY

Concerning the sounds of poetry, which are the focus of these lectures, there is of course a very long tradition of study. But here, Bunting turns out to be no more in tune with the saecular teaching of the academy than with the teachings of post-fifties aesthetics.

There has been a governing assumption that poets and readers should be able to understand, and chart, consciously, the rules by which the rhythms of poetry are constructed, because these rules (by the nature of art) are simplicities: are, in their very essence, simple number.

The sound-form of poetry, from the classical era to the Renaissance, was taken to be a subdivision of music, which was seen (in the Pythagorean-Platonist manner) as a manifestation of cosmic laws whose very essence was simplicity, exactitude, mathematical purity, and stability. To have proposed organic suppleness in rhythm (Bunting's terms) to an ancient Greek thinker would have been like proposing muddy clarity.

Platonizing theories of harmony had a great influence on the Italian and then on the English Renaissance, as is well known: the treatises on verse and on music of the English sixteenth century are full of the beauties of divine regularity. But Bunting is certainly right in supposing that theorists at most stages in this tradition were not overmuch concerned with actually listening to verse. They had other preoccupations: mainly, with building metaphysics. [47]

Strangely, when (in the early twentieth century) the forgotten scores of the Elizabethan madrigals were examined once more in the originals, their rhythms turned out to be of great complexity, or apparent irregularity. Such was this irregularity that it was only by dint of the most devoted training that modern singers were able to master the songs of Weelkes, Byrd, and their colleagues.[48] Yet those Elizabethans who theorized, theorized in the Pythagorean manner about divine simplicities.

It was in the phase of the rediscovery of those irregular rhythms in the Elizabethan manuscripts that Bunting got his musical training. His teacher was W. G. Whittaker, a friend and neighbor (as Anthony Flowers has now discovered) of the Bunting family.[49] Whittaker was a distinguished conductor and composer who had helped Fellowes with the editing of the lute music. In 1919, Fellowes rediscovered, at Durham Cathedral, part-books for the Great Service of Byrd, and "the first complete service after an interval of nearly 300 years took place in Newcastle Cathedral on May 31st, 1924, when it was sung by the Newcastle Bach Choir under Dr. W. G. Whittaker."[50] Bunting, aged twenty-four, sat in on rehearsals—no doubt because his aunt was in the Bach Choir.[51]

It seems likely that his rhythmic sense was clarified by these contacts. When in 1936 he commented on Persian prosody, his model was the rhythms of Elizabethan lute songs, where "the music is evidence, the grammar only cast-iron theory."[52]

The intricacies of Elizabethan rhythmic practice did not survive the catastrophe of the Civil War. When Dr. Burney, friend of Garrick and Johnson and author of an influential history of music, encountered the rhythmical oddities of the surviving madrigals, he considered them merely "*false accent.*"[53] The ecstasies of the Pythagorean-Platonic cosmic vision had faded in the seventeenth century, to be replaced by a moralism. Writers now seemed to cling to the regularity implied by the term *numbers* (= verse), not because of its intellectual beauty but because it intimated that the cosmos was not overcomplex, was thus knowable, thus (to our apprehension) stable.[54] *Harmony* came to mean regularity of rhythm itself; steady alternation of stresses was true harmony—was indeed a duty, for the "order" of poetry was also a moral example. Milton, benighted contemporary of the great Waller, was to be excused as best one might.

A yen for the predictable is one of the constants in Western prosodic theories: it is just as strong in Augustine and Puttenham as in Dr. Johnson. But Bunting despises safety. He is for dance, the unexpected, the off-balance:

> each dancer alone
> with his foolhardy feet[55]

And therefore, in verse, he prefers (he tells us in these lectures) "subtle and unsteady" rhythms.[56] This foolhardiness, one of Bunting's emotional centers, is the equivalent of going beyond the permitted, the "patrolled bounds"—as did Epicurus in the philosophical explorations that Lucretius celebrated, and which are indirectly recelebrated in Bunting's *Briggflatts*. In his taped verse readings, Bunting dwells with evident delight on those balancing lines in Wyatt where the syllable is poised between a pulse and a space.

There is no reason why a critic or a reader should merely borrow Bunting's anarchic metaphors and pass off their values as self-justifying; still less as deciding what is, and is not, present in the rhythms of Shakespeare or of *Beowulf*. But we should also avoid seeing these questions as merely setting regularity (simple numbers) against freedom, with a free choice between the two according to one's preferences. There is no doubt that order, rules, and number underlie; for they underlie the chaos of the straw lying about this loft, just as much as they underlie the clear-cut symmetries of the stink bug that walks across it. The question is, what kind of number and order?

It may be held—contrary to one argument in these lectures—that the central fact about poetry in the English iambic pentameter tradition is a terribly simple and regular one: the alternation of weak stress position and strong stress position through ten units. Unlike Bunting, I believe it is so. And unlike Bunting, I think this is a functioning fact even in the best poems of the tradition, from *The Tempest* to Bunting's own "I am agog for foam."[57] (Only, a position is an expectation, established in some manner within the poem: it is not an actualization.)

But when traditional prosodists have referred to this simple frame, they have fostered the illusion that the traditional or regular verse forms were *applied to English words* in accordance with rules that they themselves could formulate. This has never been so. Dr. Johnson berates Donne for his waywardness with accents; yet he himself could not have formulated the rules that the admired Pope adhered to and that Donne had broken. (To put it another way: he could not have given any systematic description of the irregularities Pope allowed himself, or have distinguished them, systematically, from those we find in Donne.) Nor could Saintsbury, one hundred thirty years later. Since the 1960s a number of "deepseated regularities" in the poets' use of words in pentameters have been discovered. They are still imperfectly understood, and it is possible that they will always remain so; but there is no doubt that they operate.[58] But they relate to facts of phonology and syntax so complex that only specialists can retain them and that (for obvious historical reasons) a poet like Shakespeare, who exploited them, cannot have been conscious of. Poets work with the sound systems of their linguistic heritage, which they apply in part by intuition; and the present lectures show that Bunting well understood this.

Yet the assumption seems to remain, in many quarters, that poets and readers should simply be able to elicit, from words in verse, simple proportions, of a kind that anyone can count on his fingers. Hence the Augustan scorn of a critic like Donald Davie for a poet like William Carlos Williams, who confesses that he cannot elicit such simplicities from his verse—who knows, according to these definitions, that he does not understand his own meters.[59]

Hence also, no doubt, the strange respect still found in some quarters for characters like Gascoigne and Puttenham.[60] Bunting rightly names Puttenham's *Arte of English Poesie* (1589) the chief seed of "the heresy" (his phrase) "of scansion."[61] Puttenham marshals various methods of discovering simple patterns in English verse, yet shows himself ignorant of every detail of what was making the verse of his great predecessors and contemporaries work—was making it, precisely, rise above a Puttenhamish doggerel.

It is not that Puttenham does not recognize the principle of metrical tension (which is the exploiting of differences between a position and an actualization). No one then did. Nor is it that he does not consciously notice instances of it where they occur. The problem is that he has a fully effective set of devices for deleting such instances, for altering them into something else before they can impinge on the sensibilities of the reader. Puttenham's supposed quantity scansions exist largely for the purpose of imposing a uniformity of pattern, which pattern nevertheless turns out to be essentially a pattern of accent.[62]

When this program is actuated, we are going to lose the phrasal stress tensions that the *Shepheardes Calender* had already been using:

And singe of sorrow and deathes dreeriment

and that poem's pulls against the meter by word stress:

Thy Muse to long slombreth in sorrowing

—though these may be no more than Italianately pleasing variations for variety's sake. We shall delete those highly directed and emotive "mis-bracketings" (where words straddle foot-boundaries) that Marlowe had already built into his *Tamburlaine* by 1587:[63]

And measure every wand'ring planet's course

. . . .

And always moving as the restless spheres

A couple of decades after Puttenham, Ariel's games with stress groups that shift against the foot, and against the syntax group, would have been as sandcastles to Puttenham's steamroller:

the fire and cracks

Of sulphurous roaring the most mighty Neptune

Seem to besiege, and make his bold waves tremble,

Yea, his dread trident shake.[64]

And still at the present time we find scholars usurping the classical term *scansion* to denote a process whereby they flatten stress sequence to a level of regularity they deem normal for the Renaissance:

Makes black night beauteous, and her old face new

Why this particular "scansion," offered by Professor Wright? Because "only very rarely" are there real spondees in Elizabethan verse.[65] This is in fact an aesthetic decision, inclining to the view that the desirable pattern is a prominent-and-simple one: that x / should never be too far from physical audibility, lest the ear get fuddled. (Hanmer in 1744 made similar decisions about *The Tempest,* and imposed them by discovering errors in the text.)[66]

This gives a clue to the kind of conscious knowledge a poet can offer when, like Bunting, he undertakes to describe the functioning of sound in verse. A poet "has to know," Bunting says, "he dare not leave it to chance: that is, the language, those aspects grammar as taught cant deal with." The language includes its sound systems: phrase stress, lexical stress, contrastive stress, other modification of stress by semantics, and the rest.

A prosodist tries to grasp the accentual systems of the English language—in their interaction with syntax, if he has an intelligent grasp of the subject. But prosody also interacts with semantics. Semantics can shift stress: this is obvious. And a shift of stress, conversely, implies a semantic shift. If *black* is supposed to receive more stress here than *night*, the meaning of the utterance is changed:

> Makes bláck nìght beauteous, and her old face new
> $\qquad\qquad\qquad\qquad$ (Sonnet 27)

A contrast, perhaps? (With "brown night"?) If *rules* is given more stress than *Age* here, as Professor Wright asks, there will be a similar effect on the meaning:

> Àge rúles my lines with wrinkles in my face
> $\qquad\qquad\qquad$ (Drayton, *Idea*, 22.2)

But in the context of the poem, this sense makes nonsense.[67]

A prosodist, at least by profession, has no training in semantics. A poet, on the other hand, if he is dedicated to the art, spends his life striving to reflect complex semantic nexuses accurately in the shapes of phonology. And the semantic nexuses (wholes and parts) to be reflected in the sound-shapes of a whole work, whether *Antony and Cleopatra* or Bunting's "Now that sea's over that island," are a very complicated thing.

These are reasons why prosody can be only a part of the field constituted by poetry. The very fundamental *observanda* of this supposed science (stresses, for example) are affected by interactions, not only with syntax, but also with semantics: whose subtleties the poet is much better equipped to sense than the prosodist. The poet's advantage as a prosodist ought to be that he starts out with a sense of this field as a field: a set of interactions, though known largely by the intuition alone. *That* is the poet's qualification to talk on this subject. And such are reasons, it seems to me, for giving a good deal of weight to the views on prosody of a self-conscious poet like Bunting.

Bunting was not a linguist, but he took care to be aware of some of the main linguistic gains of his day. And he knew what sort of knowledge was required at the level at which language and things interact in poems.

Neither pedantry nor ignorance will do: this is the understanding that Pound, Williams, Zukofsky, and Bunting had arrived at. And herein was the essential step forward. They knew that they had to be linguists in the popular sense: they learned foreign languages. This taught them the gristly uniqueness of any semantic package in any tongue. They knew they could not ignore linguistics in the specialists' sense: the speculations about syntax's relations with anthropology of Bunting, Pound, Zukofsky, and Zukofsky's friend Kaplan are a basic part of their development. Words ceased to be unreal accidents attached to real ideas and real things. Language was another, interacting, organism. They thus broke a dualism between consciousness and language, as deep as the dualism between consciousness and world posited by Emerson when he said things represented "spiritual facts."

Bunting's professional amateurism in the matter of literature is not only pragmatic; it is also essential to the revolution of the period 1910–20. This is the revolution that made the difference in verbal quality between any line written by Coleridge or Swinburne and almost any written by a member of the tribe of Pound. When words are not windows but are known in a selfhood that changes as the language flexes, they can be brought back to manifesting texture in themselves, and so reflecting semantic texture: not the reshufflable abstractions and symbols suggested in Coleridge's vague movement:

> Yon crescent Moon, as fixed as if it grew
> In its own cloudless, starless lake of blue

but the qualities and forces implied by the overlapping stress contours (and the phonemes that edge them) in *Briggflatts:*

> sinews ripple the weave,
> threads flex, slew, hues meeting,
> parting in whey-blue haze.

DECORATION

The reader who has been patient thus far may wish to go straight to Bunting's own words; the following explanations can be returned to, if necessary, afterward. There remains only to fill out an idea of Bunting's, important to these lectures, but for which he never here offers examples: the idea of aural decoration.[68]

Bunting posits (as I have noted) that the body of English verse must be rhythm; the main line of these lectures traces how intelligent work with rhythm rose and faded over the centuries, and where the possibilities lie now. Rhythm (in English) stands to the other sound-features of words as body to dress. And since Spenser, Bunting says, poets have been too ready to distract the reader's attention from basic weaknesses in the poem's shape by using such "decoration," which is a recurrent vice of the English tradition.[69]

This is a strong theme of Bunting's from the time he first began to set out his views of verse in essays,[70] and implies much more than a worry about oversweet sounds in verse. The oversweetness (he says) has tended to reflect and be reflected by an analogous lushness in ideation. The theme is thus part of Bunting's lifelong attack on "the magnificent tradition" in English poetry. Here I shall emphasize some of its main distinctions and offer examples of what Bunting appears to have in mind.

There exists poetry (Bunting posits) that draws a main part of its interest from accent sequence:

> Behold, Love, thy power how she despiseth
>
> > (Wyatt)
>
> From him that ere long must bed thee
>
> > (Campion)
>
> The sea's colour moves at the dawn
>
> > (Pound)

This interest, he seems to accept, has value whether it comes from strong tugs against an established blank verse movement:

> Heaven stops the nose at it, and the moon winks
>
> > (*Othello*)

or from a simple change of pattern coupled with a shift from long syllables to short:

> $\quad$ thry̅thswy̅th behe̅old
> ma̅eg Higela̅ces
>
> > (*Beowulf*)[71]

or from those tensions (so frequent in Yeats) brought out of the English language's tendency to try to keep strong stresses at equal time intervals:

> And the white breast of the dim sea

And this rhythmic play has value even where it takes the form only of gentle variations against a fairly steady pattern, as in the *Shepheardes Calender;* or of single-line "effects."

But it has far greater value when the poet can articulate it into a paragraph-long progression of changes, of shifts developed for some deep analogy—or contrast—with changing meaning. Donne achieves this sometimes; for example, in the whole of the sonnet "Thou hast made me." Pound does it in the whole of "The Return," where there is no line that is not a contributive development of the main rhythmic idea. Zukofsky described such an articulation in Pound's Canto XXX, whose "composite of internal rhyme, repetition of word, repetition of line with one word altered, delayed and rapidly extended cadence, and tendency towards wrenching of accent" results in a play where "the cadence of the word 'pity' itself is never perfectly expected."[72]

> Now if no fayre creature followeth me
> It is on account of Pity,
> It is on account that Pity forbideth them slaye.
> All things are made foul in this season,
> This is the reason, none may seek purity
> Having for foulnesse pity
> And things growne awry;
> No more do my shaftes fly
> To slay. Nothing is now clean slayne
> But rotteth away.

This art, for Bunting, is the real thing: it is that for which verse, in English, essentially exists. And one may remark that it seems to be a true contribution to the medium of language, because it does not clutter up the ideation with more detail on that plane. (A writer may choose to let it do so, as Dylan Thomas did, by allowing the rhythmic idea to dictate the ideation; but that is a choice.)

But there are other kinds of sound in words that can be patterned, too:

> And those sweete rosy leaves so fairely spred
> Upon the lips, shall fade and fall away
> To that they were, even to corrupted clay.[73]

By the time of the *Fowre Hymnes,* as this example shows, Spenser was a past master at weaving them. It is a question not only of simple matters like head-consonants echoed by midword consonants, but also developing lines of vowels. In this example one may point to Spenser's skill by mentioning the sort of banality in sound that he avoided:

> sw**ee**t ros(ie) l**ea**ves   so f**air**ly [b**are**]

(It is evident that one must break one's patterns also.) This writing is excellently mellifluous and tempting to the tongue, and the reader may follow out its weavings for himself; but the main principle is, as Bunting says in describing Spenser's art, "decorating every phrase as heavily as it will bear."

But it will be noticed that these are the very same arts that are in play in poems which, to Bunting,[74] are peaks of the Whole Art. Watch the evolution of vowels here:

> F**u**ll f**a**thom f**i**ve thy f**a**ther l**ie**s
>
> . . . .
>
> N**o**thing of him that d**o**th fade
>
> But doth s**u**ffer a s**ea**-ch**a**nge
>
> Into s**o**mething r**i**ch and str**a**nge

And

> fies nobilium tu quoque fontium,
> me dicente cavis imp**o**sitam **ili**cem
>   **s**axis, unde **lo**quaces
>   **ly**mphae de**sili**unt tuae.

Why blame Spenser for developing these skills when the art of poetry is, essentially, sound, and art is essentially form?

Shakespeare shows why:

> When summer's breath their masked buds discloses
>
>   (Sonnet 54)

This manner is as delicately brilliant as Guido Reni's way with pale yellows, pinks and dead greys; and, when the cultural cycle brings around again an age in which emotion is respectable, it becomes the model for all verse. Keats is its great reviver:

> Not in lone splendour hung aloft the night
>
> . . . .
>
> To feel for ever its soft fall and swell

It gets loaded onto it the religion of Art's mystery or arcane craft, so that the Sacred Book of the Arts that Mallarmé and Yeats dreamed must be constructed all wholly of the same; and Joyce must interlard its tricks with Newman's constructions to produce the self-praising inner utterance of the unbearable Stephen:

> A veiled sunlight lit up faintly the grey sheet of water where the river was embayed. In the distance along the course of the slow-flowing Liffey slender masts flecked the sky.

These gorgeous passages are essential to the argument of the *Portrait of the Artist,* being the demonstration of Stephen's mystic powers as an Artist (though they add little to Keats). But "Our greatest are not free of these faults," as Bunting complained.[75] Pound exercised himself in the same skills, sometimes a little clankingly:

> In the slow float of differing light and deep [76]

And where it helps the matter, as in the rich bogs of early Heaney, it is a great resource:

> Bubbles gargled delicately, bluebottles
> Wove a strong gauze of sound around the smell.[77]

The trouble is that by now it is a norm, and you are insufficiently a Writer if you don't do it always. As Bunting noted, this lushness is a strong link between Swinburne and the self-indulgent Cummings. Hopkins studied the Welsh *cynghanedd* patterns, but used them at times for a sub-Keatsian toying ("dandled a sandalled"), and Dylan Thomas used the further freedom of maneuvre offered by surrealist semantics to go head first into a pig-wallow of sound.

All this is disastrous for poetry, partly because the sound-shapes tend to act as an analogy for a vision of "what is."

Shakespeare certainly knew that a constant play of texture becomes a sensory glitter; and Bunting seems to suggest that this gave him the aural analogy he wanted for the semantic glitter of the great speeches of his later plays. When a Macbeth or an Othello expresses strong emotion, Bunting argues, he does it by running up thick hanks of semantic threads that branch intoxicatingly three ways at once, where the mind can never follow them in the full flight of the utterance.[78] He works this art together with multitudinous sound patterning because the two, aesthetically, reinforce each other. And so Shakespeare perpetuated Spenser's influence by becoming another great model for the "magnificent" (or lush) tradition in English poetry.

When this becomes the norm, things are very difficult for the writer who wants to include the nonecstatic in his verse. He may want to "keep his eye on the object," as Bunting said Wordsworth did. He may consider that a given area of existence (economics, for example, or the history of slavery, or his own childhood) is capable, by being looked at steadily, of being understood. And he may consider that—while there may be a place in this area for the most intense wrath or agony—to understand clearly, and present with clarity, segments of what happened or what is happening will not detract from those emotions but build to them the more strongly. Such a writer, reared among the monuments of our orgiastic tradition, will have to labor long to shake off (as Bunting says he had to shake off[79]) the mode of Shakespeare; will probably arrive, if at all, at the solid rhythm articulation of a Canto I only after wasted years.

One should not assume that this program of Bunting's is perfectly consistent with what he did, even when he did it successfully. In most of his criticism, Bunting adopts what looks like a solidly neoclassical posture: all is self-discipline and conscious care. The terms seem like those of a new debate between proponents of Drab and Golden poetry: as if all Bunting now wanted were sober everyday thought in a guise as plain as Gascoigne's.[80] (This pose has made him very popular with neoclassicist critics.) Were that so, Bunting might have been content with that slack revival of blank verse that (for example) Yeats thought sufficient for his versions of the Japanese Noh:

> For he grows pale and staggers to his feet

—and that Noh translators of the seventies still seem to think preferable to honest prose. Yet even when Bunting does "pentameters," they have rhythmic surprise:

> and the foam dies and we again subside
> into our catalepsy, dreaming foam [81]

But it is more important to notice that even the best of Bunting's own verse may not be the natural outcome of the aesthetic he argues for.

Zukofsky, not himself, he argues, is the one who can modulate sound into the main structure of a whole poem, without overlarding it with rich phoneme play; as perhaps here:

> Horses that pass through inappreciable woodland,
> Leaves in their manes tangled.[82]

It is obvious that the staple of *Briggflatts* is quite different, being a very prominent and extremely rich patterning of consonants, consciously modeled on both Anglo-Saxon and the Welsh *cynghanedd*. But as Bunting remarked with reference to Catullus and Manuchehri, the "magnificent" is capable of contributing great power when it modulates out to the direct-and-simple at the right moment:[83]

> Silver blades of surf
> fall crisp on rustling grit,
> shaping the shore as a mason
> fondles and shapes his stone.

And despite Bunting's own doubts, he does also develop a Zukofskian limpidity, in which deft off-balance of accent is woven with just-touched-on repeat of phonemes:

> trembling phrase fading to pause
> then glow. Solstice past,
> years end crescendo.

A Note on Texts

The first eleven lectures here are from a series given at Newcastle University in 1969–70; the last two, from a second series at Newcastle University in 1974.

The sources for the text are of two kinds: photocopies or originals of manuscript drafts of the 1969–70 series, now in the possession of Peter Quartermain; and the tape recordings surviving from both series (now in the Bunting Archive, University of Durham) made under the direction of Kelsey Thornton when the lectures were delivered. Chapters 1, 4, 12, and 13 below are transcribed from the tapes, and the remainder from the manuscript drafts, for the reasons outlined in what follows. Three of the lectures as they survive have no titles: I have here entitled them respectively "Wordsworth and Whitman," "Pound's Cantos," and "Zukofsky."

The Quartermain drafts are almost complete, on a sequence of small ($7\frac{7}{8}$" × 7") sheets of typing paper, typed double-spaced, usually with one paragraph per sheet. (One of them exists only in photocopy, for Bunting destroyed the original; and two of them also exist on tape: see below.) There is, however, a hiatus at about midpoint, centering on the passages concerning Whitman: here some of the writing is in notes and some seems to have been reworked. For this see Chapter 8, "Wordsworth and Whitman," note 1.

Of the second series of lectures (1974), the manuscripts have disappeared, five lectures were recorded (but with gaps), and three recordings, if made, have not survived. It seems clear that some of the matter in the lost lectures corresponded closely to what survives in the 1969–70 manuscripts, but other cross references show that Bunting developed in them ideas that are only sketched in what survives. Two of the surviving lectures in particular, on Pound's *Cantos* and on Zukofsky, complement and complete the line of thought of the 1969–70 series, and so I print them here.

The aim is to have an uncluttered reading text. I therefore do not draw attention to deletions or additions in the manuscripts or false starts on the tapes, except where these are of particular interest. In the lectures transcribed from manuscript, I omit Bunting's rough indications of poem titles, page references, and reading times. Any poem titles that remain are supplied by me. In the lectures taken from tapes, I omit chairpersons' introductions and exchanges about slide projection.

Where only a manuscript draft is extant, I follow it literatim, preserving Bunting's characteristic spelling and punctuation: "couldnt," "the poets business." I make two exceptions to this rule. Obvious typing mistakes I silently correct, and the titles of poems or books—which Bunting almost always left unmarked—I put in quotation marks or italics. I have silently normalized Bunting's spelling of names and poem titles where these are (as frequently) misspelled by him, but not where he chooses an authentic form, such as "Campian" or "Wyat," no longer in common use.

In the case of the two lectures here for which only a tape-recording is extant (chaps. 12 and 13), I transcribe what I hear, making no attempt to incorporate Bunting's usual written forms.

But in two cases (chaps. 1 and 4) we have both a manuscript draft and a tape. Naturally they differ. For the oral occasion, Bunting added ideas and information to his written text, rather than cutting; therefore I take the tapes here for my base text. Apart from such additions, variants are almost never substantive; I list them only when they seem noteworthy. In transcribing the tapes of these two lectures, I aim strictly at a sense of the oral occasion and avoid any attempt at a mongrel text: if the manuscript punctuates, spells, or paragraphs differently from my hearing of the tape, I take no heed. Thus also in these two cases, I no longer follow Bunting's private conventions of spelling and punctuation: his audience would have heard "Provençal" not "Provenzal," and so I leave it.

Throughout, editorial insertions are indicated by square brackets. In the taped lectures, inaudible passages are indicated by a space between brackets, thus: { }; doubtful transcriptions are marked thus: {cagey}.

In the manuscript draft, Bunting does not normally include the poems that he intends to read out to his audience: he notes only their titles or first lines. Here I have thought it helpful to insert the poems. In some cases it is clear which edition of the given poem he used, and I give the text of that edition without comment. Elsewhere there may be doubts or no clue at all; in these cases I remark on its status in a note.

Where Bunting's text has been determined, but he strays from it, I print the words as Bunting reads them.

In certain cases, the passage that Bunting reads appears in the photo-copies (now in the Bunting Archive) prepared for Bunting's reading for his anthology of verse recorded at Newcastle University. In these cases I can assume Bunting approved of the text, and I insert it here from the photocopies whether or not the source edition has been determined. In other cases, the passage appears in the typescript draft for his pro-jected poetry anthology (now in the Bunting Archive). Here I use the source edition if it has been determined; but the typescript text itself is no guide to Bunting's intentions, for the typist clearly was not Bunting. Passages are often garbled in such a way as to show that the typist had little comprehension of what he was typing.

For other passages there is not enough evidence; but there is no profit in elaborate conjecture. Given his main argument about the nature of poetry, Bunting would certainly have had a strong preference for texts with no editorial emendation, preferring the risk of scribal or printer's error to the probability of metrical bowdlerization by editors. On the other hand, he would probably have cared a good deal less about accu-racy in lexis and not at all about spelling or punctuation. Thus he prob-ably chose Masson's 1874 edition of Milton merely because it was not obviously an editorially "improved" text; the availability of critical edi-tions of the same would not particularly have interested him.

All notes are mine. I do not normally annotate matters dealt with in standard one-volume companions to literature, unless Bunting's infor-mation seems to require correction. Dates attached to Bunting's poems are the dates of writing as given in the editions of his poems that he supervised.

Abbreviations

B:SV:	Peter Makin, *Bunting: The Shaping of His Verse* (Oxford: Clarendon Press, 1992).
Bunting, *Briggflatts* (etc.):	Basil Bunting, *The Complete Poems*, ed. Richard Caddel (Oxford: Oxford UP, 1994).
Tape (1974) *incipit* "Well, I see" (etc.):	Tape-recording of lecture from the 1974 series at Newcastle University, beginning "Well, I see" (etc.).
Pound, Canto XXXI, 157 [etc.]:	Ezra Pound, *The Cantos* (London: Faber, 1964), 157 (Canto XXXI) (etc.).

The following abbreviations are used in notes for the libraries holding Basil Bunting manuscript material quoted: these manuscripts are used by kind permission of these libraries as owners of the material.

Beinecke:	The Yale Collection of American Literature, Beinecke Rare Book and Manuscript Library, Yale University
Buffalo:	The Poetry/Rare Books Collection, University Libraries, State University of New York at Buffalo
Bunting Archive:	The Basil Bunting Archive, Durham University Library
HRC:	Harry Ransom Humanities Research Center, The University of Texas at Austin
Indiana:	The Lilly Library, Indiana University
Washington:	George Marion O'Donnell Papers, Special Collections, Washington University Libraries.

BASIL BUNTING ON POETRY

ONE

The Codex

I hope that I'm not here under false pretences—I'm no sort of scholar, and I don't want anybody to rely on anything I say.

It seems to me that the language of criticism, the language of grammar and prosody, in this country and perhaps in all countries, is full of words imported from Latin, Greek and other learned languages, such as men normally use when they want to make vague statements sound precise, or when they want to make remote generalities seem relevant. Generalisation of course is the method of mathematics, and has been so successful in its proper place that people seem to expect it to succeed wherever it's possible to apply it, with whatever violence. But the arts are recalcitrant to generalisation. All you can usually say about a poem or a picture is, 'Look at it, listen to it.' Whether you listen to a piece of music or a poem, or look at a picture or a jug, or a piece of sculpture, what matters about it is not what it has in common with others of its kind, but what is singularly its own. It's not conformity to a type that makes the work of art valuable, but its difference from other works of art.

You think of all the weary attempts that poets have made to imitate Greek tragedies—I was reading one of Swinburne's the other day: *Hamlet* is a great play because it's not a bit like any work of Aeschylus'; it's not even like any other work of Shakespeare; Joyce's *Ulysses* is a good book because it would never have come into Dickens's head to write it; yet if you try to define tragedy, you must lump *Hamlet* and *Lear* with the *Oresteia*, and also with *Maria Marten: Or, The Murder in The Red Barn;*[1] and you must class *Great Expectations*, and *Ulysses*, and *Don Quixote*, and *Uncle Tom's Cabin*, all as novels, and you get nowhere by doing so.

I think it was a bad poet who is now forgotten, Sir John Squire,[2] who once pointed out that the old London Omnibus Company displayed on every vehicle an excellent English hexameter: 'Never step off the bus with your back to the oncoming traffic.' It may not be quite the classic hexameter that Vergil wrote, but it's every bit as good as those that many poets of the last century and the beginning of this wrote and called English hexameters.[3] But there's nothing significant in what Vergil and the London Omnibus Company, and let's say Robert Bridges, have in common; we've learned nothing about their quality as poets when we've discovered that they all wrote a rhythm that can be made to conform, more or less, to a pattern which certain grammarians in Alexandria two thousand years ago decided to call a hexameter.[4]

There are, however, a few—only a few—things which can be said about the arts in a general way. I don't think they can be reached by classifying works of art according to any a priori principle; but perhaps they may by looking at the history of the various arts, examining the earliest specimens, and perhaps carrying back the argument a little further, by—further into the past, that is—by analogy with what primitive people do today in remote parts of the world. I'm not going to do this for you—I'm not enough of a scholar to do it convincingly, though a number of people have been working on it in recent years—but I'll try to indicate a part of what I mean.

The earliest poet whose work we know in any detail is Homer, and we cannot get much further back by including whoever wrote *Gilgamesh;* our knowledge of music isn't anything like as ancient as that. But there are paintings in caves of extreme antiquity, and other paintings, just like them, made the other day by Bushmen in South Africa, or Australian aborigines. The more primitive the pictures are, the more they resemble the dances that primitive people hold from time to time, and I don't think I'm misrepresenting the views of scholars of art who are anthropologists, if I say that they think almost all the arts originate in the dance. Perhaps they would except sculpture, which is obviously a close relation to pottery and basket-making, but these too interact with the dance.

The anthropologists used to tell us—perhaps they still do—that the primitive dance has a purpose. It exists to compel the rain to fall, or the crops to grow, or for some other useful end. I don't quite agree with them. I think perhaps the wild men danced at first just for the fun of it, or out of habit. Primitive people are not so much obsessed with utility and reasons for doing things as we are, {but} when at last they ask themselves, or the ethnologist comes along and asks them, 'Why are you dancing?', they think out a plausible reason. Why, after all, does a bird sing when it isn't calling its mate or giving warnings to its young? It sings because that's what birds do, and people dance because that is what is natural for human beings to do.

Some of you perhaps know Ezra Pound's story about the desert Arab. I don't know what explorer he got it from, he knew a number of Arabian explorers.[5] The earnest visitor says to the Arab, 'Let us talk about God.' The Arab says, 'I must milk my camels.' When the camels are milked, the visitor says, 'Let us discuss God.' The Arab replies, 'I must drink my milk.' At last the milk is gone, and the visitor says, 'Sir, have you time at last to talk about God?' The Arab says, 'I must dance.'

That I think is a dance done just for the dance, it's a time when you {want to} feel like dancing, you've got a tummy full of food at last after a hungry day, and so on. It's just a purely natural reaction.

The movements of the human body dancing dictate a rhythm. It is not at all difficult to see how music is born.

I think possibly some of you have heard me tell about a time when I was coming down the Zagros mountains from Persia into Iraq.[6] The Kurds live there, some of them are migrant shepherds. And as I was coming down the mountain I met a tribe of Kurds on the move, going up the mountain, hundreds of them, in little groups, with their animals. And as my car approached I became aware of a sound like the sound you hear when the tread is coming off your tyre—flap, flap, flap. I stopped the car and examined the tyres. They were alright. Then I noticed that the sound went on even while the car was stopped. A group of Kurdish women was approaching me. They wore the usual smock, fastened with a brooch at the neck and fastened again below the navel, but all in between is open, and the sound that I'd heard was their long, slack dugs beating against their belly as they walked: beating out a kind of march tune, steadily.

Well now you think of some of the coloured ladies you have seen on television dancing, in Central Africa. They are the same shape and must make the same sound when they dance. They have no need of castanets or drums. Their bodies supply the music. Such sounds of course give a very direct hint to percussive music, which I daresay nobody will dispute is the beginnings of all music.

I don't need to elaborate, or to try to show how all the elements of music arise. The fundamental one is there, dictated by the human body doing what it is natural for it to do. Poetry must arise very similarly, from the grunts and cries of the dancers. It is very closely related to music from its birth, and both are tied ultimately to the body and its movements. That can be traced out in more detail than I want to go into, and a lot of the detail is unconvincing. But the general proposition I think is a true one.

Poetry and music are both patterns of sound drawn on a background of time. That's their origin, and their essence. Whatever else they may become, whatever purpose they may sometimes serve, is secondary. They *can* do without it, in case of necessity. Whatever refinements and subtleties they may introduce, if they lose touch altogether with the simplicity of the dance, with the motions of the human body and the sounds natural to a man exerting himself, people will no longer feel them as music and poetry. They will respond to them {as meaning}, no doubt, but not with the exhilaration that dancing brings. They'll not think of them as human concerns; they will find them tedious.

I think that is what happened to poetry a good deal in the last century: a lot of Victorian poetry, a lot of the poetry contemporary with it in France, [and] other countries, lost touch with music, and with the simplicity of bodily movement, and became merely a rather puzzling way of setting down facts on the page, whereas it really has no fundamental connection with facts at all.

The graphic arts, of course, begin with the dance frozen, and perhaps also from the decoration of pottery and weaving; though the repetitive patterning of most primitive decoration, on pottery especially, suggests that it, too, may have a connection with the dance. I don't intend to talk about that, it's not my business, but I think that all the arts can be used to illustrate each other. Rhythm can be as visible in space as it is audible in time; and symmetry, and proportion, are as discernible in time as they are in space. So the arts have in common at least their close connection with the dance, and the fact that they need no justification. Whether they serve any useful purpose or not doesn't matter; their first purpose was to be enjoyable, no more, and if they fulfil that, they've got nothing to apologise for.

That's why I'm going to talk about a piece of graphic art rather than a poem, at the moment. Northumberland has not produced very many poets. But it has produced some of the greatest graphic artists who have ever lived. And I think it's worthwhile for poets, and people who write about poetry, to examine the work of these artists, and see how much of their processes can be brought over into their own art of poetry.

The central masterpiece of Northumbrian art, and also of all the art of the Dark Ages, except what you find in Byzantium, is the *Codex Lindisfar-*

nensis, the Lindisfarne Book.[7] The Book itself is in the British Museum, where the Keeper is a little {cagey} of showing it; but he will if you insist. There's a splendid facsimile of enormous expense in a few libraries.[8] One copy is in the University here. I don't know whether the Free Library has one, but it ought to have.

There are perhaps half-a-dozen books in the world comparable to the *Codex Lindisfarnensis.* They were all produced by Northumbrians, or by people under the immediate influence of Northumbrians. The Book of Durrow, which is in Ireland, is believed to have been made in Northumberland. The Echternach Book, which is, I forget whether it's [in] Germany or Luxembourg,[9] was made there by Northumbrian missionaries. The Book of Kells, which is about a century younger than these, was made in Ireland, at a time when Ireland was chock full of Northumbrian scholars and monks.[10] They're all of them copies of the Gospels, with pages of decoration, decorated initials, and, usually, portraits or symbols of the Evangelists. And two things strike you immediately about them: the art is utterly abstract, as abstract as any art ever was; and it is complex to an extraordinary degree, without ever losing its unity and its proportion.

The Lindisfarne Book was written and drawn by Eadfrith, or Eadfrith,[11] Bishop of Lindisfarne, at Holy Island, a little before the year 700.

This [slide] is from the Gospel of St Matthew, Chapter 1, Verse 18,[12] which begins, in the Vulgate's Latin, 'Christi autem generatio sic erat'. The abbreviation for Christ's name, 'chi rho iota', occupies the whole top of the page, more than half the page, and the three letters are woven together into a single monogram, very irregular in its shape, and yet perfectly balanced. The page here appears to be slightly incomplete; the slide's not quite taking it in, all, so that there is a very slight appearance of imbalance there. But it's perfectly balanced if you look at it on the page itself [fig. 1]. Every millimetre of the letters in the monogram is occupied by an enormously complex system of ribbons and spirals, and knots, and circles, and they spill over at the corners and in the loops of the letters and at the cross of the 'chi' [fig. 2], yet without disturbing either the clarity of the writing or the proportions of the design.

There must be hundreds of elements in this one monogram. They repeat, and they echo and they balance one another, and yet I think none is ever repeated without some variation; and often, when you compare two figures that seem alike at first, you find them proceeding by quite different methods to quite different ends, though still related to each

FIG. 1. Lindisfarne Gospels (BL Cotton Nero D.IV), fol. 29r: Initial page for the opening of the genealogy of Christ (Matthew 1.18). By permission of the British Library.

FIG. 2. Lindisfarne Gospels (BL Cotton Nero D.IV), fol. 29r (detail).
By permission of the British Library.

other. You look at it, close up with a magnifying glass, and it seems rather florid, rather chaotic. You stand back and look again, and it's as classical, as perfectly placed on the page, as simple in essence, as those Japanese prints with a single spray of cherryblossom.

And beneath this extremely rich monogram, and combined with it into a single design, covering the whole page, there's another [work of art], no less striking, though quite different in character.[13] You see the four lines of text there, one large—here—two middle-sized, and one small, at the bottom. They give a perfect base, on which the monogram can stand. They give scale to it, as well as contrasting with it. All that wild dream of curves is gone. These letters are very angular. There is a place where there are three identical esses in one line, but no other letter is repeated in the same form in which it first appeared. Each has been separately designed, perfectly recognisable, yet always different. There are some ligatures: U and T are combined into a single letter; so are E and M; and the first four letters of 'generatio' are linked into one single form.

The angular letters are in complete contrast to the monogram. The one is all legato, the other staccato, yet they do seem to have something in common: not merely that they combine well, and contrast well, but the letters, being different, and yet seeming to repeat, and the elements of the decoration on the monogram seeming to repeat without ever being really alike, {is} much the same principle. So the letters combine into a pattern subordinate to the design, just in the way the elements of the monogram are; and no less meaningful, no less satisfying, than the monogram, though so completely different.

I think one of the few people writing today whom you can identify with certainty as a poet who is going to last is David Jones. He is also a designer, and particularly a designer of lettering. He maintains that the whole quality of a civilization, or a culture, can be shown in a very short inscription, or derived even from a single letter. Letters are not, to him, just an approximate notation of sound to be set down more or less automatically and read as fast as decent articulation permits. A year or two ago I had tea with David Jones while he was engaged on a piece of lettering in the Roman manner [fig. 3]. He'd got the letter T at the beginning of one line. As we talked, he suddenly fell silent. A look of abstraction came into his face. And he set down his teacup and his piece of cake, fiddled about till he got a pencil, and stood up to his easel, and slowly, slowly, very carefully, drew in the letter H. Then he sat down again; with a sigh, he said, "I'll have the E by Friday!"

F1G. 3. David Jones, title page for *The Tribune's Visitation* (London: Fulcrum Press, 1969). By permission of the Trustees of the David Jones Estate and the National Library of Wales; copyright by the Trustees of the David Jones Estate.

Well, I think that Eadfrith worked in some such spirit. There must have been days of thought in each of the letters on this page, and even on the pages which have no illumination.

This [second slide] is a different monogram—a different initial letter, {rather}.[14]

You'll find something which {at first sight looks very} unbalanced there. But when it's combined with the other letters on the page, the total design has an extreme solidity {about it}. On the pages of the text, the thing is done in what I think is called half-uncials, but the letters are rarely alike; you'll find C made in one line in half-a-dozen different ways. And so on. And every letter was drawn with much preliminary cogitation, much considering how its shape would affect the shapes of the rest of the letters on the page.

That is the way you've got to write poetry, you know: every word has got to be thought of with all that care.

If this seems rather complicated, there is more complication to come. Each of the gospels in the Lindisfarne book is preceded by a couple of pages,[15] one of which has a portrait of the evangelist; we'll not discuss that one here. The other is a page entirely filled with interwoven patterns—which I believe the writers call a carpet page. In these carpet pages, what you see at first sight is usually only the perpetual crisscross of lines, or perhaps some elements of the design, which may be mere ribbons, or may be forms that suggest the forms of birds, animals, foliage, extraordinarily simplified and changed [fig. 4].

One of the commonest elements is a cormorant. Someone, probably Eadfrith, has worked long on evolving this form, which stands for the cormorant, seeing how much could be left out while still keeping all that's essential to recognise the creature. He has brought it down to two or three lines; but these lines are so specific, so certainly the needful ones, that he can afford to fill in the body of the bird, which is naturally a very sombre creature, with all sorts of colours which contradict the natural appearance. It's often as bright as a parrot, though black and white are the only colours it has in nature; but the outline is so definite, as far as it goes, that you're not likely to make any mistake. I have tried to suggest, in my poem *Briggflatts,* how the light reflected from the water at certain times does seem to clothe the cormorant's shining body in a variety of colours—I have seen it often in quiet harbours about dawn.[16] But you needn't necessarily believe that Eadfrith had any such effect in mind. He was so sure of the elements of his drawing that he could afford to play with the rest.

Fig. 4. Lindisfarne Gospels (BL Cotton Nero D.IV), fol. 94v: "Cross-carpet" page for the opening of Mark (detail). By permission of the British Library.

In spite of the brilliant coloured hatching, in spite of the impossible attitude in which most of the cormorants are stretched, in spite of all these violent outrages on natural history, the lines on the page seem distilled essence of cormorant, more real than the living bird itself.[17]

Well, I won't worry you with other details. But as you gaze at one of these so-called carpet pages, little by little, the confusion of ornament sorts itself out, you notice how carefully balanced the whole thing is, and a great cross emerges from the welter of ornament [fig. 5]. There are occasions when the cross is made conspicuous, but usually it requires a good look at the page before you identify the cross. I fancy this must have been Eadfrith's way of implying that if you looked steadily at all the innumerable details which are all we ever see of the world you might detect amongst them a symbol of unity which, for him, was the symbol of Christianity.

What would have astonished later artists of a different tradition is that Eadfrith does not emphasise this cross, or very rarely does. He doesn't force it on the beholder. He leaves him to find it, to discover it for himself, to learn what holds the page together, and discovering it in this way, it stays far more firmly in your mind than a great contrasty cross thrown at you, so to speak.[18]

There's a tomb in Hexham Abbey which is known as the tomb of King Aelfwald [fig. 6].[19] Some archaeologists say that it's nothing of the sort, that it really belongs to a much later age. I think they are wrong, but even if they are right, it still shows how a good tradition can permeate everything and endure. Unfortunately the canopy over the tomb prevents us taking photographs of the whole design, which is one of the vine as the tree of life. The particular vine in question is very clear and unencumbered, very symmetrical, although when you look carefully you find that no two leaves are alike: there are small differences in all of them. But near the top of the vine there are four leaves which group themselves into a little, inconspicuous cross, which it's quite easy to overlook. The same trick done in a different element that Eadfrith has been playing on the readers of his Gospels.

Well, at this point I am going to disappoint any of you who may happen to have neat, efficient, academic minds. I'm not going to explain the bearing of all this on poetry. I think that if you need definitions and words derived from Greek to demonstrate what the Lindisfarne Book has in common with the best of music and poetry you are not very likely to understand the arts at all profoundly anyway.

FIG. 5. Lindisfarne Gospels (BL Cotton Nero D.IV), fol. 94v. By permission of the British Library.

FIG. 6. Tomb cover, Hexham Priory
(from Charles Clement Hodges, *Ecclesia
Hagustaldensis: The Abbey of St. Andrew,
Hexham* [Edinburgh: privately printed,
1888]).

But if you will look long and carefully at the Lindisfarne Book and then turn to—oh, let's say Edmund Spenser's *Fowre Hymnes,* or Ezra Pound's Cantos, I think you'll find the supposed difficulties of their very complex art have vanished. I do not mean that either Spenser or Pound has made as perfect a design as Bishop Eadfrith, but each has made something of the same nature. There seems at first to be a confusion of detail and decoration, but the balance is never lost, and the main design shows through, ultimately, without insisting on itself.

You could make a closer analogy between the frontispieces of the Lindisfarne Book and that great Northern poem, *Sir Gawain and the Green Knight.*[20] There the poet never forces his allegory. The whole thing is allegorical from beginning to end, yet he never takes you by the neck and says 'Get down to it, that's an allegory, you've got to interpret it', the way most allegorists do. The detail intertwines and repeats, and yet the richness of detail never obscures the balance, the beautiful balance and symmetry of the main design of that poem. And the detail is simplified, almost abstract, just as the cormorants on Eadfrith's page are simplified. Neither Pound nor Spenser simplifies detail any more than that.

Of course art is not always as complex as the *Codex Lindisfarnensis.* Perhaps it very seldom is. Sometimes it looks, at first glance, exceedingly simple—paintings like the Chinese geese in the British Museum, where everything seems to depend on the placing of the geese on the silk; poems like some of the Japanese *haiku;* or tunes in which one minimal shift of a key makes the whole thing memorable; some of the poems of, say, Catullus, are very simple, though Catullus can also be very formidably complex indeed. But usually, there's much more to it than the hearer or beholder realises at first. Those geese weren't placed on the silk by guess; it required some pretty complex geometry, a whole system of intricately related and balanced ratios. I don't mean that the artist could have given you a mathematical formula for them, but in some sense they were there in his mind before he dipped his brush in the dye.

Well, I've taken up a lot of your time talking about the Lindisfarne Book, partly because it seems to me to show qualities with which it is easy to draw analogies in music and poetry, and partly because Eadfrith seems to me one of the very great and very influential artists, and yet is never given his due share of attention in popular accounts of art, and partly also because Eadfrith was a Northumbrian.

I don't mean to suggest that his art had anything to do with his race. Indeed, the Angles who settled in Northumberland seem to have lived

on such easy terms with the Britons {among them}, that it would be hazardous to suggest that Eadfrith or Cuthbert or any other Northumbrian
who was not a nobleman was of purely Anglic race. Many must have had
British mothers. Even some of the kings married British women.[21] Race
{is a misty} notion anyway, and racial characteristics change with lightning rapidity.

But languages last pretty well, and cultures seem to last almost for ever.
Conquests and catastrophes bury them for ages, and yet sooner or later
they stir into life again. I don't think I am misrepresenting recent historians if I say that they believe that, race or no race, a fusion of cultures
took place in early Northumberland. What the Angles had to begin with
you can see in the finds from Sutton Hoo now in the British Museum;
there must have been similar things here; and they added the very abstract art of curving lines and great complexity which the Celtic people
developed in France and Belgium and Britain, before the Romans came
and overlaid it for some centuries with their imperial stuff.[22]

We have some of the graphic art that this fusion produced, notably
the Lindisfarne Book and its imitators, but also the cross at Bewcastle
[fig. 7]; if either *Beowulf* or *The Dream of the Rood* is a northern poem,
and both seem to be, we have some of its literature; and in Bede and
Alcuin we have some of its thought—and very striking thought it is,
when you get down to it. Northumberland failed politically. It might
have recovered from the Northmen, but after the Norman Conquest it
was governed as a conquered province of Norman England for five full
centuries, constantly repressed by the authorities at York.[23] In spite of
this at least some of the original Anglo-Celtic Northumbrian culture had
life in it for centuries. You can see it in the sepulchral crosses built into
the wall of the church at Bywell, a dozen miles up the Tyne;[24] it's twelfth
or thirteenth century work [fig. 8], still rich with the same impulse that
made the Bewcastle Cross, and that made the cross-carpet pages in the
Lindisfarne Gospels; and in many of the ballads you can find a drastic
simplification, which suggests the simplification of the cormorants in the
Lindisfarne Book, or of parts of *Sir Gawain*.[25]

Perhaps I am too hopeful in imagining that the impulse of Northumbrian culture may not yet have quite vanished from the north. I think
our best hope of an art or a literature of our own does not lie in imitating what has come to us from Rome or Europe or from the South of
England, but in trying to discern what is our own, and to develop it and
fit it for 20th and 21st century conditions.

FIG. 7. Bewcastle Cross, south and east faces (from W. G. Collingwood, *Northumbrian Crosses of the Pre-Norman Age* [London: Faber & Gwyer, 1927]).

FIG. 8. Tomb covers now set in the wall of the church of St. Andrew, Bywell.

It will be a very complex art, a difficult one, but I think its results need not be difficult to the beholder or the reader. It's not easy, first, to simplify detail till only the barest essentials of the detail are left. Second, to weave an enormous number of such details into an intricate pattern which yet keeps perfect balance and proportion. And thirdly, to set your central theme with infinite care in just the right place—which is the same place it would be in if there weren't any details[26]—and to leave it there without calling attention to it, leave it there for the reader to discover for himself.

TWO

Thumps

When I spoke to you here fourteen days ago I tried to suggest to you that the arts are closely related. They have all a common ancestry. In particular music and poetry are twin sisters born of the primitive dance. By studying one, you can understand much about the other, and every art of this family can throw at least some light on the procedures of the other arts. There will be more to be said about that later.

I also tried to find, from the pages of the Lindisfarne Book, what were the most striking characteristics of Northumbrian art, and suggested that they would be found reflected in some degree in Northumbrian poetry: and a similar connection might, I think, be traced between the arts of other cultures. Giotto and Dante have much in common. There are passages in the Persian epic which call to mind, very vividly, the lovely miniature paintings made six centuries later in Persia.

I would go further, and say that the finest Persian carpets could never have been designed except in the same culture which produced the qasidas of Manuchehri.[1]

But there are, of course, limits to the resemblances between the arts, even within a single culture. Painting and sculpture make their designs in space; music and poetry make theirs in time. It is the succession of sounds that traces an outline on the background of time.

Poetry and music part company at a later stage. Music begins with the repetitive noises, the stampings and flappings and clappings, made by the human body dancing, and imitates them at first with percussive instruments and then with others, including the human voice singing.

Poetry begins with the grunts and cries of the dancers, but as soon as it is conscious of itself it organises those noises into articulate words and sentences. Various scholars have collected some of the songs wild men sing at their dances. The famous anthropologist Boas set down a few. Sir Maurice Bowra has assembled many from the writings of the anthro-

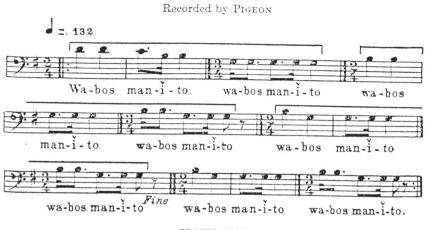

Recorded by PIGEON

TRANSLATION

Wa'bos (rabbit)   manIto' (spirit)

FIG. 9. A Menominee song (from Frances Densmore, *Menominee Music* [Washington, D.C.: U.S. Govt. Printing Office, 1932]).

pologists.[2] I have, or I used to have, at home, a little volume with many of the songs of the Menominee Red Indians.[3]

They dont make much sense. Some just repeat one phrase endlessly. Some suggest a mood, but have no other coherence. All the phrases are sad, or all are cheerful, but there is scarcely any other way in which they hang together apart from the form—all fit one tune, so all must share the form it dictates [fig. 9]. They are a convincing demonstration that poetry can exist without troubling itself to have any meaning at all, let alone a valuable one.

Those of you who enjoy the Blues will know that the same kind of thing still goes on. Some Blues songs have nothing in common between their stanzas except that they all suggest a gloomy outlook. They are none the worse for that. There is one that begins:

> What you goin' a do when the meat gives out
>   Ma honey?
> What you goin' a do when the meat gives out
>   Ma honey?
> What you goin' a do when the meat gives out?
> Goin' to sit on de stoop wiv ma mouf in a pout
>   For some time.

I forget what misfortunes are foreshadowed in the other verses, but they have nothing in common except the tune, the form the tune dictates, and the mood. And each shows in the first three lines the repetition which I just mentioned as a characteristic of Menominee Indian and other primitive poetry.

But the portrait of a mood is a convincing one. The words are still related very closely indeed to music; and it may be that the wretched singer gets some comic relief from the sounds which recall, rather remotely, the exhilaration of the dance.

From evoking moods to portraying character is a short step, but one that removes poetry a lot further from music. Music can manage moods, perhaps better than words can, but it makes a muff of drawing character, or of satire. There is a fine example in Ezra Pound's book, *Culture*. Pound translated the poem from the German of a nineteenth century collector of folklore, who found it in Siberia.

Praise Song of the Buck-Hare

I am the buck-hare, I am,
The shore is my playground
Green underwood is my feeding.

I am the buck-hare, I am,
What's that damn man got wrong with him?
Skin with no hair on, that's his trouble.

I am the buck-hare, I am,
Mountaintop is my playing field
Red heather my feeding.

I am the buck-hare, I am,
What's wrong with that fellow there with his eye on a girl?
I say, is his face red!

I am the buck-hare, I am,
Got my eyes out ahead
You don't lose me on a dark night, you don't.

I am the buck-hare, I am,
What's wrong with that bloke with a poor coat?
Lice, that's what he's got, fair crawlin' he is.

I am the buck-hare, I am,
I got buck teeth.
Buck-hare never gets thin.

I am the BUCK-HARE, I am,
What's that fool got the matter with him?
Can't find the road! Ain't got no road he CAN find.

I am the buck-hare, I am,
I got my wood-road,
I got my form.

I am the buck-hare, I am,
What ails that fool man anyhow?
Got a brain, won't let him set quiet.

I am the buck-hare, I am,
I live in the big plain,
There's where I got my corral.

I am the buck-hare, I said so.
What's wrong with that loafer?
He's been to sleep in a bad place, he has.

I am the buck-hare,
I live in the bush, I do,
That's my road over yonder.

I am the buck-hare, I said so,
Women that don't get up in the morning,
I know how they look by the chimney.

I am the buck-hare, I said it,
I can tell any dumb loafer
Lying along by the hedge there.

I am the buck-hare,
Women don't love their men?
I can tell by what their cows look like.[4]

There is nothing very consecutive about the buck hare's reflections,
but already they are not far from poems familiar to us in anthologies.
Compare them for a moment with a poem by that most sophisticated
Elizabethan, Sir Walter Raleigh:

The Lie

Goe soule the bodies guest
    vpon a thankelesse arrant,
Feare not to touch the best
    the truth shall be thy warrant:
Goe since I needs must die,
    and giue the world the lie.

Say to the Court it glowes,
    and shines like rotten wood,
Say to the Church it showes
    whats good, and doth no good.
If Church and Court reply,
    then giue them both the lie.

Tell Potentates they liue
    acting by others action,
Not loued vnlesse they giue,
    not strong but by affection.
If Potentates reply,
    giue Potentates the lie.

Tell men of high condition,
    that mannage the estate,
Their purpose is ambition,
    their practise onely hate:
And if they once reply,
    then giue them all the lie.

Tell them that braue it most,
    they beg for more by spending,
Who in their greatest cost
    seek nothing but commending.
And if they make replie,
    then giue them all the lie.

Tell zeale it wants deuotion
    tell loue it is but lust
Tell time it meets but motion,
    tell flesh it is but dust.
And wish them not replie
    for thou must giue the lie.

Tell age it daily wasteth,
    tell honour how it alters.
Tell beauty how she blasteth
    tell fauour how it falters
And as they shall reply,
    giue euery one the lie.

Tell wit how much it wrangles
    in tickle points of nycenesse,
Tell wisedome she entangles
    her selfe in ouer wisenesse.
And when they doe reply
    straight giue them both the lie.

Tell Phisicke of her boldnes,
    tell skill it is preuention:
Tell charity of coldnes,
    tell law it is contention,
And as they doe reply
    so giue them still the lie.

Tell fortune of her blindnesse,
    tell nature of decay,
Tell friendship of vnkindnesse,
    tell iustice of delay.
And if they will reply,
    then giue them all the lie.

Tell Arts they haue no soundnesse,
    but vary by esteeming,
Tell schooles they want profoundnes
    and stand too much on seeming.
If Arts and schooles reply,
    giue arts and schooles the lie.

Tell faith its fled the Citie,
    tell how the country erreth,
Tell manhood shakes off pittie,
    tell vertue least preferreth
And if they doe reply,
    spare not to giue the lie.

So when thou hast as I,
    commanded thee, done blabbing,
although to giue the lie,
    deserues no less then stabbing,
Stab at thee he that will,
    no stab thy soule can kill.[5]

Raleigh is less spontaneous. There is nothing in his poem as unexpected as the Buck Hare's leaps. The character he portrays is attitudinising a bit. But the form of the poem is more or less the same, and its intention is similar.

Perhaps I need not trace the stages by which poetry is elaborated any further. The Buck Hare is obviously within sight of the poetry known to anthologists and the general public of literate nations. It would be tedious to trace it step by step to the citified poetry of Pope or T. S. Eliot. You are all quite capable of doing that for yourselves, if you read enough poetry.

The adoption of articulate language differentiates poetry from music; but there are other ways in which poetry is shaped by the language it adopts.

Some of you are probably students of 'linguistics' and know a lot more than I do about the structure of languages. That study was scarcely invented, or at any rate systematised, when I was young. I have never learned its particular vocabulary, so you must forgive me if I seem to be speaking like a simpleton or teaching my grandmother how to suck eggs. Everything I have said, and everything I shall have to say is really pretty obvious, and my only intention is to remind you of things you know already. There are many features which all languages have in common, but there are also many which belong only to certain groups of languages which necessarily affect the poetry written in them.

Some languages have what Sinologists call 'tones'. You know how in Chinese

'Ciao ciao'

means something quite different from

'Ciao ciao'.

Now if your language dictates the tone relations between one syllable and the next, or between the beginning and end of one syllable, you can only sing a line to music that follows the same general pattern of tones, that is, of pitch, from note to note. This limitation does not worry us in England. Our syllables have pitch too, but it is not fixed. Sometimes we use it to indicate shades of meaning, but even then it is usually associated with stress, which we do notice, so that the change of pitch gets overlooked. We are hardly aware of it unless we are paying very special attention to it. But it was of some importance in ancient Greece: at least, that is a common opinion. The Alexandrian grammarians invented the Greek accents to indicate 'tones'. They have nothing to do with stress.

Now, Greek choruses were sung, and lyrics were sung to an accompaniment, and even the speeches in their plays and the epic itself were chanted. I have no idea whether anybody has investigated the relations between Greek accents and the music that went with Greek poetry, but some such relation must have existed and must have been at once a restriction to the poet and a beauty in the poetry he composed. The audience was meant to hear what the chorus had to say, and it could not have done so if the syllables had been sung on the wrong pitch. The words would have seemed garbled.[6]

When Alexander's conquests spread the Greek language amongst alien peoples, who took no account of pitch, pitch became meaningless in the koiné—'standard Greek'—BBC Greek. In fact, it was because of this that the grammarians invented the accents—they would have been unnecessary to a public that knew from childhood how Greek was pronounced. But people soon ceased to be aware of pitch as a necessary part of language and poetry, except the scholars; so the poets from Syria and Africa and so on, soon stopped taking any notice of it as an element in their poetry.

Again, very many languages distinguish quantity, that is, the relative time it takes to pronounce a syllable. I think most English people are hardly aware of it, for reasons I will explain presently. But in German, as it is spoken by poor Berliners, for instance, quantity is very noticeable, even exaggerated. Berliners drawl the long syllables and clip the short ones. The distinction of long and short is important in many languages. Most of you have met it in Greek or Latin. In Latin it is fairly crude, a rough and ready distinction. The Greeks seem to have distinguished three lengths of syllable, though not consistently enough for the grammarians to frame rules for the middle length. Persian and Arabic describe their prosody in different terms, but if you were to adapt it into the terms used for Greek and Latin, you would find them distinguishing four different lengths of syllable—though quantity is rapidly disappearing from contemporary Persian speech.

Here again the words and their music have to be matched. It will not do to sing a long syllable to a short note or stretch out a short syllable to a long note. A Persian or Roman poet was free from worry about pitch, which nobody noticed in his language, but quantity was an important part of the spoken language: roughly as important as the length of a note is in music. Consequently it became the most prominent feature in their versification.

Quantity exists in English too, and poets who admired Latin and Greek poetry have tried to use quantity in English. There is nothing impossible about it, nor is it especially difficult, but in English quantity is not a fixed characteristic of the syllable. A syllable may be short when there is no stress on it but long the moment it is stressed. Consequently the pattern is easily lost. One reader may put his stresses in a different place from the other, and so disturb the sequence of long and short.

In Persian one of the easiest effects for a poet to get is to arrange the stress on the short syllable. That is possible, but very difficult in English, for by stressing the syllable you almost always lengthen it, thus destroying the pattern.

But in spite of the difficulties very many English poets have been constantly conscious of quantity, and a few have tried to write in it, in adaptations of classical metres. One of the best was Campian,[7] a poet who was even more of a musician than a poet. Probably the best example of all was written by Edmund Spenser.[8]

You must distinguish between these poets who were trying to use quantity in English, and the much larger number of poets who have tried to transfer patterns used with quantity by Greek or Latin poets to a pattern of stresses in English. Victorian hexameters are almost all stress patterns following the scheme of a quantity pattern. Spenser's attempt has been anthologised quite a lot recently, but I hope you will forgive me for reading it now. True quantity, not stress, is what he aimed at.

Iambicum Trimetrum

Vnhappie Verse, the witnesse of my vnhappie state,
    Make thy selfe fluttring wings of thy fast flying thought,
    And fly forth vnto my Loue, whersoeuer she be:

Whether lying reastlesse in heauy bedde, or else
　　Sitting so cheerelesse at the cheerfull boorde, or else
　　Playing alone carelesse on hir heauenlie Virginals.
If in Bed, tell hir, that my eyes can take no reste:
　　If at Boorde, tell hir, that my mouth can eate no meate:
　　If at hir Virginals, tel hir, I can heare no mirth.
Asked why? say, Waking Loue suffereth no sleepe:
　　Say, that raging Loue dothe appall the weake stomacke:
　　Say, that lamenting Loue marreth the Musicall.
Tell hir, that hir pleasures were wonte to lull me asleepe:
　　Tell hir, that hir beautie was wonte to feede mine eyes:
　　Tell hir, that hir sweete Tongue was wonte to make me mirth.
Nowe doe I nightly waste, wanting my kindely reste:
　　Nowe doe I dayly starue, wanting my liuely foode:
　　Nowe doe I always dye, wanting thy timely mirth.
And if I waste, who will bewaile my heauy chaunce?
　　And if I starue, who will record my cursed end?
　　And if I dye, who will saye: *this was, Immerito?*[9]

I wish Spenser had found time to write much more of this sort, for the movement of the lines I have just read seems to me a very lovely one. Many modern English poets have had a go at quantity, but I imagine most of them were counting the syllables on their fingers rather than hearing them, so that most of the results seem pretty crabbed or take refuge in queer 'poetical' diction. Here is one early attempt of my own.

Dear be still! Time's start of us lengthens slowly.
Bright round plentiful nights ripen and fall for us.
Those impatient thighs will be bruised soon enough.

Sniff the sweet narcotic distilled by coupled
skins; moist bodies relaxed, mild, unemotional.
Thrifty fools spoil love with their headlong desires.

Dally! Waste! Mock! Loll! till the chosen sloth fails,
huge gasps empty the loins shuddering chilly in
long accumulated delight's thunderstorm.

Rinsed in cool sleep day will renew the summer
lightnings. Leave it to me. Only a savage's
lusts explode slapbang at the first touch like bombs.[10]

An English poet may not wish to use quantity as the organising element in his verse: but he should keep his ear open for it—it is part of the language, and cannot be altogether left out of account, as 'tone' is.

The Romans, like our own poets, had a public which was at first scarcely aware of quantity. The oldest Latin verses we can find are written by stress with a heavy decoration of alliteration, like our own most ancient verse. The first Roman poets to imitate Greek quantitative measures must have had a difficult time. Yet they did at last succeed, so well that some people, myself for one, think that a certain translation of Sappho by Catullus is better in Catullus's version than in Sappho's original.[11] Nevertheless stress was always noticed, and Vergil often arranged his stresses in a pattern that formed a sort of counterpoint to the quantitative pattern. And later stress reasserted itself and threw quantity out, except amongst academic poets such as Ausonius or Claudian. The church hymns are more stress patterns than quantity patterns as a rule.

It may seem strange to say that Latin poetry first comes to life after the Roman Empire had disintegrated. It is not strictly true, for there were poets of far greater genius in classical times than in the sixth and seventh centuries. Yet the best of them have something academic about them, something imitative, and perhaps this is a result of the cramping effect of writing in a system of quantity which was foreign to their language. By comparison, there is a noble freedom and directness both of diction and of rhythm which gives extraordinary splendour to the early Christian hymns and wonderful freshness to lay songs from the dark ages. They were written in harmony with the language, not against its grain.

Our language, so far back as we can trace it, has taken account mainly of stress. Quantity, when we are aware of it, and tone, which we are hardly ever aware of, are constantly altered and adapted to the pattern of stress, as much in conversation as in poetry. The *measure,* that is, the correspondence between the verse and whatever music the poet had in mind, is reckoned from stress to stress—bar to bar. This is obvious enough if you are reading Old English, though some scholars seem to obscure it. But later, men became acquainted with Latin metrics, and then with French. There is no real stress at all in French, so that the French count syllables—a very crude kind of reckoning by quantity—and English poets writing for a nobility that spoke French more readily than English tried to imitate them.

In Old English poetry there are usually four thumps to a line, and between the thumps, or in front of them or behind them, the poets were free to cram as many less emphatic syllables as they could pronounce without gabbling, or as few as they liked—even none at all. If you read the sections on metre in your Old English grammars without letting the authors technical terms hypnotise you, you will see that the description I have just given fits exactly. In addition, there was usually a pause of some sort between the second thump and the third. There are exceptions—three thumps instead of four, sometimes five—and minor variations, but that is the general pattern: thump, thump, pause, thump, thump; with the unstressed syllables trooping around in considerable disorder. That disorder is the seed of variety, and gives the old verse its liveliness and suppleness.

The moment poets began to count syllables, their difficulties began too—or the difficulties of the prosodist who tried to explain what the poet was doing. The notion was of a regular alternation of stressed and unstressed syllables, or of one stressed and two unstressed. But that is not the way the English language comes to our lips. If poetry is to fit such a pattern, one of two things must happen: either the language becomes stilted and cramped, or you introduce a polite fiction according to which syllables that have no real stress, or only the faintest, are counted as stressed. In theory the line of ten syllables imported from France should run

> Ti-tum ti-tum ti-tum ti-tum ti-tum

or

> Tum-ti tum-ti tum-ti tum-ti tum-ti

or some combination of these.

In practise it is continually reverting to the four stresses of Old English.

> Whán that Aprílle with hir shóures sóte

or

> To bé or nót to be, thát is the quéstion

I'm sure none of you think Shakespeare meant to be read:

> To bé or nót to bé, that ís the quéstion

I leave it to you to trace this reversion to Old English measures, through English heroic verse and blank verse. If you pronounce it naturally, you will find the reversions far commoner than the supposed pattern of five stressed, five unstressed, even when you allow the pairs of syllables to be turned around whenever the poet fancies. A few poets, mainly in the XVIII c managed to stick close to the theoretical pattern.

Dr Johnson once said something to the effect that Mark Akenside, the Newcastle poet, wrote perfect blank verse, by which Johnson meant ti-tum ti-tum etc. But Dr Johnson did not recommend anybody to imitate Akenside, or even to read him. He said, I think, that it was impossible to read him. I am quoting from memory.[12]

Allow the words to take their natural stresses and forget the theory altogether, and you will find a far more interesting and varied rhythmic structure than any that could be derived from or fitted into the fancied pattern.

> Of mán's fírst disobédience and the frúit
> of that forbídden trée whose mórtal táste
> brought déath into the wórld, and all our wóe

Notice where Milton has put three stressed syllables together in a row — taste brought death — and how you get four stresses with a pause between second and third if you read 'mortal taste brought death', making a line you might find in *Beowulf*. Milton is full of energetic rhythms of this sort, which almost make up for his inversions and latinisations of English.

The line of four stresses is not confined to English. There is something very like it in the oldest Welsh or proto-Welsh or British poem, the *Gododdin* of Aneurin,[13] though the stresses are less marked and alliteration is used more sparingly than in *Beowulf*. But I think these are the oldest examples of it. You find something very like it again in the splendid Spanish epic fragment, the *Cantar del Cid*.[14] It is not absent from Norse poetry. Even the Persian epic, which stands with Homer above all other poetry, though [it] is organised on a very different system, a system of quantity, yet a very large number of its lines fall into a pattern of four stresses.

Perhaps four stresses is about as much as a man can utter quite comfortably without taking a minimum breath. Then the four stress line would be on a par with the theme four bars long which is so common in music, because four bars is about as much as an untrained singer can do at one mouthful with perfect comfort.

I do not want to make too much of this. There are many languages in which stress plays no part worth mentioning, and whose poetry would show no trace of a four-stress pattern.[15] But it so permeates English poetry that I think it possible to take the four-stress line as the normal one, one from which to vary, one with which others may be compared or contrasted.[16]

Pound spent many years of his youth in what he called 'breaking the pentameter'[17]—that is, getting rid of the tiresome drone of blank verse read by the supposed rules, and very often, in Victorian England, written with only a slight modification of those supposed rules. It cast its blighting shadow back onto the great poetry of former ages, inducing people to read it, not as it was written, by the poet's ear, but by the inept notions of prosodists.

But I think if Pound had read Shakespeare, or that marvel of beautiful end-stopped blank verse, *Arden of Feversham*,[18] by the natural movement of the words, he would not have found a pentameter, a line of five feet, but a line of four measures infinitely variable, and much nearer his own free style than he supposed. Some critics have complained that Pound uses too many spondees—that is, two stressed syllables side by side, and the same objection has been raised to my own verse: but I've shown you that it could be made just as freely against Milton if people read Milton naturally, and not, as I'm afraid most of them do, in a mechanical, dull sing-song.

And anyway, English is full of spondees. You will find them in all the liveliest poets. The effort to avoid them weakens the movement of the lines of XVIII c poets.

I am trying to suggest that poets should bear the peculiar features of their own language in mind, even when they are engaged in trying to naturalise some excellence they have found in a foreign poet. Greek patterns, French patterns, dont fit English words at all smoothly. And if you want the fit to be free from wrinkles, even American patterns should be used very gingerly.

THREE

Ears

I think I proposed last time that English poets should bear in mind the length of time it takes to speak a syllable—its quantity—even though quantity, in English, is not constant enough to be used very often with confidence as the main means of organising a verse.[1] Stress often lengthens a short English syllable and sometimes the absence of stress shortens a long one; so the reader doesnt always know how to pronounce the line, if there is no music with it to help him.

Of course, long ago, there usually was music. Songs were sung and verse tales were chanted. In Persia at the present day, if you want to hear the classical poets properly you go to a recital, where two or three instruments and a learned singer keep the tradition alive. If you listen to them frequently, you are not likely to write such silly things about, say, Hafez, as some English orientalists do.[2]

The radio day begins in Persia with a canto of the epic, chanted in a way which may have changed in detail down the ages, but is the same in essence as it always was.

I have seen a miniature which shows how the artist, four or five centuries ago, thought the epic was chanted nine centuries ago. The singer, the ravi or jongleur who reads for the poet,[3] has the book open in front of him. There is an orchestra in one corner of the room, accompanying the chant. In the centre of the room dancers are miming the action, while the king looks on from his throne; and Firdosi himself, the author of the epic, is conducting. That is how a poetry reading ought to be arranged, but it cannot be done for five pounds and your train fare, with no time for rehearsal.

The Persian poet in the middle ages moved about with a whole company of highly paid helpers and their servants, and even when times

---

The title of this lecture is given as "Ears" on the first page and "Ear" on all others.

degenerated and kings had less to spare for civilised entertainment, the poet needed his ravi, his singer. You all know, of course, how the Provenzal poets, the troubadours, had each his jongleur, who played the lute and sang the principal's verses.[4] By the end of the middle ages times were harder still for poets, and they took to playing their own accompaniment and singing their own poems. When Wyat says: 'my lute, awake!' he is not just making a conventional noise. The lute was real, and he really played it. We have no independent evidence of Wyat doing so, but there is no reason to doubt it.[5] Other poets did. He lived in a court where music and poetry were expected of everyone, where King Henry VIII himself wrote good music and fairly good poems, some of which are extant, and played not the lute only but the recorders as well. He had a fine collection of instruments.

It sometimes amuses me to see the strange figure Ann Boleyn makes in popular history books (of all sects), a kind of cinema vamp, or a figure of physical beauty. She was not a bad looking lass, but her charm for Henry was that she was a most civilised person. She had been taught at the court of Margaret of Navarre, that learned poetess and story teller, who gathered all the intellect of France under her roof.[6] I imagine Ann was a protestant or something close to it (it was the latest fashion) before she ever met Henry. Her first intimate friend when she returned to England—at about the age of 15[7]—was Wyat. He wrote verses for her even when the king had declared his interest—and Henry put up with it. I think it is worth mentioning this now that so many people regard Henry as an ogre. At any rate his court had time to cultivate music and poetry, separately and together.

The music of that age is more familiar to us now than it was at the beginning of this century. Still, its cadences are not always familiar to people who have listened perforce mainly to pop or to the standard list of German-Italian classical music. I want to play some of it for you, to accustom your ear to the trick of it. Particularly, I want you to notice the effect got when, as often happens, a long note, or sometimes a long pause, is carried on beyond the bar (or where a modern writer would have drawn a bar).[8]

If you draw out a syllable in this way the result is very puzzling to literal minded people who take prosodists seriously. It seems as though the poet had stumbled and muffed his beat.

In fact, this syncopation makes it possible to use a far larger and more varied and subtler array of rhythms. But a curious thing happened. Wyat did not print his poems, and the Elizabethan editors who did, a generation later, were neither poets nor musicians, though they must have known something about prosody. When Wyat left a long syllable to carry on over the bar,[9] or intended a pause to suppress the beat, they thought this was just his incompetence, or that he had been misrepresented by the people who copied out his verses. The editors rewrote Wyat wholesale, trying rather ineffectually to reduce his subtle rhythms to ti-tum ti-tum ti-tum etc.[10] For many years editors felt that something must be wrong, and each editor had another shot at rewriting Wyat, right down to Sir Arthur Quiller-Couch in his *Oxford Book of English Verse*.[11] Wyat's real poetry was only rescued at last after quite a bit of this century had passed by.

That is something to be remembered when you think of the efforts Pound and Yeats were making in 1910 and thereabouts to bring some subtlety to the stiff Victorian verse they inherited.[12] They had never seen Wyat's real work. They did find models at last, but in poetry much below Wyat's standard, and in some of the music I am going to ask [my assistant] to play to us now.

NOT MY <u>HEART</u>, BUT <u>MY</u> HEART[13]

When Arnold Dolmetsch began to revive old instruments and old music, Pound and Yeats were soon aware of it.[14] Pound had worked with Walter Rummel, trying to puzzle out the tunes of Provenzal poetry.[15] But I think it is possible that the music that helped them to modify their rhythms was current a little earlier. Sometime in the 1890's Frederic Keel published a collection of Elizabethan songs, and madrigals arranged as songs, with piano accompaniment modified from the lute tablature.[16] It was still usual then for people to sing and play in London drawingrooms, and Yeats and Pound were at home at many more or less highbrow teaparties, where it is almost certain that they heard people singing Keel's versions. Certainly they did not wait for the *scholarly* resurrection of the Elizabethans. Fellowes was busy with that before the end of the First World War,[17] but Yeats was letting long syllables stretch over the beat earlier than that.

It was very late in literary history before poets began to forget the origins of their art and try to do without music. I have mentioned Campian, who was writing words and music together in 1610. Edmund Waller wrote songs with very beautiful rhythms in collaboration with the musician

Henry Lawes, in the middle of that century. People we do not now associate with music were associated with music nevertheless. Ferrabosco set several of Donne's poems, and other composers also had a go at Donne.[18] How many of Shakespeare's songs are by Shakespeare it is hard to say, but some at least he must have written with the composer by his side, and certainly Ben Jonson did the same.

The French poet Malherbe, one of the finest craftsmen who ever made verse, lamented to his friend Racan that he was severely handicapped because he had never been taught to finger the lute—he had to get someone else to do it for him. This about 1630.[19]

In the end it was less the poets who threw over music than the musicians who threw over poetry. They became more interested in harmony than in the melodic line, and in the improved instruments invented between 1650 and 1750 than in the human voice. So their line became more regular and commonplace. The subtle rhythms were restrained. Long fioriture had to be sung on a single syllable, murdering whatever poetry there was.[20]

So the poets gradually lost touch with music. They lost sight of the vast variety of possible rhythms. The noise they made became monotonous, and though they tried to compensate for that by wit, the monotony was infectious—the wit, the syntax, the diction, all became stereotyped. They aimed at neatness. They achieved the sterile emptiness of a hospital corridor. There was no substitute for music as a guide. A poet must write by ear (nearly all poets compose *aloud*); if he starts counting syllables and heeding the rules prosodists invent, writing verse becomes a pedantic game on a par with crossword puzzles.

FOUR

Wyat

[When I asked you to listen to Tudor songs a fortnight ago I had two things in mind: to get you to listen for a much wider variety of rhythm than it was customary to distinguish in the XVIII and XIX centuries, and a much closer liaison between music and poetry; and to introduce you to the things which made Sir Thomas Wyat the effective founder of modern English poetry.

It is usual to give Chaucer that honour; and Chaucer was certainly a poet of much wider range than Wyat. You might almost say that he was the inventor of the English language in the same sense in which Dante was the inventor of the Italian language. He is also clearly the best or the second best narrative poet in English.[1] So I shall have to justify deposing him in Wyat's favour.

Chaucer, like Wyat, was a man of the court, which spoke a dialect of French. Like Wyat, too, he was an occasional diplomat. French must have been as familiar to him as English, so that it is not surprising that at least his earlier work was based on French verse forms, French conventions of thought, and followed French fashions. Chaucer's line is a French line—the syllables are counted.] The strength of the old English system of four stresses is so great that Chaucer often follows it more or less unconsciously, but at least he never goes further from the French count of syllables than he can excuse on the grounds of poetic licence. The texture of the verse is French. It echoes the sweetish noises of the French romance poets and does very little with the coarser, though stronger, unifying thread of alliteration, which is particularly English. The architecture, the total shape of each poem in Chaucer is French: that is, at that date, the form is a very loose fit for the matter, leaving room for all

---

This lecture is transcribed here from the tape (see "A Note on Texts"); the opening, missing from the tape, is supplied from the MS.

manner of discursiveness. That is almost always entertaining in Chaucer, who was a man of great genius, but it was a fatal invitation to the long-winded bores who imitated him.

When Chaucer went further abroad and began to use Italian stories and themes his limitations became clearer. If you read his *Troilus and Criseyde* alongside Boccaccio's *Filostrato,* of which it is partly an expansion and partly a translation, you will find that Chaucer is much slower and much wordier than his model. His elaborations and interruptions and moralisings deprive the story of the rush and drive that it has in Boccaccio, they blunt its sharp edges and muffle its impact. Of course, that suits the sentimentalists too. Chaucer's is still a great poem, but not such a great poem as Boccaccio's. Again and again Boccaccio says in a few words what takes Chaucer many lines. The tension has been let down everywhere and the hard Italian story softened into something very like French romance; a rather misty, garrulous prettiness in place of the clear and pitiless Italian. It takes all Chaucer's humour and observation to get away with it.

Chaucer had other things on his mind than cogency. He was more or less consciously creating a literary language for the class he wrote for, dipping into all the dialects of English for useful words and importing French words wholesale. Besides, he was exercising his eye for character, the comic genius which no other English writer except Charles Dickens has ever possessed to such a degree. His humour, in this sense, is almost the only thing about Chaucer which cannot be paralleled in French. It is so congenial to us that we accept him at once, without noticing how foreign he is in many other ways.

However, it wasn't really necessary for Chaucer to slow down his narrative to the French pace, or to spread his metaphors and images so wide. Just before his time the northern author of *Sir Gawain and the Green Knight* had maintained a very high tension throughout a long poem.[2] There are no wasted words in *his* story. The shape of his poem was worked out beforehand, obviously, in some detail, just as Dante's was, and he kept to the plan. Chaucer is always losing sight of his plan. He comes back again to it, but he loses sight for a while. Moreover, the author of *Sir Gawain* kept his music English, though, like everyone else who wrote for the landed class in those days, he used many French words. The sound of the words in *Sir Gawain* is knitted up with the emotion that they are to convey much more closely than Chaucer usually managed; for Chaucer was, to some extent, making use of the sound patterns of a different language. Charles d'Orléans, his contemporary, was nearer to him in such ways than Langland, or the author of *Sir Gawain*.

I think that's why Chaucer's successors failed. They were trying to write French poems in English, and that was an awkward task for anyone of less genius than Chaucer. The Scots did better. The wars with England had given them native epic material, not addressed to Norman barons; so that no Scots poet could afford to ignore Barbour or Blind Hary, however rough and ready he thought them.[3] Thus the native element was strong enough to balance the French element and tighten the verse up. Whether you read Dunbar or Douglas, you can't fail to notice that the words and their main movement are Scots, not imitation French.[4] The virtues of these Scots poets have been exaggerated a good deal lately, for different reasons, by Hugh MacDiarmid, the Scottish nationalist, [and] by Ezra Pound, wanting to hit on the head the insensitive Tudor poets, but they had certainly more life than any English poet between Chaucer and Wyat—a matter of one hundred and fifty years.

I hope nobody will think that I am trying to belittle Chaucer. He seems to me one of our three greatest poets, but his work stands rather aside from the main line of English poetry, and in some ways it ignores the natural advantages of the English tradition. On the other hand, the literary language that he created has endured, with a modest amount of change, so that his diction sounds less strange to twentieth century ears than the diction of *Piers Plowman* or *Sir Gawain;* and the music he took from French romance has attractions: it is lighter than the music of most English poetry, less sticky. Chaucer could never have written the kind of noise that Keats rejoiced in: very sticky.

Wyat was even further from the ancient tradition of English than Chaucer was, but unlike Chaucer he went directly back to the head-springs of poetry; back to song itself, to music, and perhaps to the dance.

Our history books are so eager to get on with the dramatic story of the Reformation that they leave us half unconscious of the atmosphere in which the Reformation took place. The whole splendour and freshness of the early Renascence was bursting into Henry's court, in the days when Wyat was a man about the court, a diplomat, and a close associate of the king. With Wyat for ambassador, More for Chancellor and Holbein for court painter, Henry VIII was one of the most striking patrons of the arts in an age full of great patrons. Moreover the court spoke English—not French as in Chaucer's day, and it was fashionable to make the most of English customs, real or imaginary.

The court was full of musicians. Everybody danced, and the king himself played the lute, and the recorders, and wrote admirable music, and very tolerable poetry to go with it. There are no contemporary reminiscences to tell us that Wyat played the lute, but his poems continually imply that he did, and there's no reason to doubt the implication.[5] To my ear it sounds certain that he composed most of them with the lute in his hand. When he says 'My lute, awake!' or 'My lute, be still', he suits the action to the words. The music that he played was no doubt less complicated and perhaps less supple than the music made by the great Tudor composers that you were listening to a fortnight ago. It developed a little later in the century. But if you listen to Wyat's poems, you will hear some of the same rhythmic effects that they made use of.[6]

And incidentally, [for] those of you who are interested in music, Cornish, the best of Henry's court musicians, set a number of Wyat's poems. Listen to this one:

> Longre to muse
> On this refuse
> I will not vse,
>   But studye to forget;
> Lett my all go,
> Sins well I kno
> To be my foo
>   Her herte is fermely sett.
>
> Sins my entent
> So trulye mente
> Cannot contente
>   Her minde as I doo see,
> To tell you playne
> Yt ware yn vayne
> For so small gaine
>   To lese my libretie.[7]

I think you'll find something in the shape of that stanza that should recall sounds you heard amongst the Tudor music two weeks ago.

Here's another that sounds to me rather like those Tudors:

> All hevy myndes
>   Do seke to ese their charge,
> And that that moost theim byndes
>   To let at large.

Then why should I
    Hold payne within my hert,
And may my tune apply
    To ese my smart?

My faithfull lute
    Alone shall here me plaine;
For els all othre sute
    Is clene in vaine.

(64)

And again—I'm sorry to keep you so long over some of these—

Most wretched hart most myserable,
    Syns the comforte is from the fled,
Syns all the trouthe is turned to fable,
    Most wretched harte why arte thow nott ded?

No, no, I lyve and must doo still,
    Whereof I thank god and no mo;
Ffor I me selff have all my will,
    And he is wretched that wens hym so.

Butt yete thow hast bothe had and lost
    The hope so long that hathe the fed,
And all thy travayle and thy cost:
    Most wretched harte why arte thou nott ded?

Some other hope must fede me new;
    Yff I haue lost, I say what tho?
Dyspayre shall nott throwghe it ynsew,
    For he is wretched that wenys him so.

(73–74)

You see how the last line of each stanza of that slows and lengthens out, making an ordinary rhythm into a striking one, in a way used again and again by the composers.

    I'm trying to avoid some at least of the better-known anthology poems.

What menythe thys? When I lye alone,
I tosse, I turne, I syghe, I grone;
My bedd me semys as hard as stone:
    What menys thys?

I syghe, I playne contynually;
The clothes that on my bedd do ly
Always methynks they lye awry:
What menys thys?

In slumbers oft for fere I quake;
Ffor hete and cold I burne and shake;
Ffor lake of slepe my hede dothe ake:
What menys thys?

A mornynges then when I do rysse
I torne vnto my wontyd gysse;
All day after muse and devysse
What menys this?

(99)

Sometimes you feel as though it would be no hopeless task to try to re-invent the notes of the tune. Notice the last lines of this stanza, which echoes right through Elizabethan music:

It was my choyse, yt was no chaunce
That browght my hart in others holde,
Wherby ytt hath had sufferaunce
Lenger, perde, then Reason wolde;
Syns I ytt bownd where ytt was free
Me thynkes ywys of Ryght yt shold
Acceptyd be.

(111)

And this too appears to have escaped most of the anthologies. The sounds in it are perhaps not quite so obviously made for music as some of the others', yet it is obvious enough; they make it clear that it was written to be played and sung, quite apart from the statement in it:

Blame not my lute for he must sownde
Of thes or that as liketh me;
For lake of wytt the lutte is bownde
To gyve suche tunes as plesithe me:
Tho my songes be sume what strange,
And spekes suche wordes as toche thy change,
Blame not my lutte.

My lutte, alas, doth not ofende,
 Tho that perforus he must agre
To sownde suche teunes as I entende
 To sing to them that hereth me;
Then tho my songes be some what plain,
And tochethe some that vse to fayn,
  Blame not my lutte.

(122)[8]

I daresay that you imagine that a highly cultured man, who was capable of writing such poems and spoke several foreign languages, would have been able to count up to ten, if he had a mind to: but right down to yesterday, and for all I know, to today too, the historians of literature kept on assuring us that Wyat couldn't. He tried to write by the number of syllables, French fashion, they say, or said, 'counting them on his fingers and getting the number wrong.'[9] That was written in 1929 in the *Times Literary Supplement*, when Bruce Richmond edited it and T. S. Eliot was his chief contributor. I prefer the evidence of my own ears, which tell me that Wyat wrote by the spoken sound or the sung sound of the words, not by their numbers, the number of syllables: words as they are spoken or sung, words arranged in swoops and loops of sound, not measured with a foot-rule or counted out like coins.

There are others who say: 'Poor fellow, nobody knew where the stress came in English in his day, no wonder he couldn't get stressed and unstressed to alternate properly.' But suppose he didn't give a damn about such wooden arrangements of stressed and unstressed? I don't believe that the people who spoke English about the court paused in doubt before a word, wondering what syllable to put the stress on. It's true that there was some disagreement about the stressing of the many words that Chaucer and his successors had adopted from French. Were they to be stressed as though they were English words, or as though they were still French? And the Tudor decision about that wasn't always the one that we have adopted. But they adopted it; they were in no doubt. They had made their choice between 'abundance' and 'abundance', and far oftener than not, it was the one which has, in the end, prevailed, namely, an English stress on the earlier syllable. But in any case Wyat used such a simple vocabulary, such a restricted list of words, that the problem, if there was one, didn't turn up as often for him as it did later for Shakespeare and his contemporaries.[10] In fact, there's nothing whatever to indicate that Wyat ever thought about scansion, in the critics' sense, at all. His words fitted his tune, or could be accommodated to it very easily, and that was all he required. Scansion is a heresy in English poetry, that wasn't introduced till Elizabeth's reign, and there's about half a century between Wyat's last poems and Puttenham's book that put scansion on its feet in English.[11]

I notice that [in] this edition of Wyat, the Muses' Library—{in} 1949—the editor, Kenneth Muir, seems to think that sonnets didn't have a tune. He thought that they at least had got to be written by ti-tum ti-tum methods, and he takes Wyat to task for failing.[12] But the word 'sonnet' is Italian, and means 'something sounded'—on an instrument. It was a musical form to begin with, rather like a minuet and trio: two tunes, each repeated once.[13] I don't think that had been forgotten in Wyat's day. The poets were too concerned with Petrarch to lose sight of *where* he found his favourite form. If Wyat's sonnets sometimes fail to fit exactly {into} the pattern the pedants made later on, independent of tunes and the origins of the form, it's not because he couldn't fit them, but because he didn't want to. They never contradict the form as a form, a musical pattern, only the rigid counted wooden uninteresting pattern of the prosodists.

I'd like to read a little more of his work; {amongst them} the anthology piece best known of his, but I'm afraid still often printed wrongly in anthologies.

> They fle from me that sometyme did me seke
>   With naked fote stalking in my chambre.
> I have sene theim gentill tame and meke
>   That nowe are wyld and do not remembre
>   That sometyme they put theimself in daunger
> To take bred at my hand; and nowe they raunge
> Besely seking with a continuell chaunge.
>
> Thancked be fortune, it hath ben othrewise
>   Twenty tymes better; but ons in speciall,
> In thyn arraye after a plesaunt gyse,
>   When her lose gowne from her shoulders did fall,
>   And she me caught in her armes long and small;
> Therewithall swetely did me kysse,
> And softely saide, *dere hert, howe like you this?*
>
> It was no dreme: I lay brode waking.
>   But all is torned thorough my gentilnes

Into a straunge fasshion of forsaking;
   And I have leve to goo of her goodenes,
   And she also to vse new fangilnes.
But syns that I so kyndely am serued,
I would fain knowe what she hath deserued.

                    (28)

And another {which is also in some of the anthologies}:

There was never nothing more me payned,
   Nor nothing more me moved,
As when my swete hert her complayned
   That ever she me loved.
      Alas the while!

With pituous loke she saide and sighed:
   Alas, what aileth me
To love and set my welth so light
   On hym that loveth not me?
      Alas the while!

Was I not well voyde of all pain,
   When that nothing me greved?
And nowe with sorrous I must complain,
   And cannot be releved.
      Alas the while!

My restfull nyghtes and joyfull daies
   Syns I began to love
Be take from me; all thing decayes,
   Yet can I not remove.
      Alas the while!

She wept and wrong her handes withall,
   The teres fell in my nekke;
She torned her face and let it fall;
Scarsely therewith coulde speke.
      Alas the while!

Her paynes tormented me so sore
   That comfort had I none,
But cursed my fortune more and more

> To se her sobbe and grone:
>   Alas the while!

>   (29)

> What no, perdy, ye may be sure!
> Thinck not to make me to your lure,
>   With wordes and chere so contrarieng,
>   Swete and sowre contrewaing;
> To much it were still to endure.
> Trouth is trayed where craft is in vre;
> But though ye have had my hertes cure,
>   Trow ye I dote withoute ending?
>   What no, perdy!

> Though that with pain I do procure
> For to forgett that ons was pure,
>   Within my hert shall still that thing,
>   Vnstable, vnsure, and wavering,
> Be in my mynde withoute recure?
>   What no, perdy!

>   (35)

You {will} have noticed how simple the language is. There are none of those Elizabethan mouth-filling polysyllables that mean so little. The syntax is quite straightforward; there are not many metaphors or similes. There are people who think that simplicity such as that is easy. In fact it is very difficult. You have to work hard and patiently to get rid of your long words and inside-out sentences. Look at that page, {if you can see it}.[14] That's Wyat's corrections to a fair copy of a poem which he had thought near enough finished to be written out in the book that he kept for his own choice of his poems. In 20 lines there are 37 changes, including corrections that have been themselves corrected, and whole new lines. They were made at several different times—enough to fill his spare time for weeks. And this *after* he had thought the poem finished.

I will read two more; one of them's a bit of rough satire:

> Ye old mule, that thinck yourself so fayre,
> Leve of with craft your beautie to repaire,
>   For it is time withoute any fable:
>   No man setteth now by riding in your saddell;

To muche travaill so do your train apaire,
    Ye old mule!

With fals favoure though you deceve th'ayes,
Who so tast you shall well perceve your layes
    Savoureth som what of a Kappurs stable,
    Ye old mule!

Ye must now serve to market and to faire,
All for the burden for pannyers a paire;
    For syns gray heres ben powdered in your sable,
    The thing ye seke for you must yourself enable
To pourchase it by payement and by prayer,
    Ye old mule!

                  (26)

And finally, one of the sonnets, not translated, but adapted from the Italian of Petrarch:

The longe love, that in my thought doeth harbar
    And in myn hert doeth kepe his residence,
    Into my face preseth with bolde pretence,
    And therin campeth, spreding his baner.
She that me lerneth to love and suffre,
    And willes that my trust and lustes negligence
    Be rayned by reason, shame and reverence,
    With his hardines taketh displeasur.
Wherewithall, vnto the hertes forrest he fleith,
    Leving his entreprise with payn and cry;
    And ther him hideth, and not appereth.
What may I do when my maister fereth
    But in the feld with him to lyve and dye?
    For goode is the liff, ending faithfully.

                  (4–5) [15]

That sonnet's a very free adaptation from one of Petrarch's.

{Now} Wyat has been held responsible for the spate of Petrarchian sonnets in English. He did in fact translate or adapt about 20 sonnets out of Petrarch's enormous output, and perhaps as many again from other Italians who followed some of Petrarch's habits. But the sonnets that Wyat translated are not particularly typical of the Petrarchan fashion. He left those to later {and} less able translators.

What Wyat found in Petrarch was largely what Petrarch took over from Provençal troubadour poetry. Wyat's own original poems have a strong troubadour flavour: like their poems, his were written to be sung, and he followed many of the conventions that they had first introduced—yet usually with a difference. The cruel mistress in Wyat's poems is not someone to despair over. He is quite ready to give her the chuck if she goes on refusing him.

The trouble with Petrarch and his imitators was that he would neither treat love realistically nor follow out the troubadour conception of love as a refiner of manners, nor the more exalted ideas introduced by Guido Guinizelli and Guido Cavalcanti, and carried so far by Dante, which came close to making human love merely a disguise for the love of God, and so prepared the way for Pico della Mirandola and the other neo-Platonists of the Renaissance.

To Petrarch love was mainly an excuse for displaying his skill as a versifier and his knowledge of classical mythology. He hardly ever pays any real attention to *Laura:* he focuses the reader's attention on his *own* cleverness, and that cleverness is far too often trivial, quite often a matter of puns. Petrarch's verse is from the first aimed directly at the coronation with laurel which he did indeed achieve in Rome {in later life}.[16] He had no humility. He loved neither the countess de Sade (Laura) nor God. Too many of his lines are mere perfunctory decoration.

Now all the Elizabethan sonneteers were infected more or less with Petrarch's bad example. Shakespeare breaks away from it very often and Spenser now and then; Sidney rarely; but Wyat is hardly touched by Petrarch at all. What he takes from him he brings back to the simplicity of feeling which Petrarch had lost, and a less pretentious, freer music. There is hardly ever any reason to remember where Wyat found his material; and indeed, for the most part, he found it in his own head (the translations are not so very many); or he found it in the eyes of Anne Boleyn, Elizabeth Darrell, and the other ladies who felt the force of his love and his poetry.

And I hope that many of you who've not gone beyond the anthologies of Wyat will do so; I've tried to {keep close} [   ], {amongst poems which are} [   ].

FIVE

Spenser

Last time I spoke to you I read you a few poems of Sir Thomas Wyat, and suggested that he, rather than Chaucer, ought to be regarded as the father of English poetry as we know it. Wyat went back, as Chaucer did not, to the very wellheads of poetry, in song and dance; and in spite of his interest in Italian verse, and his familiarity with French and Spanish, his vocabulary remained astonishingly simple and very English; and but for such echoes of the Provenzal troubadours as were more or less the common property of all Europe, he is uncommonly free from literary reference of any kind. Even the Troubadour echoes are faint in him. His words come in the sequence of their own music, which was also the sequence of the music they were set to, and pay hardly any attention to the imagined rules of poetry.

Because of this freedom, helped by a musician's ear, Wyat's rhythms are suppler, subtler and better wedded to the emotional sense of his words than those of nearly all other English poets, and yet he manages to keep his syntax simple and colloquial always. But only the less sophisticated of his followers preserved some of these virtues. You will find some of their work in the Elizabethan miscellanies. The men the literary histories concern themselves with, Surrey and Sackvile, chiefly, seem hardly to have understood what Wyat was up to.[1] Their lutes were not in their hands. They interested themselves in metrical regularities, such as English abhors. Blank verse, imported by them from Italy, had to be rescued from their precision and Anglicised before it was any use in this island.

So there was nothing whatever to prepare the English literary world for the sudden irruption of Edmund Spenser. I dont suppose any book in our whole poetical history has had so great and so lasting an effect as the *Shepheards Calender*.[2]

'Rude ditties tuned to shepherd's oaten reed',[3] and therefore to be sung, but not to his own accompaniment. You cant blow a pipe and sing at the same time. In fact, only parts of *The Shepheards Calender* seem intended to be sung: most of the dialogue and some of the other matter is one remove from song. But if the young Spenser lacked Wyat's supreme merit, he seemed to have all the virtues that Wyat lacked. Wyat has a somewhat narrow scope. You would never guess from Wyat's work that he was a most valued diplomat, or an accomplished linguist, or a trusted administrator. If we did not know that he was a friend of Cromwell as well as of Ann Boleyn, it would be hazardous to infer even that he was a Protestant, or inclined to be one. But Spenser, in the fancy dress of an Arcadian shepherd, manages to leave the world in no doubt about his Puritanism, his support of Leicester's party in politics,[4] his wide reading in many languages. Love, to Wyat, was the occasion for some graceful conventions and some psychological insight, but mainly for a song, words and music to delight without necessarily instructing anyone or discussing anything. To Spenser love is an emblem of man's deepest aspirations. If Spenser had a lute, he kept it in the back room. He has less rhythmic variety than Wyat; but he made words yield a music less dependent on rhythm, in which the varied pitch of vowels, the varied attack of consonants, a more marked rhythm, a much more insistent alliteration, almost drove the composer out of business. The words were their own music.

No poet in English, and not many poets in any language, have had such a lasting influence on poetry as Edmund Spenser. He made new starts in a score of different directions, and all he did he did with extreme skill; but not all he did was good for the future of English poetry. His faults as well as his virtues were and still are imitated, and have given English poetry its characteristic colour. Even the age of reason was not exempt from his influence, and from the early years of last century his influence revived and is still strong. Poets very different from Spenser have believed they were imitating him, and poets who thought they were following a system quite different from his have nevertheless used his procedures without noticing.

I think it is worth while drawing attention to the curious parallel between Spenser and Pound. Each began with a raid on the past: Pound imitated the troubadours, Spenser tried to imitate Chaucer. Each tried out a great many forms which are sometimes very elaborate and little used: each, for instance, wrote a sestina.[5] Each invented a diction of his own, which differed so much from ordinary English that Ben Jonson said Spenser 'writ no language' and the critics are never tired of saying much

the same about Ezra Pound.[6] Each liked archaisms, and neither both-
ered to distinguish between real archaisms and bogus archaisms. Each
planned a very long poem which was to mirror the world, and neither
planned it thoroughly enough, so that as time went on and their interests changed, the original plan had to be distorted to make room for new
ideas, so that the form is not easily grasped and the poem looks to impatient readers as though it were shapeless.[7] But by their endless interest in
the technical problems of poetry, each of them provided a great range
of tools other poets could make use of, a great gallery of models.

I dont mean, of course, that any poet could be successful by merely
imitating Spenser or Pound. The best of Spenser's direct imitators,
Michael Drayton, was a good poet, but not one of the really great. No, I
am thinking of poets very different in their aims who were able to choose
some process of Spenser's and use it for their own ends. Ben Jonson
might scorn Spenser's vocabulary, but he made use of sound patterns
in a way he could only have learned from Spenser. Milton owes at least
as much to Spenser as to Shakespeare. And long afterwards, it is hard
to see what would be left of Keats if we could take away what he owed to
Spenser.

It may seem as though the Eighteenth Century were a great interreg-
num in Spenser's reign; but it is not only true that Spenser's influence
did overbear that of Waller and Dryden in the end; but even Pope and
Samuel Johnson, when they wanted a great effect to end the *Dunciad* or
the *Vanity of Human Wishes,* took their note from Spenser. And I would
say that there are places where Wordsworth imagined he was imitating
Milton, but was really imitating the traces of Spenser in Milton.

The second half of Queen Elizabeth's reign is a very complicated
period in our poetical history. You might say that three new sets of ideas
were at work, as well as the ideas inherited more or less from Wyat.
Shakespeare was breaking down Italian blank verse into a very free system which was still useful to T. S. Eliot. Raleigh and Donne were importing, I think from Spain, a somewhat harsher kind of verbal music
and a system of realistic images for high-flown ideas still much used. But
even in Shakespeare, when he is not writing for the stage; and even in
Donne, it is not difficult to find lines that would never have been written
if Spenser had not been a few years earlier to show them how.

I daresay some of you are wondering why *I* make so much of Spenser.
You may have gathered that I want words to be related closely to music,
but Spenser does not seem to have written much to be sung. I want

the greatest possible economy of phrase, but Spenser takes his time. I like rhythms which are subtle and unsteady, but Spenser never strays far from the general pattern. And I like a poem with a clear form, a kind of architectural shape, while Spenser, though he can make such shapes beautifully, as you see in his hymns and epithalamiums, allows the *Faerie Queen* to sag and bulge and get lopsided.[8]

It is not *only* that he provided a set of tools which almost every poet since his time has made at least some use of. Spenser extended the range and the possibilities of poetry in very many directions. Political invective and political satire are there in *The Shepheards Calender* and *Mother Hubberd's Tale;*[9] the *Fowre Hymnes* tackle the most abstruse philosophy of his day, and not in mere imitation of Pico della Mirandola, or Ficino, but with modifications of his own. His *Amoretti* deal with love in its gentlest form, without the violence which salts Shakespeare's sonnets or much of Donne's work. There is much more variety in Spenser than people sometimes imagine.

But there is one characteristic almost always present. Almost every phrase is decorated as heavily as it will bear.[10]

Much decoration is hardly possible in verse written to be sung. The words must not compete with the notes. But Spenser handled words so as to make them their own music. Even the earliest scraps of his verse, written at school, make use of the sounds of words so fully that they leave no room for the musician to add anything to them. There is no such economy of means as Wyat had used. This abundance of decoration was Spenser's way all his life, and it has been the most persistent of his legacies to English poetry. There had been nothing of the sort in English poetry before Spenser, only a less sumptuous foretaste here and there in Chaucer. There was nothing like it in Italian and only an indication of it in French, in the poetry of du Bellay, which Spenser knew and translated, and in Ronsard.

You might say, not quite accurately, that Spenser had transferred the main interest from the rhythm of long and short, stressed and unstressed, to the succession of vowels and consonants, the alliterations, assonances and sequences which are useful helps in composing poetry but are not the fundamental things. As time went on Spenser wrote in this way more and more continuously and more and more ruthlessly. He would let his syntax stumble for the sake of an assonance or his rhythm grow mechanical for the sake of an alliteration. Some of the archaisms he used and some of the words he coined or imported from English dialects and foreign languages serve no other purpose than this of enriching the secondary music of vowels and consonants.

For this purpose too he invented or at least made free use of those doublebarrelled hyphenated adjectives which have become an addictive drug to English poets; and far too many adjectives altogether. Adjectives mostly weaken the noun they stand with and poetry with too many of them loses its energy and its touch with the world we feel and see.[11]

In short, Spenser imposed 'poetic diction' on English, more or less for the first time, and certainly for several centuries. He did it so well that it is easy to forget how fatal the example was to many lesser poets; and even in Spenser, when he grows tired or his attention wanders, its effect is wearisome.

You may consider that Milton commits worse outrages on syntax than any Spenser was capable of, but it was Spenser who gave the bad example. You may say that Pope's verse would be good to dance to if you had two wooden legs, but it was Spenser who first allowed himself to lose sight of rhythm and let mere metre take its place in the interest of secondary qualities. But the foundation of music is rhythm, and if you allow it to become monotonous or to stumble, no amount of vocal colour, no amount of urbanity or wit, will ever compensate for it.

I dont think I can be sure of showing you what I mean without reading you an example. This is early Spenser, from *The Shepheards Calender*, and it is free from the excesses of his mannerisms that you might find here and there in later work. Moreover, in this piece Spenser is far from neglecting rhythm: he plays some difficult tricks with it. The poem fulfils its function very splendidly, for though it is an elegy its mourning is a ceremony, a formality, not a cry of grief. But there is a tone of gorgeous unreality about it. It sets poetry away from the normal concerns of men and women, in a special language. It is not a stimulant, but a drug. And to the extent that later English poetry has kept this tone, it explains the indifference of the multitude to poetry.

> Vp then *Melpomene* thou mournefulst Muse of nyne,
> Such cause of mourning neuer hadst afore:
> Vp grieslie ghostes and vp my rufull ryme,
> Matter of myrth now shalt thou haue no more.
> For dead shee is, that myrth thee made of yore.
> *Dido* my deare alas is dead,
> Dead and lyeth wrapt in lead:

O heauie herse,
Let streaming teares be poured out in store:
O carefull verse.

Shepheards, that by your flocks on Kentish downes abyde,
Waile ye this wofull waste of natures warke:
Waile we the wight, whose presence was our pryde:
Waile we the wight, whose absence is our carke.
The sonne of all the world is dimme and darke:
The earth now lacks her wonted light,
And all we dwell in deadly night,
O heauie herse.
Breake we our pypes, that shrild as lowde as Larke,
O carefull verse.

Why doe we longer liue, (ah why liue we so long)
Whose better dayes death hath shut vp in woe?
The fayrest floure our gyrlond all emong,
Is faded quite and into dust ygoe.
Sing now ye shepheards daughters, sing no moe
The songs that *Colin* made in her prayse,
But into weeping turne your wanton layes,
O heauie herse,
Now is tyme to dye. Nay time was long ygoe,
O carefull verse.

Whence is it, that the flouret of the field doth fade,
And lyeth buryed long in Winters bale:
Yet soone as spring his mantle doth displaye,
It floureth fresh, as it should neuer fayle?
But thing on earth that is of most availe,
As vertues braunch and beauties budde,
Reliuen not for any good.
O heauie herse,
The braunch once dead, the budde eke needes must quaile,
O carefull verse.

She while she was, (that was, a woful word to sayne)
For beauties prayse and plesaunce had no pere:
So well she couth the shepherds entertayne,
With cakes and cracknells and such country chere.
Ne would she scorne the simple shepheards swaine,

    For she would cal hem often heme
    And giue hem curds and clouted Creame.
        O heauie herse,
Als *Colin cloute* she would not once disdayne.
        O carefull verse.

But nowe sike happy cheere is turnd to heauie chaunce,
Such pleasaunce now displast by dolors dint:
All Musick sleepes, where death doth lead the daunce,
And shepherds wonted solace is extinct.
The blew in black, the greene in gray is tinct,
    The gaudie girlonds deck her graue,
    The faded flowres her corse embraue.
        O heauie herse,
Morne now my Muse, now morne with teares besprint.
        O carefull verse.

O thou greate shepheard *Lobbin,* how great is thy griefe,
Where bene the nosegayes that she dight for thee:
The colourd chaplets wrought with a chiefe,
The knotted rushrings, and gilte Rosemaree?
For shee deemed nothing too deere for thee.
    Ah they bene all yclad in clay,
    One bitter blast blewe all away.
        O heauie herse,
Thereof nought remaynes but the memoree.
        O carefull verse.

Ay me that dreerie death should strike so mortall stroke,
That can vndoe Dame natures kindly course:
The faded lockes fall from the loftie oke,
The flouds do gaspe, for dryed is theyr sourse,
And flouds of teares flowe in theyr stead perforse.
    The mantled medowes mourne,
    Theyr sondry colours tourne.
        O heauie herse,
The heauens doe melt in teares without remorse.
        O carefull verse.

The feeble flocks in field refuse their former foode,
And hang theyr heads, as they would learne to weepe:
The beastes in forest wayle as they were woode,

Except the Wolues, that chase the wandring sheepe:
Now she is gon that safely did hem keepe,
    The Turtle on the bared braunch,
      Laments the wound, that death did launch.
        O heauie herse,
And *Philomele* her song with teares doth steepe.
        O carefull verse.

The water Nymphs, that wont with her to sing and daunce,
And for her girlond Oliue braunches beare,
Now balefull boughes of Cypres doen aduaunce:
The Muses, that were wont greene bayes to weare,
Now bringen bitter Eldre braunches seare,
    The fatall sisters eke repent,
      Her vitall threde so soone was spent.
        O heauie herse,
Morne now my Muse, now morne with heauie cheare.
        O carefull verse.

O trustlesse state of earthly things, and slipper hope
Of mortal men, that swincke and sweate for nought,
And shooting wide, doe misse the marked scope:
Now haue I learnd (a lesson derely bought)
That nys on earth assurance to be sought:
    For what might be in earthly mould,
      That did her buried body hould,
        O heauie herse,
Yet saw I on the beare when it was brought
        O carefull verse.

But maugre death, and dreaded sisters deadly spight,
And gates of hel, and fyrie furies forse:
She hath the bonds broke of eternall night,
Her soule vnbodied of the burdenous corpse.
Why then weepes Lobbin so without remorse?
    O Lobb, thy losse no longer lament,
      Dido nis dead, but into heauen hent.
        O happye herse,
Cease now my Muse, now cease thy sorrowes sourse,
        O ioyfull verse.

Why wayle we then? why weary we the Gods with playnts,
As if some euill were to her betight?
She raignes a goddesse now emong the saintes,
That whilome was the saynt of shepheards light:
And is enstalled nowe in heauens hight.
     I see thee blessed soule, I see,
     Walke in *Elisian* fieldes so free.
       O happy herse,
Might I once come to thee (O that I might)
       O ioyfull verse.

Vnwise and wretched men to weete whats good or ill,
We deeme of Death as doome of ill desert:
But knewe we fooles, what it vs bringes vntil,
Dye would we dayly, once it to expert.
No daunger there the shepheard can astert:
     Fayre fields and plesaunt layes there bene,
     The fieldes ay fresh, the grasse ay greene:
       O happy verse,
Make hast ye shepheards, thether to reuert,
       O ioyfull verse.

Dido is gone afore (whose turne shall be the next?)
There liues shee with the blessed Gods in blisse,
There drincks she *Nectar* with *Ambrosia* mixt,
And ioyes enioyes, that mortall men doe misse.
The honor now of highest gods she is,
     That whilome was poore shepheards pryde,
     While here on earth she did abyde.
       O happy herse,
Ceasse now my song, my woe now wasted is.
       O ioyfull verse.[12]

You may feel as I do that Chaucer was much nearer to the concerns of men than this is, and that Wyat was much closer to the essentials of poetry; but it seems at the same time as though all that has been most characteristic of English poetry for four centuries (with some intervals) sprang suddenly fullgrown into life when *The Shepheards Calender* was published, nine years before the Armada sailed, and a dozen before Shakespeare's first work.

SIX

After Spenser

Last time I spoke to you I tried to persuade you that Edmund Spenser gave English poetry its special characteristics. He invented so much, explored so widely and perfected so many useful processes that it was next to impossible for later poets to avoid being indebted to him. He was so much what his contemporaries called him, the Prince of Poets, that it is not surprising to find his vices as well as his virtues continually propagated by his successors. When I first considered the contents of these lectures I had some idea of demonstrating this by much reading, both of Spenser himself and of passages in later poets which show clearly the application of Spenser's patents to other men's manufactures. But on second thoughts it seemed to me useless to do so, since the evidence is there in every anthology and every general course of English literature.

Besides, an outsider like myself can be of most use when he points out something that teachers overlook, but they have never overlooked Spenser and his influence. Perhaps they are so used to it that they take it too much for granted. It is more entertaining to discuss Milton's very individual Latinisms than the debt he owes to Spenser, huge though it is. But they insist, very rightly, that Spenser must be read if you are going to understand English poetry; and if by chance you read poetry in other languages too you are not likely to miss the conclusion that the easiest way of distinguishing what is particularly English poetry from what is common to the poetry of many languages is by looking for the traces of Spenser.

Still, I dont want to exaggerate his influence, though it would be difficult to do so. Even in his own time there were poets who elaborated kinds of verse and processes within verse that Spenser never touched. Some of these have very little importance; they were fashions which soon died. Euphuism is inherently boring. Bombast is a vice of the stage, and when the theatre declined it declined too. Euphuism and bombast are merely two of the vices of bad poetry, and if they did not mar so much of Shakespeare's verse there would be no need to pay any attention to them at all. But when Lady Macbeth wants to tell us that the blood on her hands would redden the sea and says instead that it would the multitudinous seas incarnadine we have to be on our guard lest the prestige Shakespeare has earned for very different characteristics should leave us imagining that this preposterous tirade is poetry.[1]

Shakespeare wrote very effective plays. In some of them he shows an eye for human character comparable to that of Dickens, and in a few he displays a nimbleness of fancy for which it would be hard to find a parallel.[2] He was also a considerable poet. He would hardly have written *Venus and Adonis* if Spenser hadnt provided the tools, and his sonnets, though some of them are very individual, owe something to Spenser and something either to Raglegh or to whatever was the source of Ragleigh's harshness.[3] I am afraid that things like the multitudinous seas sound rather like parodies of Spenser at his most wilfully resonant moments. Shakespeare was capable of such virtuosity—akin to parody—that I suspect that somebody walked into the Mermaid one day with a poem by Donne or by Raghleigh and said: 'Just take a look at this' and Shakespeare said: 'Pooh! I can do that kind of thing in my sleep' and sat down there and then to produce 'The Phoenix and Turtle', his only piece in that manner, and the most impressive piece that manner ever produced.[4] Or again: few people would dispute that 'Full Fathom Five' is the most convincing sample we have of what can be done by the music inherent in the sound of words without much else to back it up.[5] It is so knitted together with correspondences of sound, vowel, consonant, quantity, stress, so complete in a tiny space that it quite outdoes Spenser at his own speciality of verbal music and leaves us with only two or three things in European poetry to set beside it—Goethe's 'Ueber allen Gipfeln ist Ruh' or Horace's 'O fons Bandusiae'; and I would add, one or two of Hafez's pieces.[6]

But Shakespeare did not add anything new to the methods of writing poetry except that, in common with other playwrights, he took part in the gradual modification of blank verse which took place between his young days and a time a little after his death. That is a commonplace of the schools, and I need not say much about it. The more the poets loosened the rules of blank verse set out by the people who first imported it from Italy the more the natural flow of the English language showed through, so that if you speak it as men do speak, and not in a special way reserved for blank verse, you find very often indeed that it has four stresses, not five, and is at least as much like a looser version of the old English line as like a looser version of the Italian one.

Blank verse was pushed even further in this direction when Milton took it over for his epic. Milton was at first an imitator of Spenser, both directly and through Ben Jonson. *Lycidas* is just *The Shepheards Calender* with a heavy infusion of pedantry. And Milton carries all his Spenserian habits with him into the largely four-stress blank verse lines of *Paradise Lost*. Unfortunately he added to them a peculiar syntax derived from Latin, which suited his own purposes fairly well, though it sometimes makes his page ridiculous; but it was fatal to his imitators, even in small doses and at a great distance in time, as you can see by reading Matthew Arnold.

For some reason Milton's most satisfying invention was overlooked in his time and has been very little imitated since—I mean the movement of parts of *Samson Agonistes*.

> SAMS. Oh, that torment should not be confined
> To the body's wounds and sores,
> With maladies innumerable
> In heart, head, breast, and reins,
> But must secret passage find
> To the inmost mind,
> There exercise all his fierce accidents,
> And on her purest spirits prey,
> As on entrails, joints, and limbs,
> With answerable pains, but more intense,
> Though void of corporal sense!
>   My griefs not only pain me
> As a lingering disease,
> But, finding no redress, ferment and rage,
> Nor less than wounds immedicable
> Rankle, and fester, and gangrene,
> To black mortification.
> Thoughts, my tormentors, armed with deadly stings,
> Mangle my apprehensive tenderest parts,
> Exasperate, exulcerate, and raise
> Dire inflammation, which no cooling herb
> Or medicinal liquor can assuage,
> Nor breath of vernal air from snowy Alp.

Sleep hath forsook and given me o'er
To death's benumbing opium as my only cure
Thence faintings, swoonings of despair,
And sense of heaven's desertion.

Or again:

CHOR. Just are the ways of God,
And justifiable to men,
Unless there be who think not God at all.
If any be, they walk obscure;
For of such doctrine never was there school,
But the heart of the fool,
And no man therein doctor but himself.

Or the very well known choral passage

See how he lies at random, carelessly diffused,
With languished head unpropt,
As one past hope, abandoned,
And by himself given over,
In slavish habit, ill-fitted weeds
O'er-worn and soiled.
Or do my eyes misrepresent? Can this be he,
That heroic, that renowned,
Irresistible Samson? whom, unarmed,
No strength of man, or fiercest wild beast, could withstand;
Who tore the lion as the lion tears the kid;
Ran on embattled armies clad in iron,
And, weaponless himself,
Made arms ridiculous, useless the forgery
Of brazen shield and spear, the hammered cuirass,
Chalybean-tempered steel, and frock of mail
Adamantean proof.[7]

This also is a development of blank verse, a radical change in it indeed, and one which opens up possibilities which have not been completely explored by poets since. And in this also Milton is most himself,
less like other poets, less dependent on his strange syntax and most convincing. Most condensed—he 'takes a chisel to write'.[8]

There was one other development of blank verse which passed and

still passes unnoticed. A few years before Shakespeare's time the unknown writer of *Arden of Feversham* used end-stopped blank verse with the
words of ordinary speech in their ordinary succession to create a wonderfully subtle pattern of changing rhythms.[9]

> FRANKLIN. Thus have you seen the truth of Arden's death.
> As for the ruffians, Shakebag and Black Will,
> The one took sanctuary, and, being sent for out,
> Was murdered in Southwark as he passed
> To Greenwich, where the Lord Protector lay.
> Black Will was burned in Flushing on a stage;
> Greene was hanged at Osbridge in Kent;
> The painter fled and how he died we know not.
> But this above the rest is to be noted:
> Arden lay murdered in that plot of ground
> Which he by force and violence held from Reede;
> And in the grass his body's print was seen
> Two years and more after the deed was done.
> Gentlemen, we hope you'll pardon this naked tragedy,
> Wherein no filed points are foisted in
> To make it gracious to the ear or eye;
> For simple truth is gracious enough,
> And needs no other points of glosing stuff.[10]

I do not know how it was ever possible for some critics to imagine that
Arden was written by Shakespeare or Marlowe. They must have had no
ear. It was more plausible to suggest George Peele, but I've looked again
at Peele recently and can say for sure that he had none of the sensitivity
to rhythm that makes *Arden*'s blank verse the best in the language.[11]

But no one ever imitated *Arden;* and all these efforts were not enough
to alter the Spenserian pattern of English poetry seriously or for long.

The only rival that lasted many years, and even threatened at one
time to supersede Spenser's pattern as the norm of English poetry was
provided by Denham. All the literary histories will tell you about it, and
they will all cite the same passage:

> Thames! the most lov'd of all the Ocean's sons
> By his old sire, to his embraces runs,
> Hasting to pay his tribute to the sea,
> Like mortal life to meet eternity;

Tho' with those streams he no resemblance hold,
Whose foam is amber, and their gravel gold:
His genuine and less guilty wealth t' explore,
Search not his bottom, but survey his shore,
O'er which he kindly spreads his spacious wing,
And hatches plenty for th' ensuing spring;
Nor then destroys it with too fond a stay,
Like mothers which their infants overlay;
Nor with a sudden and impetuous wave,
Like profuse kings, resumes the wealth he gave.
No unexpected inundations spoil
The mower's hopes, nor mock the ploughman's toil;
But godlike his unweary'd bounty flows;
First loves to do, then loves the good he does.
Nor are his blessings to his banks confin'd,
But free and common as the sea or wind;
When he, to boast or to disperse his stores,
Full of the tributes of his grateful shores,
Visits the world, and in his flying tow'rs
Brings home to us, and makes both Indies ours;
Finds wealth where't is, bestows it where it wants,
Cities in deserts, woods in cities, plants.
So that to us no thing, no place, is strange,
While his fair bosom is the world's exchange.
O could I flow like thee! and make thy stream
My great example, as it is my theme;
Tho' deep yet clear, tho' gentle yet not dull;
Strong without rage, without o'erflowing full.[12]

There is no doubt that these lines, and the rest of *Cooper's Hill*, had a great and long influence.[13] Waller, Dryden, Pope, Johnson, all acknowledged it.[14] The fashion it set lasted more than a century, and for nearly half that time the fashion was all but universal. But there are several remarkable things about it. First, Denham never wrote another line that I would trouble you to read: all trivialities or stiff imitations of himself. Secondly, though the great poets at the turn of the century imagined that their heroic couplets were some sort of reflection of the French alexandrines, *Cooper's Hill* was in fact written before the alexandrine had settled down to its permanent pattern.[15] Pope could imitate Boileau,[16] but Denham anticipated Boileau. And thirdly, most remarkable of all, there was no development. Denham's poem had reached in one step the limits of what that couplet can do. Of course Pope and Johnson and others made it serve for purposes Denham never dreamt of, but they did so partly by importing processes that belonged to the Spenserian mode, a crust of vowel chimes and consonant sequences that destroyed the limpidity that was, they believed, the couplets reason for existence. What they did in such passages could be done better in the Spenserian manner.

The great merit of the couplet was its compactness. You can get a lot said in a short space with the help of antithesis. Its fatal defect is monotony. So long as poets imagined that it was their business to teach, the concision the couplet forced on the poet and the clarity he aimed at served a useful purpose. But the monotony made narrative terribly stiff and heavy and description dull, as though all landscapes, all creatures and all faces were alike. It forbade singing altogether, and its own music was extremely limited, even before the poets took to trying to follow the supposed rules of prosody continually.

Perhaps I ought also to notice that the poets who practised the heroic couplet believed themselves to be followers of Spenser. Waller said he learned chiefly from Fairfax,[17] who was one of the more whole-hearted and feebler imitators of Spenser; and it is certain that both he and Denham learned something from their reading of Ben Jonson, whose couplets are a modification of Spensers. And of course the framework goes back at least as far as Chaucer. Yet the aims introduced by Denham were very different from Spenser's, and the whole movement, though it never quite banished the Spenserian sounds, is a long remission of Spenser's dominance.

There is another point. The exploiters of the heroic couplet were highbrows, and that was a new phenomenon. Elizabethan writers might address themselves to noble patrons, but most of them still expected to be read and enjoyed by a wide audience, not particularly educated. Shakespeare's patron was the populace, and if it enjoyed the bombast and bloodshed more than the good poetry in his plays, still, it could take whatever he offered. Donne's poems were set and sung, and some of them were popular. But Denham and Waller spoke only to the world of fashion, and their successors assumed an audience that knew some Latin and was fluent in French, or at least an audience that liked it to be thought that it was familiar with such things. Quite a lot of their poetry is poetry about poetry, not about life. So the divorce sets in between the wide audience and the poet. Only Dryden avoids it to some extent because he lived by writing plays.

This sort of thing is a progressive disease. Literature in general fed more and more upon itself. Poetry was written in an arbitrary, narrow form, in an arbitrary vocabulary different from that of speech, fit only to treat such desiccated subjects as theoretical morals and literary criticism.[18] Even in Pope's reign Allan Ramsay was writing songs, singable though, by comparison with the Elizabethan songs, crude. Secondary poets tried rather haplessly to escape from the fashion. And by the latter part of Dr Johnson's life the accepted highbrow poetry was quite dead, with nothing to offer but Blair and his like, or the sentimentality of Goldsmith. Such writers occupied the available sinecures and dictated university taste, while the men with life in them and in their verse ploughed or engraved for a living.[19]

I dont know whether things would have been any better for poetry if Denham had never set going the fashion that crippled it. Anyway no really great poet turned up to test the matter till the 1790s.

SEVEN

Realism

Modern English poetry started when Wyat went straight to the essentials, to what poetry has in common with music—its rhythmic structure and variety. Spenser gave modern English poetry a great kit of tools, but also its tendency to overdo ornament and sonority: but his ornament was alive. The attempt to discipline the heirs of Spenser, which Denham began, lacked life. It was a fashion, and being restricted to a class, it became a highbrow game. The public forgot the poets, and the poets were content to be forgotten by it.

Emotion does not go well with the heroic couplet: but it is a good vehicle for parody, and for a rather restricted kind of wit. I cant think of any good parodies in English before Shakespeare:

> When icicles hang by the wall,
>> And Dick the shepherd blows his nail,
> And Tom bears logs into the hall,
>> And milk comes frozen home in pail,
> When blood is nipp'd, and ways be foul,
> Then nightly sings the staring owl,
>> Tu-whit;
> Tu-who, a merry note,
> While greasy Joan doth keel the pot.
>
> When all aloud the wind doth blow,
>> And coughing drowns the parson's saw,
> And birds sit brooding in the snow,
>> And Marian's nose looks red and raw,
> When roasted crabs hiss in the bowl,

The whole of this lecture is handwritten, with the exception of the last paragraph, which is in typescript, on a separate (unpaginated) sheet.

> Then nightly sings the staring owl,
>> Tu-whit;
> Tu-who, a merry note,
> While greasy Joan doth keel the pot.[1]

But Gay made the longlasting *Beggar's Opera* out of parody. You cannot exclude it from the category of poetry, though very few anthologies seem to think it solemn enough for them.

Wit is infrequent and rather clumsy in English poetry till Butler wrote *Hudibras*. That mock epic is in 8 syllable lines, but the famous wits of the heroic couplet never went beyond what Butler had taught them. The types of all their jokes are to be found in *Hudibras,* or in the few shorter pieces he left. *Hudibras* is too familiar to need quoting, yet I think it is often overlooked. Beside it, Pope's stuff looks pretty-pretty, and Rochester lacks vigour.

> Ye smock fac'd lads, secure your gentle bums;
> For full of lust and fury, see he comes!
> 'Tis buggaring Nokes, whose damn'd unwieldy tarse
> Weeps, to be buried in his footman's arse.
> Unnatural sinner, lecher without sense,
> To leave kind whores, to dive in excrements![2]

Even Dryden, though there is great strength under his urbanity, has not the concentrated *point* Butler gets so often.

However, wit was not the principal preoccupation of the XVIII c. From first to last there is an attempt to bring poetry to terms with the unpoetical, unheroic life of England. They were in search of realism. Dryden sometimes strays into that direction: Pope had some respect for the facts and does give a rather idealised, rather prettified account of fashionable life and thought. Swift makes it ugly, but a portrait, sometimes convincing; the preoccupation with realism, the broadening of its view to include other classes besides the richest, went on steadily, though very clumsily, throughout the century.

Realism is, of course, closely tied to humour.

Chaucer's "Wife of Bath" and Dunbar's "Tua Mariit Wemen" were and are still funny today, but they had surprisingly few offspring. Skelton went off into fantasy, and fantasy took the place of observation with the Elizabethan poets except on the stage. It is surprising how slowly realism, even in its most amusing form, got a footing in English. Butler pushes fun too far for realism. There is no novel to compare with *Lazarillo de Tormes* until Fielding began to write, nearly 2 centuries later, and even Fielding left the less attractive facts of life out of his novels.[3]

Do any of you know the *Tancia*, or the *Fiera?*—two enormous plays, or sets of plays, by Michelangiolo Buonarotti the Younger.[4] I dont think the English even noticed those astonishing feats of realism. Buonarotti was a nephew of Michelangiolo the sculptor. He tried to make one day in the life of Florence into a mirror of the world; and that day in the lives of a few characters a mirror of the life of the city. The fundamental notion is so like that of *Ulysses* that I have wondered whether James Joyce had come across the *Tancia* during his Italian years.

The resemblance goes somewhat beyond the main notion, for Buonarotti uses every variety of colloquial language, from thieves' slang and the solecisms of foreigners to polite conversation, though never, I think, parody or puns. However, I doubt if the *Tancia* influenced even Italian literature—none of the Italians I have met have ever read it, and only a few have heard of it; certainly there is no trace of that kind of wholesale realism in English, verse or prose.

Instead you have a long series of timid approaches right through the XVIII c. I am not thinking of Defoe, who is more concerned to give the paraphernalia of life than a transcription of life itself. He details the circumstances, but often has nothing to put in himself. But what had poetry to set beside Richardson, Fielding, Smollett? Goldsmith takes a subject from life, but sentimentalises it and prettifies it. Burns gets a trifle nearer with 'The Cotter's Saturday Night' and a lot nearer with 'The Jolly Beggars' and 'Holy Willie's Prayer'.[5] Crabbe sticks carefully to observation; but his verse plods on, his stories drag.

Crabbe wrote 'The Village' in 1783, and nothing else for years.[6] I dont know when Wordsworth became aware of him: but two years later Wordsworth aged 15 was reading the Kilmarnock edition of Burns to his sister during the school holidays at Penrith.

With Wordsworth, realism suddenly became the main weapon of a great poet, as though all the XVIII c had been tending toward had come forward at a bound to meet it. Almost all the innovations which impressed Wordsworth's contemporaries, for or against, so powerfully, spring from the needs of realism. In many other respects he remained very much like other XVIII c poets.

He imagined that it was the poets business to improve the morals of his readers, and would bore them conscientiously in the good cause.

He understood from the admonitions of Coleridge and the example of Pope that a poet ought to propound a complete system of philosophy, and that left him rather in a hole, because while Pope had Bolingbroke to provide the philosophy (such as it was),[7] *he* had only Coleridge, who promised it but never kept his promise. So the great philosophical poem which was to be the business of Wordsworth's life dwindled to a prelude, and some skirmishing with morals by way of an *Excursion* away from the theme that never got started.[8]

All this is very XVIII c indeed: so that I find it difficult to understand how he has ever come to be classed with the Romantics. It seems to be simply because his first mark was made with the *Lyrical Ballads* bound up with Coleridge's 'Ancient Mariner'. Now the 'Ancient Mariner', 'Kubla Khan', and 'Christabel' are the foundations of English Romanticism, and it is curious to note that the idea for the 'Ancient Mariner' was supplied by Wordsworth: though he gave up trying to write it almost at once.[9] It was outside his scope. The *Lyrical Ballads* themselves were far from Romantic: they were realism at its very barest.

But even before the *Lyrical Ballads*,[10] the first of Wordsworth's poems that is much more than imitation of his elders is 'Salisbury Plain', later called by the less effective title, 'Guilt and Sorrow'. He was 21 when he wrote it.[11] Its realism is thorough, and grim. Crabbe saw the middle classes, even the lower middle classes, but Wordsworth watched the very poor, the beggars and thieves and starving labourers, gipsies, drunken wastrels, shepherds, village idiots. His imagination was as uncompromising as Hardy's. The hero of 'Salisbury Plain', if you can give him that title, was hanged, and in the first version, his body was gibbetted to rot in chains, and parents brought their children to see that edifying example. Some readers protested at the brutality, and Coleridge, whose interventions in Wordsworth's poetry were always unfortunate, persuaded him to change it and remit the gibbetting.[12]

But the country people and out of work sailors of 'Salisbury Plain' do not talk like country people. XVIII c usage forbade them to. The story holds you, but all the time you get impatient with the wooden language. It is to get rid of this disadvantage that Wordsworth conceived his celebrated notions about diction. He must use ordinary speech to keep his story real, and to keep it moving fast. When he had no story to tell, no reason to hurry, Wordsworth usually turned back to something like a mere modification of XVIII c diction. This happens even in discursive intervals in his narration.

Not very long ago poets dreaded prolixity. They suspected adjectives. They avoided parentheses. They tried to write sentences as lean as Dante's, as compact and final as La Rochefoucauld's. Their work profited by their parsimony of words, but some of them never noticed that images, incidents, reflections are often as needless as the words they omitted. The reader can supply them as readily if he likes, and the reader may also be as well read in greek mythology as the poet and impatient of parallels which increase the number of lines but do not much deepen the understanding. The terse sentence is only a small help if the series of images etc is diffuse.[13] Wordsworth, most economical of images and incidents, did not care to seem terser than a man talking and was, therefore, out of fashion, not available as an exemplar. But work can be extremely concise without straining to spare either words or images.

EIGHT

Wordsworth and Whitman

[The remarks on Whitman in this chapter present a fulcrum to the argument of both series of lectures represented here, insofar as this argument leads to Pound's *Homage to Sextus Propertius* and *Cantos* as its conclusion. But historical accidents, or perhaps emotions relating to Bunting's own poetry, have left the Whitman section of this lecture in a very unfinished state.[1] It is not even a rough first draft but notes toward such a draft: notes that Bunting himself could have used in the classroom to produce a coherent lecture but that the reader who does not know the detail Bunting associated with these terms and names may need some help with. For such help, see "Whitman: Editor's Explanatory Note" immediately following the lecture.]

[WORDSWORTH]

All the eighteenth century moved towards Wordsworth. Decade by decade, the poetry men wrote, turned away from metropolitan smartness to things that seemed more real, nearer to the common lot, more provincial. The Augustans had addressed one another. Their successors tried more and more to catch the common man's ear. Poets went on talking about reason, but provided less of it, and less, for common people are not reasonable. They look for customary pieties, and morals that sound self-evident. The poets provided these.

They turned away too from systematic discussion to embody their morals in descriptions and tales; tales and descriptions which came steadily nearer and nearer to what men experience in common life. The way is long from Parnell's 'Hermit' to Crabbe's grey narratives, but it was trodden steadily throughout the century.[2] Wordsworth brought nothing new to this steady movement of taste, but he pushed it faster and more firmly along its path. He has far more in common with the poets before him than with the romantic generation amongst which he lived.

Even the plain words Wordsworth chose to use, though they killed off a stilted habit, have more resemblance to good eighteenth century usage than to the coloured vocabulary of Keats—or of Coleridge.

What was new was Wordsworth's narrative skill. Whether he follows an immemorial pattern, as in 'The Waggoner' or 'The Idiot Boy', or complicates the telling of his story, as he does in the poem I want to read to you, he holds his reader like hardly any other poet for many generations before him. As a storyteller, he is one of the family of Chaucer, and perhaps the foremost of the family.

I think it is hardly too much to say that if the multiple ironies through which he relates the story of 'The Brothers' had occurred to Henry James or to Conrad, we would have had a thirty page preface to explain them.

The man to read it should be Norman Nicholson, who could give you the sounds Wordsworth meant you to hear. I am a Northumberland man, and all I can claim for my reading is that my vowels are nearer to those Wordsworth uttered than a Londoner's might be, and my intonation perhaps less foreign to his.[3]

Nobody had thought of 'standard English' in Wordsworth's time. He spoke as a Northerner, in spite of the years he spent in Cambridge, London and Somerset; in such a Northern way that Keats and Hazlitt found it hard to follow his conversation.[4] And though he did not compose in dialect, he composed in his own voice, aloud. His music is lost if his poems are read in Southern English, and no doubt that is why so many critics imagine he had none.

The Brothers

"These Tourists, heaven preserve us! needs must live
A profitable life: some glance along,
Rapid and gay, as if the earth were air,
And they were butterflies to wheel about
Long as the summer lasted: some, as wise,
Perched on the forehead of a jutting crag,
Pencil in hand and book upon the knee,
Will look and scribble, scribble on and look,
Until a man might travel twelve stout miles,
Or reap an acre of his neighbour's corn.
But, for that moping Son of Idleness,

Why can he tarry *yonder*—In our churchyard
Is neither epitaph nor monument,
Tombstone nor name—only the turf we tread
And a few natural graves."

         To Jane, his wife,
Thus spake the homely Priest of Ennerdale.
It was a July evening; and he sate
Upon the long stone-seat beneath the eaves
Of his old cottage,—as it chanced, that day,
Employed in winter's work. Upon the stone
His wife sate near him, teasing matted wool,
While, from the twin cards toothed with glittering wire,
He fed the spindle of his youngest child,
Who, in the open air, with due accord
Of busy hands and back-and-forward steps,
Her large round wheel was turning. Towards the field
In which the Parish Chapel stood alone,
Girt round with a bare ring of mossy wall,
While half an hour went by, the Priest had sent
Many a long look of wonder: and at last,
Risen from his seat, beside the snow-white ridge
Of carded wool which the old man had piled
He laid his implements with gentle care,
Each in the other locked; and down the path,
That from his cottage to the church-yard led,
He took his way, impatient to accost
The Stranger, whom he saw still lingering there.

'Twas one well known to him in former days,
A Shepherd-lad; who ere his sixteenth year
Had left that calling, tempted to entrust
His expectations to the fickle winds
And perilous waters; with the mariners
A fellow-mariner; and so had fared
Through twenty seasons; but he had been reared
Among the mountains, and he in his heart
Was half a shepherd on the stormy seas.
Oft in the piping shrouds had Leonard heard
The tones of waterfalls, and inland sounds

Of caves and trees:—and when the regular wind
Between the tropics filled the steady sail,
And blew with the same breath through days and weeks,
Lengthening invisibly its weary line
Along the cloudless Main, he, in those hours
Of tiresome indolence, would often hang
Over the vessel's side, and gaze and gaze;
And, while the broad blue wave and sparkling foam
Flashed round him images and hues that wrought
In union with the employment of his heart,
He, thus by feverish passion overcome,
Even with the organs of his bodily eye,
Below him, in the bosom of the deep,
Saw mountains; saw the forms of sheep that grazed
On verdant hills—with dwellings among trees,
And shepherds clad in the same country grey
Which he himself had worn.

        And now, at last,
From perils manifold, with some small wealth
Acquired by traffic 'mid the Indian Isles,
To his paternal home he is returned,
With a determined purpose to resume
The life he had lived there; both for the sake
Of many darling pleasures, and the love
Which to an only brother he has borne
In all his hardships, since that happy time
When, whether it blew foul or fair, they two
Were brother-shepherds on their native hills.
—They were the last of all their race: and now,
When Leonard had approached his home, his heart
Failed in him; and, not venturing to enquire
Tidings of one so long and dearly loved,
He to the solitary church-yard turned;
That, as he knew in what particular spot
His family were laid, he thence might learn
If still his Brother lived, or to the file
Another grave was added.—He had found
Another grave,—near which a full half-hour

He had remained; but, as he gazed, there grew
Such a confusion in his memory,
That he began to doubt; and even to hope
That he had seen this heap of turf before, —
That it was not another grave; but one
He had forgotten. He had lost his path,
As up the vale, that afternoon, he walked
Through fields which once had been well known to him:
And oh what joy this recollection now
Sent to his heart! he lifted up his eyes,
And, looking round, imagined that he saw
Strange alteration wrought on every side
Among the woods and fields, and that the rocks,
And everlasting hills themselves were changed.

    By this the Priest, who down the field had come,
Unseen by Leonard, at the church yard gate
Stopped short, — and thence, at leisure, limb by limb
Perused him with a gay complacency.
Ay, thought the Vicar, smiling to himself,
'Tis one of those who needs must leave the path
Of the world's business to go wild alone:
His arms have a perpetual holiday;
The happy man will creep about the fields,
Following his fancies by the hour, to bring
Tears down his cheek, or solitary smiles
Into his face, until the setting sun
Write fool upon his forehead. — Planted thus
Beneath a shed that over-arched the gate
Of this rude church-yard, till the stars appeared
The good Man might have communed with himself,
But that the Stranger, who had left the grave,
Approached; he recognized the Priest at once,
And, after greetings interchanged, and given
By Leonard to the Vicar as to one
Unknown to him, this dialogue ensued.
    LEONARD. You live, Sir, in these dales, a quiet life:
Your years make up one peaceful family;
And who would grieve and fret, if, welcome come

And welcome gone, they are so like each other,
They cannot be remembered? Scarce a funeral
Comes to this church-yard once in eighteen months;
And yet, some changes must take place among you:
And you, who dwell here, even among these rocks,
Can trace the finger of mortality,
And see, that with our threescore years and ten
We are not all that perish.—I remember,
(For many years ago I passed this road)
There was a foot-way all along the fields
By the brook-side—'tis gone—and that dark cleft!
To me it does not seem to wear the face
Which then it had!
    PRIEST.   Nay, Sir, for aught I know,
That chasm is much the same—
    LEONARD.   But, surely, yonder—
    PRIEST.   Ay, there, indeed, your memory is a friend
That does not play you false.—On that tall pike
(It is the loneliest place of all these hills)
There were two springs which bubbled side by side,
As if they had been made that they might be
Companions for each other: the huge crag
Was rent with lightning—one hath disappeared;
The other, left behind, is flowing still.
For accidents and changes such as these,
We want not store of them;—a waterspout
Will bring down half a mountain; what a feast
For folks that wander up and down like you,
To see an acre's breadth of that wide cliff
One roaring cataract! a sharp May-storm
Will come with loads of January snow,
And in one night send twenty score of sheep
To feed the ravens; or a shepherd dies
By some untoward death among the rocks:
The ice breaks up and sweeps away a bridge;
A wood is felled:—and then for our own homes!
A child is born or christened, a field ploughed,
A daughter sent to service, a web spun,
The old house-clock is decked with a new face;

And hence, so far from wanting facts or dates
To chronicle the time, we all have here
A pair of diaries,—one serving, Sir,
For the whole dale, and one for each fire-side—
Yours was a stranger's judgment: for historians,
Commend me to these valleys!
   LEONARD.   Yet your Church-yard
Seems, if such freedom may be used with you,
To say that you are heedless of the past:
An orphan could not find his mother's grave:
Here's neither head nor foot-stone, plate of brass,
Cross-bones nor skull,—type of our earthly state
Nor emblem of our hopes: the dead man's home
Is but a fellow to that pasture-field.
   PRIEST. Why, there, Sir, is a thought that's new to me!
The stone-cutters, 'tis true, might beg their bread
If every English church-yard were like ours;
Yet your conclusion wanders from the truth:
We have no need of names and epitaphs;
We talk about the dead by our fire-sides.
And then, for our immortal part! *we* want
No symbols, Sir, to tell us that plain tale:
The thought of death sits easy on the man
Who has been born and dies among the mountains.
   LEONARD. Your Dalesmen, then, do in each other's
   thoughts
Possess a kind of second life: no doubt
You, Sir, could help me to the history
Of half these graves?
   PRIEST.   For eight-score winters past,
With what I've witnessed, and with what I've heard,
Perhaps I might; and, on a winter-evening,
If you were seated at my chimney's nook,
By turning o'er these hillocks one by one,
We two could travel, Sir, through a strange round;
Yet all in the broad highway of the world.
Now there's a grave—your foot is half upon it,—
It looks just like the rest; and yet that man
Died broken-hearted.

LEONARD.   'Tis a common case.
We'll take another: who is he that lies
Beneath yon ridge, the last of those three graves?
It touches on that piece of native rock
Left in the church-yard wall.
        PRIEST.   That's Walter Ewbank.
He had as white a head and fresh a cheek
As ever were produced by youth and age
Engendering in the blood of hale fourscore.
Through five long generations had the heart
Of Walter's forefathers o'erflowed the bounds
Of their inheritance, that single cottage—
You see it yonder! and those few green fields.
They toiled and wrought, and still, from sire to son,
Each struggled, and each yielded as before
A little—yet a little,—and old Walter,
They left to him the family heart, and land
With other burthens than the crop it bore.
Year after year the old man still kept up
A cheerful mind,—and buffeted with bond,
Interest, and mortgages; at last he sank,
And went into his grave before his time.
Poor Walter! whether it was care that spurred him
God only knows, but to the very last
He had the lightest foot in Ennerdale:
His pace was never that of an old man:
I almost see him tripping down the path
With his two grandsons after him:—but you,
Unless our Landlord be your host tonight,
Have far to travel,—and on these rough paths
Even in the longest day of midsummer—
    LEONARD. But those two Orphans!
    PRIEST.   Orphans!—Such they were—
Yet not while Walter lived:—for, though their parents
Lay buried side by side as now they lie,
The old man was a father to the boys,
Two fathers in one father: and if tears,
Shed when he talked of them where they were not,
And hauntings from the infirmity of love,

Are aught of what makes up a mother's heart,
This old Man, in the day of his old age,
Was half a mother to them.—If you weep, Sir,
To hear a stranger talking about strangers,
Heaven bless you when you are among your kindred!
Ay—you may turn that way—it is a grave
Which will bear looking at.

    LEONARD.   These boys—I hope
They loved this good old Man?—

    PRIEST.   They did—and truly:
But that was what we almost overlooked,
They were such darlings of each other. Yes,
Though from the cradle they had lived with Walter,
The only kinsman near them, and though he
Inclined to both by reason of his age,
With a more fond, familiar, tenderness;
They, notwithstanding, had much love to spare,
And it all went into each other's hearts.
Leonard, the elder by just eighteen months,
Was two years taller: 'twas a joy to see,
To hear, to meet them!—From their house the school
Is distant three short miles, and in the time
Of storm and thaw, when every watercourse
And unbridged stream, such as you may have noticed
Crossing our roads, at every hundred steps,
Was swoln into a noisy rivulet,
Would Leonard then, when elder boys remained
At home, go staggering through the slippery fords,
Bearing his brother on his back. I have seen him,
On windy days, in one of those stray brooks,
Ay, more than once I have seen him, mid-leg deep,
Their two books lying both on a dry stone,
Upon the hither side: and once I said,
As I remember, looking round these rocks
And hills on which we all of us were born,
That God who made the great book of the world
Would bless such piety—

    LEONARD.   It may be then—

    PRIEST. Never did worthier lads break English bread;

The very brightest Sunday Autumn saw,
With all its mealy clusters of ripe nuts,
Could never keep those boys away from church,
Or tempt them to an hour of sabbath breach.
Leonard and James! I warrant, every corner
Among these rocks, and every hollow place
That venturous foot could reach, to one or both
Was known as well as to the flowers that grow there.
Like roe-bucks they went bounding o'er the hills;
They played like two young ravens on the crags:
Then they could write, ay, and speak too, as well
As many of their betters—and for Leonard!
The very night before he went away,
In my own house I put into his hand
A Bible, and I'd wager house and field
That, if he be alive, he has it yet.
    LEONARD. It seems, these Brothers have not lived to be
A comfort to each other—
    PRIEST.   That they might
Live to such end is what both old and young
In this our valley all of us have wished,
And what, for my part, I have often prayed:
But Leonard—
    LEONARD.   Then James still is left among you!
    PRIEST. 'Tis of the elder brother I am speaking:
They had an uncle;—he was at that time
A thriving man, and trafficked on the seas:
And, but for that same uncle, to this hour
Leonard had never handled rope or shroud:
For the boy loved the life which we lead here;
And though of unripe years, a stripling only,
His soul was knit to this his native soil.
But, as I said, old Walter was too weak
To strive with such a torrent; when he died,
The estate and house were sold; and all their sheep,
A pretty flock, and which, for aught I know,
Had clothed the Ewbanks for a thousand years:—
Well—all was gone, and they were destitute,
And Leonard, chiefly for his Brother's sake,

Resolved to try his fortune on the seas.
Twelve years are past since we had tidings from him.
If there were one among us who had heard
That Leonard Ewbank was come home again,
From the Great Gavel, down by Leeza's banks,—
And down the Enna, far as Egremont,
The day would be a joyous festival;
And those two bells of ours, which there you see—
Hanging in the open air—but, O good Sir!
This is sad talk—they'll never sound for him—
Living or dead.—When last we heard of him,
He was in slavery among the Moors
Upon the Barbary coast. 'Twas not a little
That would bring down his spirit; and no doubt,
Before it ended in his death, the Youth
Was sadly crossed.—Poor Leonard! When we parted,
He took me by the hand, and said to me,
If e'er he should grow rich, he would return,
To live in peace upon his father's land,
And lay his bones among us.
    LEONARD.   If that day
Should come, 'twould needs be a glad day for him;
He would himself, no doubt, be happy then
As any that should meet him—
    PRIEST.   Happy! Sir—
    LEONARD. You said his kindred all were in their graves,
And that he had one Brother—
    PRIEST.   That is but
A fellow-tale of sorrow. From his youth
James, though not sickly, yet was delicate;
And Leonard being always by his side
Had done so many offices about him,
That, though he was not of a timid nature,
Yet still the spirit of a mountain-boy
In him was somewhat checked; and, when his Brother
Was gone to sea, and he was left alone,
The little colour that he had was soon
Stolen from his cheek; he drooped, and pined, and pined—
    LEONARD. But these are all the graves of full-grown men!

PRIEST. Ay, Sir, that passed away: we took him to us;
He was the child of all the dale—he lived
Three months with one, and six months with another;
And wanted neither food, nor clothes, nor love:
And many, many happy days were his.
But, whether blithe or sad, 'tis my belief
His absent Brother still was at his heart.
And, when he dwelt beneath our roof, we found
(A practice till this time unknown to him)
That often, rising from his bed at night,
He in his sleep would walk about, and sleeping
He sought his brother Leonard.—You are moved!
Forgive me, Sir: before I spoke to you,
I judged you most unkindly.

    LEONARD.   But this Youth,
How did he die at last?

    PRIEST.   One sweet May-morning,
(It will be twelve years since when Spring returns)
He had gone forth among the new-dropped lambs,
With two or three companions, whom their course
Of occupation led from height to height
Under a cloudless sun—till he, at length,
Through weariness, or, haply, to indulge
The humour of the moment, lagged behind.
You see yon precipice;—it wears the shape
Of a vast building made of many crags;
And in the midst is one particular rock
That rises like a column from the vale,
Whence by our shepherds it is called THE PILLAR.
Upon its aery summit crowned with heath,
The loiterer, not unnoticed by his comrades,
Lay stretched at ease; but, passing by the place
On their return, they found that he was gone.
No ill was feared; till one of them by chance
Entering, when evening was far spent, the house
Which at that time was James's home, there learned
That nobody had seen him all that day:
The morning came, and still he was unheard of:
The neighbours were alarmed, and to the brook

Some hastened; some ran to the lake: ere noon
They found him at the foot of that same rock
Dead, and with mangled limbs. The third day after
I buried him, poor Youth, and there he lies!
    LEONARD. And that then *is* his grave! —Before his death
You say that he saw many happy years?
    PRIEST. Ay, that he did—
    LEONARD.   And all went well with him?—
    PRIEST. If he had one, the Youth had twenty homes.
    LEONARD. And you believe, then, that his mind was easy?—
    PRIEST. Yes, long before he died, he found that time
Is a true friend to sorrow; and, unless
His thoughts were turned on Leonard's luckless fortune,
He talked about him with a cheerful love.
    LEONARD. He could not come to an unhallowed end!
    PRIEST. Nay, God forbid! —You recollect I mentioned
A habit which disquietude and grief
Had brought upon him; and we all conjectured
That, as the day was warm, he had lain down
On the soft heath, —and, waiting for his comrades,
He there had fallen asleep; that in his sleep
He to the margin of the precipice
Had walked, and from the summit had fallen headlong:
And so no doubt he perished. When the Youth
Fell, in his hand he must have grasped, we think,
His shepherd's staff; for on that Pillar of rock
It had been caught mid-way; and there for years
It hung; —and mouldered there.

    The Priest here ended—
The Stranger would have thanked him, but he felt
A gushing from his heart, that took away
The power of speech. Both left the spot in silence;
And Leonard, when they reached the church-yard gate,
As the Priest lifted up the latch, turned round, —
And, looking at the grave, he said, "My Brother!"
The Vicar did not hear the words: and now
He pointed towards his dwelling-place, entreating
That Leonard would partake his homely fare:

The other thanked him with an earnest voice;
But added, that, the evening being calm,
He would pursue his journey. So they parted.

 It was not long ere Leonard reached a grove
That overhung the road: he there stopped short,
And, sitting down beneath the trees, reviewed
All that the Priest had said: his early years
Were with him:—his long absence, cherished hopes,
And thoughts which had been his an hour before,
All pressed on him with such a weight, that now,
This vale, where he had been so happy, seemed
A place in which he could not bear to live:
So he relinquished all his purposes.
He travelled back to Egremont: and thence,
That night, he wrote a letter to the Priest,
Reminding him of what had passed between them;
And adding, with a hope to be forgiven,
That it was from the weakness of his heart
He had not dared to tell him who he was.
This done, he went on shipboard, and is now
A seaman, a grey-headed Mariner.[5]

 I think it is still usual for people to speak of Wordsworth and perhaps even to think of him as one of the so-called Romantic poets. Then they are disappointed, because it is no use looking in Wordsworth's poems for anything at all like what they are used to finding in Shelley or Byron, or even in Landor and Southey and Scott. Perhaps they are misled because they know that Wordsworth and Coleridge were very close friends at one time, and Coleridge certainly did give a great impetus to the Romantic fashion with his 'Kubla Khan' and his 'Ancient Mariner'.[6]

 Wordsworth made no such breach with the Eighteenth Century. His chief interests were realism in speech and in matter, and moral edification. Poets had been making more or less clumsy approaches to realism for almost a century before Wordsworth's time. Goldsmith had a go at it, and Burns achieved it now and then. Crabbe looked at the shopkeepers and schoolteachers of his day, which was also Wordsworth's day, with an undeceived eye, but tried to describe them in such a wooden literary language that their reality escaped from the page. Wordsworth tried to keep to spoken English, a real language to describe real people, and it enabled him to fulfil at last an Eighteenth century ambition in poems such as 'The Old Cumberland Beggar'.

WHITMAN[7]

So all the XIX c brought was minor variations on the general Spenserian model of English poetry:

except for Walt Whitman.

Whitman very uneven, too fond of Hugo-esque words like Freedom, Democracy, Life, Death—large and empty (as Swinburne after him): but its his best that matters.

Sea Drift, especially.[8]

Not new, nothing ever is.

The notion of escaping from the Alexandrine—Baudelaire & 'prose poetry'. French prose poetry generally vague & *pretentious*

That *may* have been one root.[9] The idea was in the air— —

But a tradition in English of *cadence*—a musical notion: plain song, where you have a lot of freedom until the 'cadence'.[10]

This in prose—where it joins forces with Hebrew parallelism because of Coverdale's psalms & Song of Songs.[11]

Cranmer—collects.[12] Latymer, sermons[13]

(why Donne & Andrewes when you have Latymer?)[14]

Burton—Anatomy of Melancholy
Browne—Religio Medici & Hydriotaphia
Macpherson, Ossian, a crude example
not Smart, because his unfinished madhouse experiments were unknown.

Swift—*Tale of a Tub*[15]

What Whitman adds to this is to make *all* the words part of the machinery which causes them to cohere into a poem. The echoes & repeats are not confined to cadences.

But he usually avoids immediate repeats or repeats that are too exact & obvious. Yet the taking up of a sound or rhythm again & again in a poem has just the same effect as taking up a theme, more or less transformed, has in music.[16]

Onomatopeia [*sic*] — 'Out of the cradle' —

$$- \cup \cup - \cup$$

Again and again through the poem: and then spondees 'Out of the ninth month midnight' —

etc

This differs from prose because of

1. the constant repeats, however modified
2. the greater use of *poetic* ornament (I mean, alliteration, assonance, vowel sequences & so on)
3. The onomatopeia [*sic*], rarely direct, but frequently emotional
4. The way each line's rhythm grows from that of the line before — no break, no new start, as usual in prose

Out of the Cradle Endlessly Rocking

[Transcribed from Bunting's Marked Copy]

Out of the cradle/ endlessly rocking,
Out of the mocking-bird's throat, the musical shuttle,
Out of the Ninth-month midnight,
Over the sterile sands^ and the fields beyond, where the child/
    leaving his bed/ wander'd alone, bareheaded, barefoot,
Down from the shower'd halo,
Up from the mystic play^ of shadows/ twining and twisting/ as if
    they were alive,
Out from the patches/ of briers and blackberries,
From the memories^ of the bird^ that chanted^ to me,
From your memories/ sad brother, from the fitful risings and
    fallings I heard,
From under that yellow half-moon/ late-risen and swollen/ as if
    with tears,
From those beginning notes/ of yearning and love^ there in the
    mist,
From the thousand responses of <u>my</u> heart/ never to cease,
From the myriad thence-arous'd words,
From the word^ stronger and more^ delicious than any,
From such as now they start^ the scene revisiting,
As a flock, twittering, rising, or overhead passing,
Borne hither, ere all eludes me, hurriedly,
A man, yet by these tears/ a little boy^ again,

Throwing myself on the sand, confronting the waves,
I, chanter of pains and joys, uniter of here and hereafter,
Taking all hints to use them, but swiftly^ leaping^ beyond them,
A reminiscence sing.

Once Paumanok,
When the lilac-scent was^ in the air^ and Fifth-month grass was
    growing,
Up this seashore/ in some briers,
Two feather'd guests^ from Alabama, two together,
And their nest, and four light-green eggs/ spotted with brown,
And every day the he-bird/ to and fro/ near at hand,
And every day the she-bird/ crouch'd on her nest, silent, with
    bright eyes,
And every day I, a curious boy, never too close, never disturbing
    them,
Cautiously peering, absorbing, translating.

Shine! shine! shine!
Pour down your warmth, great sun!
While <u>we</u> bask, we two^ together.

Two together!
Winds blow south, or winds blow north,
Day come white, or night come black,
Home, or rivers^ and mountains/ <u>from</u> home,
Singing <u>all</u> time, minding <u>no</u> time,
While we two^ keep together.

Till of a sudden,
May-be kill'd, unknown to her mate,
One forenoon^ the she-bird^ crouch'd <u>not</u> on the nest,
Nor return'd that afternoon, nor the next,
Nor ever appear'd again.

And thenceforward^ <u>all</u> summer/ in the sound of the sea,
And at night/ under the full of the moon/ in calmer weather,
Over the hoarse surging of the sea,
Or flitting^ from brier to brier/ by day,
I saw, I heard^ at intervals/ the remaining <u>one,</u> the he-bird,
The solitary guest^ from Alabama.

Blow! blow! blow!
Blow up^ sea-winds^ along Paumanok's shore;
I wait^ and I wait^ till you blow^ my mate^ to me.

Yes, when the stars glisten'd,
All night long^ on the prong^ of a moss-scallop'd stake,
Down^ almost^ amid the slapping waves,
Sat the lone singer/ wonderful/ causing tears.

He call'd^ on his mate,
He pour'd forth^ the meanings^ which I^ of all men^ know.

Yes^ my brother^ I know,
The rest might not, but I have treasur'd^ every note,
For more than once/ dimly^ down to the beach gliding,
Silent, avoiding the moonbeams, blending myself with the
    shadows,
Recalling now^ the obscure shapes, the echoes, the sounds^ and
    sights/ after their sorts,
The white arms^ out in the breakers^ tirelessly tossing,
I, with bare feet, a child, the wind^ wafting my hair,
Listen'd/ long and long.

Listen'd to keep, to sing, now translating the notes,
Following you^ my brother.

Soothe! soothe! soothe!
Close on its wave^ soothes the wave^ behind,
And again^ another behind/ embracing and lapping, every one close,
But my love soothes not me, not me.

Low^ hangs the moon, it rose late,
It is lagging—O^ I think^ it is heavy^ with love, with love.

O madly the sea/ pushes upon the land,
With love, with love.

O night! do I not see^ my love/ fluttering out/ among the breakers?
What is that^ little black thing/ I see/ there in the white?

Loud! loud! loud!
Loud I call^ to you, my love!
High and clear/ I shoot my voice/ over the waves,

Surely you must know^ who is here, is here,
You must know^ who I am, my love.

Low-hanging moon!
What is that dusky spot/ in your brown yellow?
O^ it is the shape, the shape^ of my mate!
O moon/ do not keep her/ from me/ any longer.

Land! land! O^ land!
Whichever way I turn, O^ I think^ you could give me^ my mate back
*   again/ if you only would,*
For I am^ almost^ sure I see her/ dimly^ whichever way I look.

O^ rising stars!
Perhaps^ the one^ I want so much/ will rise, will rise^ with some of you.

O^ throat! O^ trembling throat!
Sound clearer/ through the atmosphere!
Pierce the woods, the earth,
Somewhere^ listening/ to catch you/ must be the one^ I want.

Shake out/ carols!
Solitary here, the night's carols!
Carols of lonesome love! death's carols!
Carols^ under that lagging, yellow, waning^ moon!
O^ under that moon^ where she droops/ almost down/ into the sea!
O^ reckless/ despairing carols.

But soft! sink low!
Soft! let me just murmur,
And do you^ wait a moment/ you husky-nois'd sea,
For somewhere^ I believe/ I heard my mate/ responding to me,
So faint, I must be still, be still^ to listen,
But not altogether still, for then/ she might not come/ immediately/ to me.

Hither my love!
Here I am! here!
With this^ just-sustain'd note^ I announce^ myself^ to you,
This gentle call^ is for you^ my love, for you.

Do not be decoy'd^ elsewhere,
That is the whistle^ of the wind, it is not my voice,

That is the fluttering, the fluttering/ of the spray,
Those are the shadows^ of leaves.

O^ darkness! O^ in vain!
O^ I am very sick^ and sorrowful.

O^ brown halo^ in the sky/ near the moon, drooping^ upon the sea!
O^ troubled reflection/ in the sea!
O^ throat! O^ throbbing heart!
And I/ singing uselessly,/ uselessly/ all the night.

O^ past! O^ happy life! O^ songs^ of joy!
In the air, in the woods, over fields,
Loved! loved! loved! loved! loved!
But my mate^ no more, no more with me!
We two together^ no more.

The aria sinking,
All else continuing, the stars shining,
The winds blowing, the notes of the bird^ continuous^ echoing,
With angry moans the fierce old mother/ incessantly moaning,
On the sands^ of Paumanok's shore/ gray and rustling,
The yellow half-moon^ enlarged, sagging down, drooping, the
    face of the sea^ almost^ touching,
The boy ecstatic, with his bare feet the waves, with his hair the
    atmosphere^ dallying,
The love^ in the heart^ long pent, now loose, now at last/
    tumultuously bursting,
The aria's meaning, the ears, the soul, swiftly depositing,
The strange tears/ down the cheeks^ coursing,
The colloquy there, the trio, each uttering,
The undertone, the savage old mother^ incessantly^ crying,
To the boy's soul's questions/ sullenly timing, some drown'd secret
    hissing,
To the outsetting bard.

Demon or bird! (said the boy's soul,)
Is it indeed^ toward your mate/ you sing? or is it really/ to me?
For I, that was a child, my tongue's use sleeping, now I have heard
    you,
Now^ in a moment^ I know^ what I am for, I awake,

And already^ a thousand singers, a thousand songs, clearer,
    louder^ and more sorrowful^ than yours,
A thousand warbling echoes/ have started to life/ within me,
    never to die.

O^ you singer solitary, singing by yourself, projecting me,
O^ solitary me/ listening, never more^ shall I cease^
    perpetuating you,
Never more^ shall I escape, never more^ the reverberations,
Never more^ the cries/ of unsatisfied love/ be absent from <u>me</u>,
Never again^ leave me to be^ the peaceful child I was/ before
    what/ there in the night,
By the sea/ under the yellow^ and sagging moon,
The messenger there arous'd, the fire, the sweet hell^ within,
The unknown want, the destiny of <u>me</u>.

O^ give me the clew! (it lurks in the night/ here/ somewhere,)
O^ if I am to <u>have</u>^ so much, let me have more!

A word^ then, (for I <u>will</u> conquer it,)
The word final, superior^ to all,
Subtle, sent up—what is it?—I listen;
<u>Are</u> you whispering it, and have been^ all the time, you^
    sea-waves?
Is that it^ from your liquid rims^ and wet sands?

Whereto answering, the sea,
Delaying not, hurrying not,
Whisper'd me/ through the night, and very plainly/ before
    daybreak,
Lisp'd to <u>me</u>^ the low^ and delicious word/ death,
And again death, death, death, death,
Hissing melodious, neither^ like the bird/ nor like <u>my</u>^ arous'd^
    child's heart,
But edging near/ as privately/ for me/ rustling at my feet,
Creeping thence^ steadily/ up to my ears/ and laving me^ softly^
    all over,
Death, death, death, death, death.

Which I do <u>not</u> forget,
But fuse^ the song^ of my dusky demon^ and brother,

That he sang/ to <u>me</u>/ in the moonlight^ on Paumanok's gray
  beach,
With the thousand responsive songs^ at random,
My own songs^ awaked^ from that hour,
And with them^ the key, the word^ up from the waves,
The word of the sweetest song^ and all songs,
That strong and delicious word/ which, creeping to my feet,
(Or like some old crone/ rocking the cradle, swathed in sweet
  garments, bending aside,)
The sea whisper'd me.[17]

Whitman's imitators were mere catchers at ideas & vague words—
Edward Carpenter—with no understanding of what made him a poet.[18]

Nothing comes of it: and Whitman is out-of-mind even in US till Pound
rereads him about 1912 or 14.[19]

WHITMAN: EDITOR'S EXPLANATORY NOTE

That Bunting never returned to clarify these notes is particularly regret-
table. As we shall see, a main trajectory of thought in the 1969 series of
lectures leads toward Pound's *Homage to Sextus Propertius,* whose achieve-
ment it attempts to explain. But that peak itself has significance for
Bunting because it enabled him to start climbing toward his own further
summit: the poems he designed as sonatas. The present lecture places
Whitman as a stage that led to the *Sextus Propertius.* Here may lie the
reason why the Whitman section was left as the sketch of a sketch: why,
though for years Bunting dropped hints about these connections, when
the opportunity came to set them all down together, he did not take it.
It may have approached too near to his own central struggle, to things
that, like any artist still working, he might want to keep free of the dis-
secting eye and the demand for more clarification that any explanation
would bring.

Here I try to clarify the main terms by bringing together Bunting's
scattered hints—more frequent as the writing of *Briggflatts* receded into
the past—in interviews, reviews, and odd notes. One of the most important of the sources consists of the materials Bunting assembled toward
his two verse anthologies, the one recorded on tape by him at Newcastle
University and the other drafted in typescript (now held in the Bunting
Archive at Durham). This latter has a section entitled "The Growing

Stem," which clearly sets out to illustrate the same line of development as Bunting describes in the present lecture. These materials are eked out by some guesses of my own as to Bunting's intentions, which I shall try to justify as I proceed.

It is fundamental to Bunting's idea that the word-sound it concerns is a shaping not of the prettier glitterings of aural surface (consonant patterns and the like) but of what is much more basic in the English language: rhythm. Thus Pound's *Propertius* was a springboard for real development because its aural shaping was essentially rhythmic. The reason why this matters will have been clear in the foregoing lectures wherever they refer to the influence of Spenser.

In the notes reproduced above, Bunting states tersely the ultimate target of his line of thought:

> Yet the taking up of a sound or rhythm again & again in a poem has just the same effect as taking up a theme, more or less transformed, has in music.

The return to earlier-stated melodic themes, "more or less transformed," is one of the builders of major structure in post-Renaissance Western music. Thus the concluding event in classical sonata form is the return of a melodic motif or motifs in a changed key. If a rhythm motif in poetry can do what a melodic theme does in music, rhythm ceases to be mere texture and becomes structure maker: as Bunting will note at the start of the penultimate lecture in this collection, "Pound's Cantos."[20] Structure by rhythm is thus the ultimate target; the main stages on the way are as follows.

1. Outside the dominant tradition of English verse (a patterning of strong stresses more or less stiffened by habits of syllable counting), you may have a verse texture built up in these steps:

a. "A tradition in English of *cadence . . .* in prose." That is, in otherwise rhythmically unpatterned prose, you may have a recurrent rhythm motif at the *end* of clause or sentence:

> From all evil and mischief, from sin, from the crafts and assaults of
> the devil, from thy wrath, and from everlasting damnation,
> > Good Lord, deliver us.
> From blindness of heart; from pride, vain-glory, and hypocrisy;
> from envy, hatred, and malice, and all uncharitableness,
> > Good Lord, deliver us.

From fornication, and all deadly sin; and from all the deceits of the world, the flesh and the devil,

   Good Lord, deliver us.

From lightning and tempest. . . .

(*Cranmer's Liturgy of 1544, from a passage selected by Bunting for "The Growing Stem"*)

  b. There may be rhythmic recurrences created by Hebrew parallelism that are not confined to the ends of clauses or sentences:

O stonde vp my loue, my beutyfull, and come (my doue) out of the <u>caues of the rockes</u>, out of the <u>holes of the wall</u>: O let me **se thy coun**tenaunce and **heare thy voyce**, for <u>**swete is thy voyce**</u> and <u>**fayre is thy face.**</u>

(*Coverdale's version of the* Song of Songs, *from a passage selected for Bunting's tape anthology*).[21]

Here I think Bunting's term *cadence* requires particular attention. He tells us that he is using the analogy of musical cadence. In music, a cadence is strictly a piece of melody or harmony that seems to resolve tensions and is thus usually found at the end of a phrase, or section, or piece. It will often have the quality of a set formula, as it does in the example of plainsong (Gregorian chant), mentioned by Bunting here. Bunting makes it clear that he is using this analogy from music to describe only certain recurring, quasi-fixed phrases that form parts of lines, as in "plain song, where you have a lot of freedom until the 'cadence.' " In a 1974 lecture he speaks of "poetry that is chanted, that is, poetry that can take great freedoms within the line, until it reaches a cadence, a pattern of sound repeated more or less exactly, and easily recognisable." [22] *Free* here of course means not merely "flexible"—Bunting would assume that all elements of verse should be that—but "unpatterned." It is the "cadence," only, in this kind of writing, that is rhythmically patterned.

  c. A writer may use both these rhythmic patternings; for in prose the tradition of cadence "joins forces with Hebrew parallelism because of Coverdale's psalms & Song of Songs":

To see a man roll himself up, like a snow ball, from báse béggary

to <u>Ríght Wórshipful</u> and <u>Ríght Hón</u>ourable titles, únjustlý to scréw

himself into <u>hónóurs and óffi</u>ces; another to stárve hís génius, damn his soul, to gather wealth, which he shall not enjoy, which

his prodigal son melts and consumes in an instant!

(*Burton's* Anatomy of Melancholy, *specified in the present lecture*)

Certain stress groups are brought to relative prominence by syntax-repeat: "starve his genius / damn his soul"; or by being semantic foci (as in the same phrases); or by being at the same time semantically connected or contrasted ("base beggary / Right Worshipful"); or by being all these together. (The deep principle is much as that of Hebraic parallelism as described by Hrushovski, where the parallel can be in semantics or syntax or rhythm, yet no one of these is indispensable.) And in this example we see the *overlaps* of rhythm groups, the *transitions* between them, and the *ambiguities* that are both inevitable and desirable in this view.[23]

d. But both these methods may still leave considerable portions of the utterance rhythmically unpatterned, which is to say, not contributing to the writing considered as aural form. Comes now nineteenth-century music (Whitman, Bunting says, may or may not have been conscious of the examples of Liszt and Berlioz).[24] It inspires Whitman to use both the above kinds of patterning, but to add the trick of constantly (though subtly) *modifying* each rhythmic motif introduced by them. He can thus make many more of the phrases in his lines refer to his rhythmic motifs, without becoming rhythmically repetitive (as Macpherson had in his Ossian poems).[25] One motif can be introduced, and then modulate; it can fall into silence, while another is brought in and changed; the poet can then bring back the first motif after a silence, or even modulate two motifs till they fuse or (a key idea to Bunting) "marry."[26]

This kind of writing will differ from prose-with-cadences. In the latter, each new sentence begins with a rhythmically slack piece and falls into pattern only at the end; or else patterned phrases will be scattered more frequently but dropped more or less as soon as the writer tires of them. Here, the line will be much more dominated by rhythmic shapes, which, however new, should in principle be related to those of the line before. Bunting's markings, in the copy of Whitman that he prepared for his tape reading, help us to distinguish:

> Out of the cradle / endlessly rocking,
> Out of the mocking-bird's throat, the musical shuttle,
> Out of the Ninth-month midnight,
> Over the sterile sands^ and the fields beyond, where the

> child / leaving his bed / wander'd alone, bareheaded,
> barefoot

Whitman underscores the key rhythm motif for the first verse-paragraph by repeating it to form the entire first line. He then repeats it many times more ("musical shuttle," and so forth) but also gives it a good many modified forms. Thus ╱ x x ╱:

> leaving his bed
> (of) yearning and love
> there in the mist

Likewise ╱ x x ╱ x ╱

> over the sterile sands

But Bunting's markings seem to suggest that in the second long verse-paragraph, a different motif family dominates. Its center may be the double trochee: ╱ x ╱ x

> Up this seashore
> in some briers
> two together

Eventually the first motif becomes dominant again (though its content has changed drastically: "incessantly moaning," "sullenly timing"). But in between, a great number of modifications—and perhaps, depending on how one takes them, interventions by other families—have appeared.[27]

At this point in his logic Bunting calls in aid what has seemed, in preceding lectures, to be a set of the devil's devices. He says "What Whitman adds to this [tradition] is to make *all* the words part of the machinery which causes them to cohere into a poem"; and this is done, not only with the kinds of rhythm modulation and repeat I have mentioned but with a "greater use of *poetic* ornament (I mean, alliteration, assonance, vowel sequences & so on)," and with onomatopoeia, "rarely direct, but frequently emotional."

Now it seems to me that Bunting sees these further fine cross-knittings as necessary because he knows that the fundamental method in this tradition cannot rhythmically pattern all the words in all the lines and that its great strength is that it does not.

My understanding of Bunting's intention is that he sees a great deal of rhythmic play between phrases that more or less dominate their lines, often constituting the greater part of their lines, and sometimes the whole of it, but never being required to form—to constitute—the whole of each line of a continuous passage.

If this view of Bunting's ideas is right, they may well have owed something to Duhamel and Vildrac's concept of a *constante rhythmique,* as described in 1910.[28] This *constante* is a "fixed numeric body," whose recurrence ties the lines together but which may or may not recur in the same part of the line, the rest being "variable" and giving the line its individual character:

> des cadences *de marteaux géants* dans des forges
> hantées *de chanteurs athlètes*
> s'allument, frissonnent, sonnent et s'estompent
> pour faire place *aux chants doux des harpes.*[29]

Duhamel and Vildrac held that "two unequal *constantes rhythmiques* can combine, either by following each other, or by overlapping. The *constante* may impose itself from the beginning of the strophe; at other times it makes itself felt only during or at the end of the poetic paragraph; for, by the values of its consonants and its vowels, by the presence and the number of its mute *e*s, it can become more or less solid, or efface itself." Alliteration, by its placing, can "launch" a rhythm for the rest of the strophe; and all the subtleties of alliteration and lapse of alliteration will have their effect on the relative strength of a motif. For "we are not revealing a formal intention in these poets," they insist. "We are observing the presence of a phenomenon."[30]

Here lies the intelligence of their idea. These rhythmic motifs may rise and fade, leaving other phrases unpatterned (musically neutral). They are not items to be charted back to back against other rhythmic units, counting from the beginning of every line and working through to the end of it.[31] That whole-line approach has been used by almost every prosodist who has attempted to account for stress patterns in this tradition, whether in the Psalms or in Whitman; it always forces the prosodist into arbitrary "scannings," and far more important, it reduces terribly the scope for ambiguities, overlaps, tensions between the possibility of one motif and another. Such tension is at the base of all Bunting's interest in rhythm, and, I should have thought, of all sensitive interest.

And this, finally, makes clear why it is essential to cleave to Bunting's musical sense of the word *cadence.* There have been valiant attempts to understand the rhythms of Wyatt and even of Chaucer, starting from the linguistic sense of this word.[32] But in the linguistic sense, every phrase

in every sentence has a cadence, and this cadence of the phrases constituting it is a feature of the whole of the utterance, omitting nothing.
Bunting's remarks about "a lot of freedom until the 'cadence'" would
here have no meaning.

2. Still we have been talking so far only about the function of rhythm
as texturer. But if the rhythmic motifs—or families of them—are distinct
enough to register themselves on the aural memory as having *their own
character;* and if particular ones are made (after an absence, during which
others dominate) to return; this will, as Bunting says here, "have just the
same effect as taking up a theme, more or less transformed, has in music."

And that effect in music, as we have noted, is strong enough to constitute one of the main structural devices of post-Renaissance Western
music. It is one of the devices by which a composer makes us feel that
the work is more than a continuing sequence of interesting fibers, nicely
knitted: it has main directions, to which the conclusion is somehow a re-
sponse.

The renewal of verse must be in sound; in sound, the foundation must
be rhythm; and now it seemed that rhythm could use a full range of
resources together with an intensive contrasting and modulating organization to provide the main shape for the most ambitious kind of poetic
work. This is the starting point for all Bunting's works using sonata form
for their main structure: that is, for all but one of his major poems.

He inherited the necessary mechanisms in 1919, when, he tells us,
Nina Hamnett the painter handed over to him Pound's demonstration
(the *Sextus Propertius*) of what could be done in the twentieth century with
Whitman's devices.[33] But this was still only texture. Pound himself never
developed it into elements for building main structure. As Bunting explains below in his lecture on Pound, the *Cantos* are structured as fugue,
which requires multiple voices, and these voices Pound suggests by the
ply of *ideational* motifs, not rhythmic ones.[34] Bunting opts for a form that
allows fewer and sharper contrasts: sonata form. And this form, as a plan
of *rhythm*-motifs, underlies (at least in intention) all his longer poems except "Chomei at Toyama."

Bunting does not set out this structural program in the present lectures. He considered it his own, possibly unique, contribution to twentieth-century English-language poetry, and his own poetry is not a topic
here. But he makes a clear allusion to it, as an extension of his argu-
ments here, when he comes to outlining Pound's plan for the *Cantos*. At
that point I explain its elements in more detail.[35]

NINE

Wordsworth and the XIX Century

I want to be very summary in what I have to say today, because I think you would like to find out what bearing all we've been discussing has on recent and contemporary poetry. But first I have to clear the whole XIX century out of our way. Fortunately, that wont take us long.

It would be easy to fill a whole year with Wordsworth, I think. He was as singular as he was excellent, and it seems to me that the customary view of his work is still beset by misconceptions and irrelevancies. I have tried to suggest that his poetry is rather the completion and clarification of XVIII c. tendencies than an early move towards Romanticism. Like other generalisations about such a prolific and many-sided poet as Wordsworth, this observation is subject to plenty of minor exceptions and modifications; but it is still true of the general colour of his work, & the root of much that astonished his contemporaries.

In particular, he completed, with great energy, the XVIII c. drift towards realism. This is not merely true of his subject matter — labourers, tramps, and the things about him. It is also the root of his vocabulary. He used English words instead of Johnsonese latinisms, as everybody is told at school; but only in the realistic part of his work. When he speculates or grows didactic, when he tries to be rather clumsily Gothic, he uses an un-realist language like his predecessors, though rarely as extreme as theirs.

Yeats complained that Wordsworth had tried to clean up the vocabulary, but had forgotten the syntax. His work is full of clumsy inversions and ill-placed parentheses or adverbial phrases. Yeats said that poetry required a living syntax even more than a living vocabulary,[1] and much of the pains he took with his own poems was an effort to get the syntax of common speech without the diffuseness that often goes with it.

This lecture is handwritten throughout. On its repeats from "Wordsworth and Whitman," cf. chap. 8, n. 1.

Wordsworth does quite often let his words hang in a loose, disorderly tangle that could surely be made neat by taking pains. But concision is not entirely a matter of diction and grammar.

You know how people who have something to tell you are apt to obscure it by all sorts of needless detail, explaining carefully things which are either irrelevant or self-evident. Even the television comedians laugh at it. But a good deal of ambitious writing is made tedious by exactly the same fault—the desire to be perfectly explicit in every detail, to leave nothing untold. They do not trust their readers to notice anything that has not been carefully pointed out.

Wordsworth is not entirely free of this fault; but in general he does leave out, very boldly, whatever he thinks the reader can supply for himself. When he does seem to be dwelling on irrelevant details, it is very often part of the technique of realism, the corroborative detail that guarantees less obvious statements, the trick Defoe used so often. The final lines of 'The Brothers', which I read last week, are of this kind. They say, in effect, 'This story seems astonishing, but it is part & parcel of everyday life'. But for this, they would seem irrelevant.

On the whole, Wordsworth is a very concise poet, in spite of fairly frequent untidiness of language. His kind of concision works well in narrative, and in lyrics with a narrative content. You know, I believe, that I think him the most skilful, and the most complex, of narrative poets in English. I tried to demonstrate that by reading 'The Brothers', but if there had been time I could have done it only slightly less effectively by reading 'The Waggoner' or 'The White Doe of Rylstone', or any of several other poems in which a story is told with great skill. I will be content to show it in little in 'The Sailor's Mother'

The Sailor's Mother

One morning (raw it was and wet—
A foggy day in winter time)
A Woman on the road I met,
Not old, though something past her prime:
Majestic in her person, tall and straight;
And like a Roman matron's was her mien and gait.

The ancient spirit is not dead;
Old times, thought I, are breathing there;
Proud was I that my country bred

Such strength, a dignity so fair:
She begged an alms, like one in poor estate;
I looked at her again, nor did my pride abate.

When from these lofty thoughts I woke,
"What is it," said I, "that you bear,
Beneath the covert of your Cloak,
Protected from this cold damp air?"
She answered, soon as she the question heard,
"A simple burthen, Sir, a little Singing-bird."

And, thus continuing, she said,
"I had a Son, who many a day
Sailed on the seas, but he is dead;
In Denmark he was cast away:
And I have travelled weary miles to see
If aught which he had owned might still remain for me.

"The bird and cage they both were his:
'Twas my Son's bird; and neat and trim
He kept it: many voyages
The singing-bird had gone with him;
When last he sailed, he left the bird behind;
From bodings, as might be, that hung upon his mind.

"He to a fellow-lodger's care
Had left it, to be watched and fed,
And pipe its song in safety;—there
I found it when my Son was dead;
And now, God help me for my little wit!
I bear it with me, Sir;—he took so much delight in it." [2]

Wordsworth spends some time establishing the woman's grand appearance; but none at all in pointing the contrast between that appearance and the fact that she was begging, unless 'I looked at her again' is meant to imply that he was startled. The begging establishes her poverty; the harshness poverty breeds is shown only by the fact that her journey was undertaken to get whatever trifle of money her son might have left: but there was none—she must beg her way home—only the bird in its cage. You are left to infer this. The hardness [3] of the poor is insisted on again by her apology for keeping the bird: 'God help me for my little wit', and it is only in the last half line that the whole force & pathos of her motherhood takes charge, suddenly, of all the previous detail. You could hardly make the point more economically.

But there is much more to Wordsworth than narrative skill or realism. I think most critics get lost in chasing his supposed philosophy or his very vague mysticism. I dont think he had any philosophy. That is why we have a *Prelude* and an *Excursion,* but not a word of the philosophic poem they were to have adorned.[4] As for mysticism, whenever that word turns up those who use it can find support in anything or nothing.[5] It is by definition an unreasonable belief. There is no arguing about it. You like what Plotinus tells you, or you dont: there is no room for evidence, and hardly any for discussion.

Fortunately, it doesnt matter to a literary critic, for what poetry professes to tell us is scarcely relevant. The poetry is in the sound, the shape of the poem; in its rhythmic variety and power, in the emotional suggestiveness of its vowels and consonants set out in complex patterns, in the symmetry of the line the sound seems to draw in the air, or in the proportion between one loop of sound and another. The people who chase real or imaginary quirks of mysticism through Wordsworth's output miss the point of his work completely; and I am afraid that is true of nearly all the Wordsworth criticism I happen to have seen.

Written in March while Resting on the Bridge at the Foot of Brother's Water

> The Cock is crowing,
> The stream is flowing,
> The small birds twitter,
> The lake doth glitter,
> The green field sleeps in the sun;
> The oldest and youngest
> Are at work with the strongest;
> The cattle are grazing,
> Their heads never raising;
> There are forty feeding like one!
>
> Like an army defeated
> The snow hath retreated,
> And now doth fare ill
> On the top of the bare hill;

> The Ploughboy is whooping—anon—anon:
>> There's joy in the mountains;
>> There's life in the fountains;
>> Small clouds are sailing,
>> Blue sky prevailing;
> The rain is over and gone! [6]

There hadnt been anything like that in English since the Elizabethans when Wordsworth wrote it in 1802.[7] Burns, Ramsay, Blake, however good their work, however singable, used well-worn rhythms and sound effects that were part of the common stock. Their songs were new examples of an old mode. Wordsworth made his music new.

His great contribution to the range of English sound has usually been overlooked, partly because the critics were chasing a will o' the wisp philosophy, and partly because many of them could not hear it. Two hundred years ago Standard English had not been invented and there was neither a BBC nor a system of education determined to make us all talk alike. Wordsworth spoke as men spoke where he was born, with broad accents and a marked R. He kept his native tongue in spite of Cambridge & London & Somerset and Leicestershire. Southerners found it hard to follow his conversation—Keats and Hazlitt and Coleridge all mention this.[8]

Wordsworth did not write dialect; but he composed aloud, very loud according to the anecdotes, in the language he spoke, and that was not the Koiné we are all taught to use now. Read him aloud, with R's and broad vowels. Remember that the word 'water' was unknown to him. He rhymes it with 'chatter' and 'shatter' because he pronounced it 'watter'; and though he spells Yarrow with OW, as the map does, he rhymes it with the word he (and we) pronounce 'marra', and rhyme with 'Jarra', down the river there.[9] Bear such things in mind when you read 'The Solitary Reaper' or the 'Ode on Immortality' and you will hear a music of great sonority and variety, differing a good deal from both the then available standards, the XVIII c, and the Spenserian derivatives, a singular music of his own which I dont think anyone has recaptured since his time.

With that I mean to leave Wordsworth. He had no successors. Neither his narrative subtlety nor his original sound seems to have had any effect in the XIX c. Even his realism vanished in the romantic orgy. Narrative? Byron was content with the slapdash manner of Scott's 'Lays',[10] spiced up with a few jokes & rhymes in the manner of Butler. Browning tried to give his stories life by colloquialisms. It worked sometimes.

Rhythm & sound? Keats went straight back to Spenser, and overdid Spenser. Tennyson tried out a more flexible rhythm, and lighter vowels, but had nothing to stiffen the prettinesses, so that the effect is rather like barley-sugar—nice enough for one mouthful, but not what you want to make a meal of. The poetry of the whole century is in the main a set of variations on Keats & Byron, Browning & Tennyson. It is hard to distinguish the Preraphaelites, though Rossetti had studied Dante.[11] Only Swinburne showed some real curiosity about rhythm.

The one poet of that century to add something substantial to the outfit of English poetry (as distinct from repeating, with variations, what had been often done) was Walt Whitman.[12]

Whitman is a very uneven poet.[13] His worst is pretty poor stuff, and even his best is disfigured by the devotion to very empty abstract words such as Freedom, Democracy, Life, Death, which was a characteristic of the middle of last century. You find the same excessive use of them in Victor Hugo, in Swinburne & others.

But Whitman brought something quite new to English poetry. I dont mean 'free verse', whatever that is. Lots of people had tried loose, unrhymed rhythms before him: Blake and Christopher Smart, Milton, the translators of the *Psalms* and the *Song of Songs*. Some kinds of heavily rhythmed prose make an approach to poetry—Browne and Burton, Latymer and Cranmer.

TEN

Precursors

I have spent too much time reviewing the general history of English poetry to spread myself very widely over its more recent developments. Still, I dont think the time has been misspent. I hope I have indicated what I think the main character of English poetry has been and what can be a foundation for its future. I have tried to show the persistent beat of English verse derived from Old English, and, from the same source, the tendency to alliteration: the close union of poetry and music in Wyat and Campion: the vast array of forms and ornaments Spenser introduced: Wordsworth's insistence on realism, which dictates his reform of diction and at least some of his narrative virtuosity; and the way Whitman discovered of holding verse together without a rigid or repetitive pattern.

But the XIX century poets neglected both Wordsworth and Whitman. Keats turned back to direct imitation of Spenser, and the rest followed him so far as their skill sufficed to take them. Most of them turned to one degree or another of prettiness, and even the most original of them, Robert Browning, who usually dodged prettiness, seems to have imagined that energy was mainly a matter of vocabulary, so that though he often uses colloquial words, and sometimes colloquial syntax, he lets them flood the page, loses his effect by repeating it or expanding it, and mistakes dramatic violence for realism. He did, however, develop the form which has since been called the 'persona', the monologue in an assumed character, which survived into this century and still has possibilities.[1] But the bulk of Victorian poetry dealt with trivial themes in a new version of poetic diction. Tennyson's version of the Arthurian cycle is very close to what the XVIII c would have called namby-pamby.[2] It is essentially nursery stuff, and you cannot say much more for Morris and Rossetti. Even Swinburne, who had more contemporary interests, never managed to climb down from his empty abstract words—freedom, love, pain and what not.

It was a mess.

In recent years it has become a commonplace of the schools to talk of a kind of revolution in poetry which is usually attributed to Ezra Pound, T. S. Eliot, and perhaps W. B. Yeats, about the time of the first world war. Sometimes those who talk about it forget the premonitory rumblings. Sometimes they fail to realise what the change really was and try to include a lot of old leftovers among the poetry that followed. Or, trying to trace history in too narrow a way, they resuscitate experimental work which never had life enough to effect anything permanent, instead of remembering the work that really did change taste.

The earliest of the rebels against the Victorian mode was certainly Thomas Hardy. He was writing poems in the 1860's which would have shocked his contemporaries pretty thoroughly if they had ever noticed them; but he made no definite appearance as a poet until the 90's, and his influence dates only from then—or much later. Hardy did not believe that God was in his heaven and all right with the world; on the contrary. He did not find it a pretty world at all. Like Wordsworth, he tried hard for realism; but unlike Wordsworth he did not think realism would be best achieved by using common speech. He uses awkward syntax and unfamiliar, often jawbreaking words, not for lack of skill, but because he thought people let poetry come in one ear and out of the other. He wanted to make them pause and think about it.

Gerard Manley Hopkins began 20 years after Hardy, and had even less influence, because his poetry was never published until his innovations in vocabulary and metre had become more or less irrelevant.[3] Others had tackled the same problems as Hopkins, more effectively, meanwhile. He, like Hardy, made his verse difficult and required his readers to pause and think; and another who followed a similar path was Charles Doughty. I am not going to suggest that anybody should read Doughty's *The Dawn in Britain* unless they are going in for research, but it was certainly a symptom of dissatisfaction with the age of Tennyson, written in a difficult, craggy language.[4] Doughty and Hopkins were both, I think, as mellifluous as most of the Tennysonians, but in a different way;[5] at any rate, they disturbed the tranquil surface of Victorian poetry as violently as they knew how. Poetry, for them, was serious, not a branch of the entertainment industry. However, none of these poets had ever much effect on what happened to English poetry. Even Hardy, much the best of them, had no outstanding followers.

The first un-Victorian voice that the British public actually heard was that of Rudyard Kipling. Like his cousin, Ford Madox Ford, he was one of the third generation of pre-Raphaelites by birth, and here and there there are marks of his origin in his writings.[6] But he, like Hardy, wanted to put realism and a poetry of his own time in place of the prettiness and mediaeval leanings of his predecessors. People are often puzzled by the uncertainty of Kipling's taste. He prints some very bad poems among the good ones. I think it was because he was so utterly isolated, exploring new regions of fact, alone, and ransacking all known poetic forms to find the right ones for his matter. Small wonder that he made many mistakes. They were not made carelessly or for lack of pains. Hardly any poet for the past century has worked so hard to attain economy and finish as Kipling did. Here is a poem published in one of his earliest books, which shows his power of condensation.

The Victorians had been tormenting themselves for half a century to find some way of keeping the unifying power of Christianity though they had ceased to believe its myths. They wrote 'about it and about, and evermore came out by that same door wherein they went,' as Fitzgerald says.[7] But what they fumble at at great length, Kipling gets into eighteen lines not easy to forget.

L'Envoi

The smoke upon your Altar dies,
        The flowers decay,
The Goddess of your sacrifice
        Has flown away.
What profit then to sing or slay
The sacrifice from day to day?

"We know the Shrine is void," they said,
        "The Goddess flown—
"Yet wreaths are on the altar laid—
        "The Altar-Stone
"Is black with fumes of sacrifice,
"Albeit She has fled our eyes.

"For, it may be, if still we sing
        "And tend the Shrine,
"Some Deity on wandering wing
        "May there incline;

"And, finding all in order meet,
"Stay while we worship at Her feet."[8]

Early in his career Kipling tried out Browning's style of 'persona', and I think 'McAndrew's Hymn' and 'The Mary Gloster' explore realms that were closed to Browning: but they are too long to read here, and in form, at least, they were not innovations. Some of Kipling's searching for the right form led him to kinds of pastiche, but pastiche done as well as he did it is poetry in its own right.

Cities and Thrones and Powers

Cities and Thrones and Powers
    Stand in Time's eye,
Almost as long as flowers,
    Which daily die:
But, as ncw buds put forth
    To glad new men,
Out of the spent and unconsidered Earth
    The Cities rise again.

This season's Daffodil,
    She never hears
What change, what chance, what chill,
    Cut down last year's;
But with bold countenance,
    And knowledge small,
Esteems her seven days' continuance
    To be perpetual.

So Time that is o'er-kind
    To all that be,
Ordains us e'en as blind,
    As bold as she:
That in our very death,
    And burial sure,
Shadow to shadow, well persuaded, saith,
    "See how our works endure!"

(484–85)

He tried sestina, ballad—everything you can think of—as Pound did later; and some of his forms are discoveries of his own.

Song of the Galley-Slaves

We pulled for you when the wind was against us and the sails
were low.

> *Will you never let us go?*

We ate bread and onions when you took towns, or ran aboard
quickly when you were beaten back by the foe.

The Captains walked up and down the deck in fair weather
singing songs, but we were below.

We fainted with our chins on the oars and you did not see that we
were idle, for we still swung to and fro.

> *Will you never let us go?*

The salt made the oar-handles like shark-skin; our knees were cut
to the bone with salt-cracks; our hair was stuck to our
foreheads; and our lips were cut to the gums, and you whipped
us because we could not row.

> *Will you never let us go?*

But, in a little time, we shall run out of the port-holes as the water
runs along the oar-blade, and though you tell the others to row
after us you will never catch us till you catch the oar-thresh
and tie up the winds in the belly of the sail. Aho!

> *Will you never let us go?*

(675)

Again

Harp Song of the Dane Women

What is a woman that you forsake her,
And the hearth-fire and the home-acre,
To go with the old grey Widow-maker?

She has no house to lay a guest in—
But one chill bed for all to rest in,
That the pale suns and the stray bergs nest in.

She has no strong white arms to fold you,
But the ten-times-fingering weed to hold you—
Out on the rocks where the tide has rolled you.

Yet, when the signs of summer thicken,
And the ice breaks, and the birch-buds quicken,
Yearly you turn from our side, and sicken—

Sicken again for the shouts and the slaughters.
You steal away to the lapping waters,
And look at your ship in her winter-quarters.

You forget our mirth, and talk at the tables,
The kine in the shed and the horse in the stables—
To pitch her sides and go over her cables.

Then you drive out where the storm-clouds swallow,
And the sound of your oar-blades, falling hollow,
Is all we have left through the months to follow.

Ah, what is Woman that you forsake her,
And the hearth-fire and the home-acre,
To go with the old grey Widow-maker?

                                        (528–29)

Almost always Kipling sticks to the words we all use and keeps them in the usual order, and almost always he combines economy of words with economy of matter.

The Way through the Woods

They shut the road through the woods
Seventy years ago.
Weather and rain have undone it again,
And now you would never know
There was once a road through the woods
Before they planted the trees.
It is underneath the coppice and hearth,
And the thin anemones.
Only the keeper sees
That, where the ring-dove broods,
And the badgers roll at ease,
There was once a road through the woods.

Yet, if you enter the woods
Of a summer evening late,
When the night-air cools on the trout-ringed pools
Where the otter whistles his mate,
(They fear not men in the woods,
Because they see so few.)

You will hear the beat of a horse's feet,
And the swish of a skirt in the dew,
Steadily cantering through
The misty solitudes,
As though they perfectly knew
The old lost road through the woods. . . .
But there is no road through the woods.

(487–88)

A good deal of Kipling's verse was written to be sung and is sung effectively: not merely the hymns such as 'Recessional', but some of the *Barrack-Room Ballads*. Yet it must be admitted that Kipling's foot is heavy —his rhythms have something coarse in them that prevents the subtleties you can find in Wyat before him or in his contemporary Yeats. I find the same defect in Eliot.[9]

The other offspring of the pre-Raphaelites, Ford Madox Ford, was somewhat younger than Kipling, and much slower in finding his own voice.[10] He too was uncertain of his way, and published bad poems—perhaps more bad than good: yet Pound is not merely being loyal to a friend when he insists on the part Ford played in changing English poetry in the earlier years of this century. Ford at his best uses language that is not merely current but conversational. Ford at his best names *things* and lets them evoke the emotion without mentioning it.[11] He had not the gift of monumental brevity, but he uses repetition for a kind of hypnotic effect:[12] uses it quite consciously, without trying to disguise it.

The Starling

It's an odd thing how one changes . . .
Walking along the upper ranges
Of this land of plains,
In this month of rains,
On a drying road where the poplars march along,
Suddenly,
With a rush of wings flew down a company,
A multitude, throng upon throng,
Of starlings,
Successive orchestras of song,
Flung, like the babble of surf,
On to the roadside turf—

And so, for a mile, for a mile and a half—a long way,
Flight follows flight
Thro' the still grey light
Of the steel-grey day,
Whirling beside the road in clamorous crowds,
Never near, never far, in the shade of the poplars and clouds.

It's an odd thing how one changes . . .
And what strikes me now as most strange is:
After the starlings had flown
Over the plain and were gone,
There was one of them stayed on alone
In the trees; it chattered on high,
Lifting its bill to the sky,
Distending its throat,
Crooning harsh note after note,
In soliloquy,
Sitting alone.

And after a hush
It gurgled as gurgled a well,
Warbled as warbles a thrush,
Had a try at the sound of a bell
And mimicked a jay . . .
But I,
Whilst the starling mimicked on high
Pulsing its throat and its wings,
I went on my way
Thinking of things,
Onwards and over the range
And that's what is strange.

I went down 'twixt tobacco and grain,
Descending the chequer-board plain
Where the apples and maize are;
Under the loopholed gate
In the village wall
Where the goats clatter over the cobbles
And the intricate, straw-littered ways are . . .
The ancient watchman hobbles

Cloaked, with his glasses of horn at the end of his nose,
Wearing velvet short hose
And a three-cornered hat on his pate,
And his pike-staff and all.
And he carries a proclamation,
An invitation,
To great and small,
Man and beast
To a wedding feast,
And he carries a bell and rings . . .
From the steeple looks down a saint,
From a doorway a queenly peasant
Looks out, in her bride-gown of lace
And her sister, a quaint little darling
Who twitters and chirps like a starling.
And this little old place,
It's so quaint,
It's so pleasant;
And the watch bell rings, and the church bell rings
And the wedding procession draws nigh,
Bullock carts, fiddlers and goods.
But I
Pass on my way to the woods
Thinking of things.

Years ago I'd have stayed by the starling,
Marking the iridescence of his throat,
Marvelling at the change of his note;
I'd have said to the peasant child: 'Darling
Here's a groschen and give me a kiss'. . . I'd have stayed
To sit with the bridesmaids at table,
And have taken my chance
Of a dance
With the bride in her laces
Or the maids with the blonde, placid faces
And ribbons and crants in the stable . . .

But the church bell still rings
And I'm far away out on the plain,
In the grey weather amongst the tobacco and grain,

And village and gate and wall
Are a long grey line with the church over all
And miles and miles away in the sky
The starlings go wheeling round on high
Over the distant ranges.
The violin strings
Thrill away and the day grows more grey.
And I . . . I stand thinking of things.
Yes, it's strange how one changes.[13]

Finally, in this context, Yeats must be considered as two persons. The younger Yeats, almost exactly Kipling's contemporary, was far less of an innovator than Kipling. He seemed, by and large, content with the general structure and general tendency of Victorian poetry: his matter, like theirs, was far away in a never-never land: Irish myth instead of Arthurian romance or Morris's denatured Vikings, but Irish myth tamed and smoothed from its native savagery to something that differed very little from the never-never lands of Tennyson and Morris.

It is true that Yeats's first long poem, *The Wanderings of Oisin,* moves much faster than Tennyson ever did, and suggests an atmosphere far better than Morris could; but its superiority is only the superiority of greater talent: it is not different in any fundamental way. Similarly, his early lyrics have very little that is new in them. They are good specimens of late Victorian, and very little more.

However, even in his earliest work Yeats had *something* that was new.

He had considered Wordsworth's preface to the 2nd edition of *Lyrical Ballads,* and concluded that it was incomplete. Wordsworth had insisted on the plain words of ordinary men, but he had said nothing about the plain syntax of ordinary speech. Yeats thought the syntax more important than the vocabulary.[14] He was not consistent in his practise—but very early he declared war on inversions and treated attributive adjectives with distrust.

The Meditation of the Old Fisherman

You waves, though you dance by my feet like children at play,
Though you glow and you glance, though you purr and you dart;
In the Junes that were warmer than these are, the waves were
    more gay,
When I was a boy with never a crack in my heart.

The herring are not in the tides as they were of old;
My sorrow! for many a creak gave the creel in the cart
That carried the take down to Sligo town to be sold,
When I was a boy with never a crack in my heart.

And ah, you proud maiden, you are not so fair when his oar
Is heard on the water, as they were, the proud and apart,
Who paced in the eve by the nets on the pebbly shore,
When I was a boy with never a crack in my heart.[15]

Beyond this, he had heard something about the theories of French poets a bit older than himself: about Verlaine, who treated poetry as sound, primarily; and Mallarmé, who, amongst the curious rigmaroles of his 'symbolism', never lost sight of the idea that poetry is essentially the same as music. Some of this he incorporated in his lyrics. I dont imply that Yeats was the only poet in the nineties, nor even the first, to bring French practise in to elucidate and reinforce the precepts of Pater,[16] nor even the earliest: but the results of what a man of genius like Yeats does are far more lasting, have far more bearing on what comes after him, than the work of other men.

Who Goes with Fergus?

Who will go drive with Fergus now,
And pierce the deep wood's woven shade,
And dance upon the level shore?
Young man, lift up your russet brow,
And lift your tender eyelids, maid,
And brood on hopes and fear no more.

And no more turn aside and brood
Upon love's bitter mystery;
For Fergus rules the brazen cars,
And rules the shadows of the wood,
And the white breast of the dim sea
And all dishevelled wandering stars.[17]

Very Victorian: but how many Victorians had the *musical* precision of a line like

'For Fergus rules the brazen cars'?

And when this skill is raised to great concentration—

The Folly of Being Comforted

One that is ever kind said yesterday:
'Your well-beloved's hair has threads of grey,
And little shadows come about her eyes;
Time can but make it easier to be wise
Though now it seems impossible, and so
All that you need is patience.'
                                Heart cries, 'No,
I have not a crumb of comfort, not a grain.
Time can but make her beauty over again:
Because of that great nobleness of hers
The fire that stirs about her, when she stirs,
Burns but more clearly. O she had not these ways
When all the wild summer was in her gaze.'

O heart! O heart! if she'd but turn her head,
You'd know the folly of being comforted.[18]

You cannot forget a poem like that: so that whatever technical skill is
in it, even though it is not easy to sort it out, takes a permanent place
in the reader's mind. So Yeats too was one of the premonitory signs of a
change to come, though in 1900 he had far less notion of the need for a
change than Kipling, Doughty, Hardy or Ford.

So much has been written in recent years about Yeats and Pound, Eliot
and Joyce; people have looked out so many facts, and so many of the
facts they have looked out are irrelevant or even misleading, that I sometimes have difficulty in recognising the men I knew when I was young.

And even those men themselves, when they write about their youth,
seem often to be more concerned with amusing or picturesque exploits
than with the real roots of what happened. We hear a lot about the
Imagists, and about F. S. Flint or T. E. Hulme or other people of no importance. Pound and Yeats, Joyce and Eliot, picked up ideas from everything around them. If here and there a notion reached them via Flint or
Aldington or Arthur Symons, what does it matter?

The notion was ineffective in such hands, and in any case, it was transformed and married to other fruitful notions by the great poets, and only
then did it begin to mould our poetry. But between themselves, the new
ideas bred rapidly. I suppose we must begin with the meeting of Pound
and Yeats.

Yeats had learned as much of his trade as he could at that time in the Rhymers Club, which met at the Cheshire Cheese for a few years in the 90's. Lionel Johnson, Dowson, Davidson, Victor Plarr and so on[19] — they dont matter. Even Davidson, the most intelligent of them, has left very little worth preserving, but their criticism kept Yeats on his toes at a time when perhaps he needed it.

ELEVEN

1910—20

Looking back from 1970 at the poetry written before 1910 and the poetry written after 1920 by first class poets in English, what strikes me most is an enormous increase of interest in music and, as is to be expected, in the analogies between musical form and the form of poetry. Compared with this, the so-called 'movements' which historians of literature bother themselves about were momentary and insignificant. Of course, the people who took part in them look back on them through the haze of memory, all tinted with the gaiety of their own youth, and dwell on notions which were never very convincing and have become less convincing still as they have grown old, because that is what they were aware of at the time. They were called symbolists or imagists or vorticists, and the names were good excuses to meet and argue in teashops and pubs; but most of those who met and argued left very little trace of themselves in what seems likely to be permanent poetry.

There is not much to be gained by reading the work of Edgar Jepson or Selwyn Image or Victor Plarr,[1] or that of Amy Lowell and her friends, except perhaps the matter for a footnote to some line in Pound's Cantos. Who cares whether F. S. Flint or T. E. Hulme or Ezra Pound invented the word 'imagism'? Or whether the vorticists were just Anglicised versions of Marinetti or had some margin of new ideas of their own?[2] All this was just froth on the river. You know how all that detergent foam gets caught in the eddies and the slow edges of the stream and draws your attention away from the set of the current and hides the look of the water.

Yeats and Pound and Eliot made their mark mainly because they worked much harder at their art than other men were doing, and thought more about it. All three of them had no doubt either read Mallarmé or heard his ideas discussed, but so had plenty of other men who made no effective use of what might be learned from Mallarmé. Pound sat for a while amongst the audience of T. E. Hulme, but none of Hulme's other auditors turned out to be first class poets. Pound was attracted by the violent energy of Wyndham Lewis, but it cannot be shown that Vorticism had any effect at all on his poetry.

Hulme wrote five elegant little epigrams:

Autumn

A touch of cold in the Autumn night—
I walked abroad,
And saw the ruddy moon lean over a hedge
Like a red-faced farmer.
I did not stop to speak, but nodded,
And round about were the wistful stars
With white faces like town children.

Mana Aboda

Beauty is the marking-time, the stationary vibration, the feigned ecstasy of an arrested impulse unable to reach its natural end.

Mana Aboda, whose bent form
The sky in archèd circle is,
Seems ever for an unknown grief to mourn.
Yet on a day I heard her cry:
"I weary of the roses and the singing poets—
Josephs all, not tall enough to try."

Above the Dock

Above the quiet dock in mid night,
Tangled in the tall mast's corded height,
Hangs the moon. What seemed so far away
Is but a child's balloon, forgotten after play.

The Embankment

The fantasia of a fallen gentleman on a cold, bitter night.

Once, in finesse of fiddles found I ecstasy,
In the flash of gold heels on the hard pavement.
Now see I
That warmth's the very stuff of poesy.
Oh, God, make small

The old star-eaten blanket of the sky,
That I may fold it round me and in comfort lie.

Conversion

Lighthearted I walked into the valley wood
In the time of hyacinths,
Till beauty like a scented cloth
Cast over, stifled me. I was bound
Motionless and faint of breath
By loveliness that is her own eunuch.
Now pass I to the final river
Ignominiously, in a sack, without sound,
As any peeping Turk to the Bosphorus.[3]

They do not exemplify his assertion that poetry, in his time, would tend to resemble sculpture.[4] There is an amusing twist to the idea and an elegant way [of] expressing it, but that wasnt new in 1914. The same qualities can be found in many of the shorter prose paragraphs in Samuel Butler's Notebooks, published a year or two earlier. I cannot say whether Hulme had read them, but I think it likely.[5] Pound had. At any rate, there is nothing here on which to found a 'movement', and nothing to justify the name Imagism, which seems to imply some connection with drawing or painting. I have read as much as I could find of Hulme's work, and cannot imagine why anybody ever took him seriously. His philosophy seems to be a deliberate rejection of reason wherever reason conflicted with Hulme's temperament, which was violent and arbitrary. It is full of weak little echoes of Nietzsche and Sorel.[6] But he is said to have been a fascinating talker, and it is quite possible to be that even when your ideas are secondhand and secondrate. He seems to me about as important to literary history as some of the witch-doctors Yeats consulted about magic or Rosicrucianism.

But the revival of a taste for music was something that went on without noticing or being noticed by the movements and coteries. It began in a small way and didnt reach a really wide public until Edward Clark took over the BBC's music about 1925 or 6 and deliberately gave the public what it didnt want until it changed its mind and did.[7]

I find it hard to get people to realise what a squalid state music was in in England before that. As late as the middle twenties I remember a respected critic excusing Beethoven's late quartets on the ground that the poor chap was deaf and couldnt hear the ghastly noise they made. Caruso sang 'The Yanks are Coming' and Dame Clara Butt never gave a concert without 'Home Sweet Home' and 'Love's Old Sweet Song'.[8] Even the cultured few limited their pleasures to Beethoven's successors or to Wagner and Verdi. Only the real intellectuals could put up with Debussy. Stravinsky was to be endured, but Schoenberg was merely a mad pedant. Mozart was not often heard, Handel only in edited versions: and musical history began with Bach, who was to be put up with in spite of his dryness and terrible difficulty.[9]

No doubt there were people who really enjoyed music and knew something about it, but they had not much public existence and hardly amounted to more than a clique of highbrows, suspect to most people, not only to the Philistines. Those of you who have read E. M. Forster's novels will have noticed that the badge of the good, sensitive, intellectual people in them is that they go to concerts. The baddies dont. Forster's people were the cream of society in the well-educated and wealthy class in Bloomsbury and South Kensington, and the Home Counties, in the years just before the first world war.

But Arnold Dolmetsch was in the midst of his researches into old instruments and old music and a few people had noticed his work.[10] (It wasnt widely recognised even in 1926.[11] He was 'that cranky archaeologist'). Dr Fellowes and others were working, though not yet noticed, at earlier music still,[12] and a few overspills from this activity did reach a rather limited public. Walter Rummel, the pianist, was able to help Ezra Pound to reconstruct, somewhat shakily, some of the music of the Troubadours; and a man called Frederick Keel had published a volume of Elizabethan songs which gradually circulated.[13] Keel's work was crude compared to that of later editors. He mistook a couple of madrigals for single-voice songs, and he frisked up piano accompaniments which sometimes muddy the lute parts, but the songs were singable and beautiful and deserved their success. Before 1910 I think they must have been well enough known to be heard now and then at the tea parties to which Kensington and Bloomsbury ladies attracted the poets and painters and novelists of London.

Some of these ladies have left a legend. Lady Ottoline Morrell tried to take possession [of] D. H. Lawrence, among others.[14] She was the most masterful of them. Lady Cunard also collected potential celebrities.[15] Somewhat later the Sitwells did much the same. But the most sagacious, the most intelligent, and the best liked of the hostesses was Mrs Shakespear.[16] Olivia Shakespear was a very close friend of Yeats. Ezra Pound became her son-in-law. The most constant of her visitors was Wyndham Lewis. Now it so happens that years later, when I met Mrs Shakespear, she made me sing to her, and I sang a song of Campian's which is given in Keel's book. She knew it, and it did not take her long to bring the volume out from amongst her books. So at least one of these hostesses was probably getting people to sing Elizabethan music in the years when her influence on young poets was at its greatest.

These Elizabethan song writers were the heirs of Wyat. Like him they often carried on the sound of a syllable over the beat, getting, in that way, a much greater variety of rhythm than Victorian poetry ever showed.[17] No real edition of Wyat existed in 1910—only poems corrected to fit acknowledged metres, as you will find them in the *Oxford Book of English Verse*.[18] As for Hopkins, Dr Bridges was still sitting on his manuscripts.[19] Keel's book of Elizabethan songs is the only place I can think of where the poets could find the rhythms which began to reappear in English, and the first poets to use them were frequenters of Olivia Shakespear's drawing room—Yeats and Pound.

When Helen Lived

We have cried in our despair
That men desert,
For some trivial affair
Or noisy, insolent sport,
Beauty that we have won
From bitterest hours;
Yet we, had we walked within
Those topless towers
Where Helen walked with her boy,
Had given but as the rest
Of the men and women of Troy,
A word and a jest.

I

The Witch

Toil and grow rich,
What's that but to lie
With a foul witch
And after, drained dry,

To be brought
To the chamber where
Lies one long sought
With despair?

II

The Peacock

What's riches to him
That has made a great peacock
With the pride of his eye?
The wind-beaten, stone-grey,
And desolate Three Rock
Would nourish his whim.
Live he or die
Amid wet rocks and heather,
His ghost will be gay
Adding feather to feather
For the pride of his eye.[20]

These poems were collected in 1914. There are others in the 1910 volume. The Victorians had been used to extra syllables: not to syllables left out. I dont suggest these are good poems. Such a trick takes time and practice to perfect.

Pound says in the Cantos: 'To break the pentameter, that was the first heave.'[21] A great deal of his early work has a heavy blankverse movement, sometimes disguised by cutting the lines up into different lengths before printing them. But the intention is not to break the pentameter merely, but to escape from the hampering measures imposed by our memory of several centuries of English verse written to models imported from other lands. Pound was helped by his essay in Old English versification. 'The Seafarer' isnt meant to reproduce the measures of its original, but to suggest them:

The Seafarer

From the Anglo-Saxon

May I for my own self song's truth reckon,
Journey's jargon, how I in harsh days
Hardship endured oft.
Bitter breast-cares have I abided,

Known on my keel many a care's hold,
And dire sea-surge, and there I oft spent
Narrow nightwatch nigh the ship's head
While she tossed close to cliffs. Coldly afflicted,
My feet were by frost benumbed.
Chill its chains are; chafing sighs
Hew my heart round and hunger begot
Mere-weary mood. Lest man know not
That he on dry land loveliest liveth,
List how I, care-wretched, on ice-cold sea,
Weathered the winter, wretched outcast
Deprived of my kinsmen;
Hung with hard ice-flakes, where hail-scur flew,
There I heard naught save the harsh sea
And ice-cold wave, at whiles the swan cries,
Did for my games the gannet's clamour,
Sea-fowls' loudness was for me laughter,
The mews' singing all my mead-drink.
Storms, on the stone-cliffs beaten, fell on the stern
In icy feathers; full oft the eagle screamed
With spray on his pinion.
                              Not any protector
May make merry man faring needy.
This he little believes, who aye in winsome life
Abides 'mid burghers some heavy business,
Wealthy and wine-flushed, how I weary oft
Must bide above brine.
Neareth nightshade, snoweth from north,
Frost froze the land, hail fell on earth then,
Corn of the coldest. Nathless there knocketh now
The heart's thought that I on high streams
The salt-wavy tumult traverse alone.
Moaneth alway my mind's lust
That I fare forth, that I afar hence
Seek out a foreign fastness.[22]

He makes his escape with 'The Return':

The Return

See, they return; ah, see the tentative
> Movements, and the slow feet,
> The trouble in the pace and the uncertain
> Wavering!

See, they return, one, and by one,
With fear, as half-awakened;
As if the snow should hesitate
And murmur in the wind,
> and half turn back;
These were the "Wing'd-with-Awe,"
> Inviolable.

Gods of the wingèd shoe!
With them the silver hounds,
> sniffing the trace of air!

Haie! Haie!
> These were the swift to harry;
These the keen-scented;
These were the souls of blood.

Slow on the leash,
> pallid the leash-men! [23]

None of this had anything to do with symbolism or imagism. But it may have had something to do with music.

Yeats used his new tool only now and then for a single line in [a] poem otherwise capable of being scanned in the traditional manner. Pound tried to use his constantly, but at first he could not make it hang together for anything much longer than an epigram.

The Lake Isle

O God, O Venus, O Mercury, patron of thieves,
Give me in due time, I beseech you, a little tobacco-shop,
With the little bright boxes
> piled up neatly upon the shelves
And the loose fragrant cavendish
> and the shag,

And the bright Virginia
        loose under the bright glass cases,
And a pair of scales not too greasy,
And the whores dropping in for a word or two in passing,
For a flip word, and to tidy their hair a bit.

O God, O Venus, O Mercury, patron of thieves,
Lend me a little tobacco-shop,
        or install me in any profession
Save this damn'd profession of writing,
        where one needs one's brains all the time.[24]

Turn from Pound and Yeats for a moment to Pound's university friend Hilda Doolittle, H.D. She was deep in Greek. The movement of Greek verse had such possession of her mind that she was never in danger of reproducing stiff, worn-out English metres. What Pound was working towards with difficulty, she did with ease, with facility. The trouble with Hilda Doolittle was not lack of a supple enough measure, but that she could not think of anything much to do with it.

Her poems do not seem to have anything to do with the world, ancient or modern. Even when she translates from Greek the reality goes out of it: none of the humour, the observation of men, is left; hardly any of the conflict, even in this fragment of the *Hippolytus* of Euripides.

III

PHAEDRA.
Lift my head, help me up,
I am bruised, bone and flesh;
chafe my white hands, my servants:
this weight about my forehead?
Ah, my veil—loose it—
spread my hair across my breast.

TROPHOS.
There, do not start,
child, nor toss about,
only calm and high pride
can help your hurt:
fate tries all alike.

PHAEDRA.

Ai, ai! to drink deep
of spring water
from its white source;
ai, ai! for rest—black poplars—
thick grass—sleep.

TROPHOS.

What is this you ask,
wild words, mad speech—
hide your hurt, my heart,
hide your hurt
before these servants.

PHAEDRA.

Take me to the mountains!
O for woods, pine tracts,
where hounds athirst for death,
leap on the bright stags!
God, how I would shout to the beasts
with my gold hair torn loose;
I would shake the Thessalian dart,
I would hurl the barbed arrow from my grasp.

TROPHOS.

Why, so distraught,
child, child, why the chase
and this cold water you would ask:
but we may get you that
from deep rills that cut the slopes
before the gate.

PHAEDRA.

Artemis of the salt beach
and of the sea-coast,
mistress of the race-course,
trodden of swift feet,
O for your flat sands
where I might mount
with goad and whip
the horses of Enetas.[25]

But her verse had its use, as an example to Pound, who knew what it came from and could try to emulate it, and to the third of the friends at Pennsylvania University, Carlos Williams, who took it without reference to its Greek origin, brought it down to the domesticities, and made it a naturalised American.[26]

In spite of Flint and Hulme, what was alive amongst the Imagists came from the Greek, via HD, or from the Chinese, very deviously, via Ezra Pound.

I think more than enough has been said by Eliot and others, about Pound's 'Cathay'. 'He invented Chinese poetry for our time', said Eliot.[27] For those who imitated the Chinese-Fenollosa-Pound it was a street without an exit.[28] Undistinguished poets, learned translators, are still churning out such poems like so much butter, smooth, bland etc etc but with very little flavour. They have not Pound's skill to turn a pause in the rhythm into emotion, nor his daring to supplement or alter the original to clinch the movement into a poem.

Lament of the Frontier Guard

By the North Gate, the wind blows full of sand,
Lonely from the beginning of time until now!
Trees fall, the grass goes yellow with autumn.
I climb the towers and towers
            to watch out the barbarous land:
Desolate castle, the sky, the wide desert.
There is no wall left to this village.
Bones white with a thousand frosts,
High heaps, covered with trees and grass;
Who brought this to pass?
Who has brought the flaming imperial anger?
Who has brought the army with drums and with kettle-drums?
Barbarous kings.
A gracious spring, turned to blood-ravenous autumn,
A turmoil of wars-men, spread over the middle kingdom,
Three hundred and sixty thousand,
And sorrow, sorrow like rain.
Sorrow to go, and sorrow, sorrow returning.
Desolate, desolate fields,
And no children of warfare upon them,
            No longer the men for offence and defence.

Ah, how shall you know the dreary sorrow at the North Gate,
With Riboku's name forgotten,
And we guardsmen fed to the tigers.

By Rihaku (Li T'ai Po)[29]

But sometime during the war—I've forgotten the exact year and my copy has no date—Pound published a remarkable book. I dont think any of the writers about Pound or about poetry in those years has taken the measure of it, or given it its true importance. It is called 'Quia Pauper Amavi' and it contains four sections.[30] The second, 'Moeurs Contemporaines', is more or less what might be expected, poems of the time, satirical, with a taste much like some of Eliot's work of the same years. But the third section is three cantos towards the great poem we know so well now; cantos later rejected or recast, but using already most of the devices that make *The Cantos* what they are, a most unpredictable contribution in 1915 or 1916. The First section, 'Langue d'Oc', shows Pound suddenly master of the music words have in them, as he had tried to be before.

Alba

When the nightingale to his mate
Sings day-long and night late
My love and I keep state
In bower,
In flower,
'Till the watchman on the tower
Cry:

"Up! Thou rascal, Rise,
I see the white
Light
And the night
Flies."[31]

Wordsworth has a poem as spontaneous in sound, though perhaps also as carefully wrought,[32] but there is very little else of the kind for more than two centuries before Pound. There's not much meaning to it, if you want a prose meaning. Neither is there to 'Full Fathom Five'. It is like the poets shout of joy to discover that at last he has mastered words.

The last section of the book, dated 1917, is *Homage to Sextus Propertius*.[33] It is a long satirical poem, an extension of Browning's notion of the Persona,[34] the poem spoken in the character of someone not the author, to throw light on the character, or on the world by seeing it through that character's eyes. A lot of nonsense has been written about it by people who imagined it to be a translation from the Latin of Propertius. The Latin is called in aid, pretty frequently, but without sequence, and often more as a source of learned puns than of direct matter. From that angle it has a bearing on what James Joyce tried to do a decade later in *Finnegans Wake*. But what I want to notice now is the freedom of its rhythmic movement. Here at last is a long poem which has no relation at all to the movement of blank verse.

> *IV*
>
> *Difference of Opinion with Lygdamus*
>
> Tell me the truths which you hear of our constant young lady,
>   Lygdamus,
> And may the bought yoke of a mistress lie with
>   equitable weight on your shoulders;
> For I am swelled up with inane pleasurabilities
>   and deceived by your reference
> To things which you think I would like to believe.
>
> No messenger should come wholly empty,
>   and a slave should fear plausibilities;
> Much conversation is as good as having a home.
>   Out with it, tell it to me, all of it, from the beginning,
> I guzzle with outstretched ears.
> Thus? She wept into uncombed hair,
>   And you saw it.
> Vast waters flowed from her eyes?
>   You, you Lygdamus
> Saw her stretched on her bed, —
>   it was no glimpse in a mirror;
> No gawds on her snowy hands, no orfevrerie,
> Sad garment draped on her slender arms.
> Her escritoires lay shut by the bed-feet.
> Sadness hung over the house, and the desolated female attendants
> Were desolated because she had told them her dreams.
>
> She was veiled in the midst of that place,
> Damp woolly handkerchiefs were stuffed into her undryable eyes,
> And a querulous noise responded to our solicitous reprobations.

For which things you will get a reward from me,
        Lygdamus?
To say many things is equal to having a home.
And the other woman "has not enticed me
              by her pretty manners,
"She has caught me with herbaceous poison,
         she twiddles the spiked wheel of a rhombus,
"She stews puffed frogs, snake's bones, the moulted feathers of
   screech owls,
"She binds me with ravvles of shrouds.
        "Black spiders spin in her bed!
"Let her lovers snore at her in the morning!
       "May the gout cramp up her feet!
"Does he like me to sleep here alone,
       Lygdamus?
"Will he say nasty things at my funeral?"

And you expect me to believe this
       after twelve months of discomfort?

VI

When, when, and whenever death closes our eyelids,
Moving naked over Acheron
Upon the one raft, victor and conquered together,
Marius and Jugurtha together,
           one tangle of shadows.
Caesar plots against India,
Tigris and Euphrates shall, from now on, flow at his bidding,
Tibet shall be full of Roman policemen,
The Parthians shall get used to our statuary
         and acquire a Roman religion;
One raft on the veiled flood of Acheron,
      Marius and Jugurtha together.

Nor at my funeral either will there be any long trail,
        bearing ancestral lares and images;
No trumpets filled with my emptiness,
Nor shall it be on an Atalic bed;
      The perfumed cloths shall be absent.
A small plebeian procession.

Enough, enough and in plenty
There will be three books at my obsequies
Which I take, my not unworthy gift, to Persephone.

You will follow the bare scarified breast
Nor will you be weary of calling my name, nor too weary
        To place the last kiss on my lips
When the Syrian onyx is broken.

                "He who is now vacant dust
                "Was once the slave of one passion:"
Give that much inscription
                "Death why tardily come?"

You, sometimes, will lament a lost friend,
        For it is a custom:
This care for past men,

Since Adonis was gored in Idalia, and the Cytharean
Ran crying with out-spread hair,
        In vain, you call back the shade,
In vain, Cynthia. Vain call to unanswering shadow,
        Small talk comes from small bones.[35]

At the end of last term I read to you a piece or two of Walt Whitman, and
asked you to reread 'Out of the Cradle endlessly rocking' in the light of
what I had been saying.[36] I had been trying to show how Whitman at his
best makes the rhythm of each line grow out of the line before it, so that
the two make a kind of figure of their own, and each is linked to each
in a perpetually altering pattern: and now and then a rhythm recurs to
tie the whole closer together. There is a kind of onomatopoeia too, an
imitation of the rhythms of things in movement or of the human breath
under various emotions.

  I dont think it is possible to miss the connection of such a poem as the
one I have just read to you with Whitman. I remember once in Rapallo
Louis Zukofsky and myself had somehow come to talk about this poem
with Pound. Louis asked Ezra to read it. Now in those days there wasnt
much to choose between Pound's reading and Yeats's. Pound was more
resonant. He drew himself up into the posture of the bard; you could
easily imagine the absent toga; filled his chest two or three times to get
it well filled and boomed out a kind of chant which astonished Zukofsky.

He'd never heard anything like that before, and he complained about it. So Pound got him to read it, and finally the book was handed to me. They both disapproved of me, so, to justify myself, I said something about quantity—the conjunction of long syllables puts a kind of swing in the rhythm—and to show what I meant I began reciting 'Out of the Cradle endlessly rocking'. I broke down, and to my surprise Pound took up where I left off and finished the Whitman poem from memory. Pound was always very cagey, even evasive, about his debt to Whitman, but he never denied it. And I am as sure as anyone can be who has nothing but circumstantial evidence, that he had reread Whitman not long before he wrote 'Homage to Sextus Propertius'.[37]

So here, in 1917, before Eliot had had time to assert himself, in Pound's volume 'Quia Pauper Amavi' you had all the main characteristics of XXc poetry displayed in a high degree of development. The movement is musical, not metrical. The language is the language of civilised men, not only in vocabulary but in syntax. There is an irony based on an assumed familiarity of all civilised men with the literature of many countries—in this case, Latin mainly. There is the irony of describing the British Empire in terms of the Roman Empire.[38]

TWELVE

Pound's Cantos

[Bunting's words begin abruptly:] sheer presumption, and extremely foolish, to attempt to deal with a poem the length of Pound's *Cantos* in a single lecture. All I can hope to do is to make one or two points that might be useful to you, because I don't think that they have all been dwelt on by the many people who have written about the *Cantos*. They tie up with what we've been saying in the other lectures, to some extent.

A short poem or a short piece of music can exist and endure mainly by its texture, the sound of a few lines, or a few lines at a time. Even so, you usually have something more general, a shape that begins with the poem or the piece and doesn't complete itself satisfactorily till the poem is finished. We're all used to that idea in music, where we specify a piece by the name of the particular shape, sequence, symmetry, or whatever it has: fugue or minuet, toccata or symphony or sonata, or whatnot. And add to that where necessary its key and its number amongst the composer's works, and so on. Some poetical forms are equally familiar: sonnet, rondeau, hokku, or hokkai, or whatever you call it, but others are less definite, at least they've got no name, a lot of them.

In the last century Browning invented something that we've taken to calling the 'persona', but it's hardly really a form.[1] A persona is a mask, that is the meaning of the word, and Browning's form has been imitated by Kipling, by Ezra Pound and T. S. Eliot, and some other people, but as I say, it's not really a form at all in the sense I'm speaking of. It merely is the poet imagining some other person speaking, and that person's words are the poem: Bishop Blougram, or {McAndrew},[2] or Bertran de Born, or Prufrock. But the words just go on falling out till everything has been said without necessarily being shaped by anything more definite than the poet's taste.

Now, a poem of any length whose parts are not related to each other by something more precise than taste is apt to sag or lose proportion. One or two poets before and after 1920 who had understood the notion of modifying and combining rhythmic themes in the way Whitman had sometimes done and Pound did in his *Propertius,* as I explained in a previous lecture, and who found that a satisfactory way of conducting the verse from line to line or over a few pages, began to wonder whether music could furnish them with an overall shape as well as with a tissue or texture or whatever you might call the local shape of the verse.[3]

Eliot in *The Waste Land* stumbled by sheer accident on something very closely analogous to the form that musicians call the sonata but he was surprisingly slow to realize what he had done—though in the end he proclaims it in the title of the *Four Quartets,* a quartet being normally a sonata written for violins, viola and a cello.[4] Pound, however, and Zukofsky after him, was fascinated by the close texture of the fugue and by its somewhat spurious air of logicality. They wanted to know whether the design of the fugue could be transferred to poetry. A short but incomplete answer is that it can't. A fugue is essentially contrapuntal, several voices imitating each other, yet free of each other, all talking simultaneously, whereas poetry is written for one voice at a time or, at most, for voices in unison. But Bach had set an example. He wrote at least two fugues for unaccompanied violin.[5] Of course they are not really fugues. No amount of double stopping can get three or more voices to sing simultaneously on the violin. The entries in Bach's unaccompanied violin fugues wait till the last entry is done or nearly done before they start. Yet he manages to convey a rather teasing sensation of a fugue, never really satisfied. Similar sequences of notes are thrown up time and again, but they never mesh together as those of a true fugue do.

Zukofsky wrote a fugue of this sort for unaccompanied voice. It's Part 7 of his long poem "*A*". It is not a fugue, but it does suggest one, suggests it very strongly. I hope to read it to you next week. But Pound, thinking out his *Cantos* a full decade before Zukofsky, was not looking for a form that fulfils itself in a page or two. Whatever suggestion he took from fugal writing must be capable of being sustained through 120 cantos, some of which proved to be very long. Canto LXXII [i.e., LXXIV], I think it is, lasts for about an hour and a half. I know because Denis Goacher and myself read through it at a celebration of the first anniversary of Pound's death, and an hour and a half is what it took the pair of us to read it.[6]

Obviously Pound was going to need many themes, not just one or two or three or four. He was going to involve himself in a polyphony far beyond anything that Bach contemplated or even the great Flemish composers of the fifteenth century who occasionally have as many as forty parts going at a time. And yet it could never be a true polyphony because poetry has only one line at a time. Pound wanted something that would carry on a theme, a sequence, in the hearer's mind since he couldn't provide it actually in his ear. And so he had to go beyond the musical elements of poetry, which are what we've been discussing in these lectures, and rely on ideas or images. That's what he did. The *Cantos* are so long and were written over such a long time — more than fifty years — that they are not wholly consistent, but right through them there are images and ideas that perpetually recur, combine and recombine, and that stay in the reader's mind, half-noticed, while some other idea or image is being announced, making a huge, polyphonic pattern of images. 'Polyphonic' is obviously the wrong word since we are no longer speaking of sound, but ideas. But I didn't know what word I could invent to take its place. This is quite consistent with composing the actual words according to the rhythmical notions he had derived through Whitman from nineteenth-century music.[7]

Moreover, this use of images fell in with ideas he'd picked up from Fenollosa's theory of the Chinese written character.[8] I am told that Ernest Fenollosa was wrong as a philologist,[9] but his notion was certainly fruitful for poetry and criticism. He thought that by putting together two or more very simple images you could show, graphically, a meaning different from either of them which they added up to. A picture of the sun set behind a picture of a tree makes a Chinese character, evidently the sun shining through the branches which, in a normal countryside, must be either sunrise or sunset, and that is the meaning of the character. A man standing beside a mouth with something issuing from it must be a man standing by his word, keeping his promise, therefore faithful, trustworthy, and all that sort of meaning. In poetry, men commonly put two images together, either explicitly or implicitly, and it's called metaphor. From each metaphor the hearer can get something more than what is meant by either image alone, or even by both of them if they were not presented together. That's a great gain in concision.

Of course this is a very old practice and a very old commonplace of criticism,[10] but Pound enlarged it enormously. He found it possible to leave out far more than is usually left out in between the separate images which combine together to produce a meaning. He deals not so much in single images set against one another as in whole families of images. For him Helen of Troy whose beauty caused wars ties up at once with Eleanor of Aquitaine whose similar beauty caused similar war and with certain less celebrated ladies of Provence and with a President's wife who caused political dissension and with a whole array of goddesses.[11] After all, Helen is the Attic form of the older Greek Selene,[12] a goddess, goddess of the moon, Artemis, Diana, Latona—who presides over child-birth—and several other goddesses, all tying up with the moon, with each other and with Helen. Diana caused Actaeon to be chased by his own hounds, and a certain Provençal lady caused, accidentally, her poet-lover to be chased by dogs too.[13] There is no end to the ramifications of the image of which Helen, Eleanor, Artemis, and so on, are all facets.

Now, he has many such bundles of images and it's these great bundles that Pound plays with, and the bundles are not permanently tied to-gether. He can always take a few sticks from one faggot and a few from another to make yet a third, so that there's an extraordinarily complex system of related images, changing as fluidly as the data of life and thought themselves, and yet never losing touch with each other. I sup-pose that's what baffles critics who are used to rigid systems in which one image always implies another, but not to one in which the relationships are so multiple that before you reach the end of the poem you may be inclined to think that each image implies all the rest. That was no doubt what Pound intended. I think he falls short of it, but he comes near enough to make a most wonderfully intricate work of art which I think will keep the scholars busy for generations and delight readers more and more as the principles on which it is composed become more familiar to them, as the little part you happen to be reading more and more seems to imply the whole poem.

And that's probably all I have to say about the *Cantos* which hasn't been said by others. A good many people have had a go at explaining them but all of them seem to be thinking rather of what the *Cantos* say than of how they say it. That's a mistake, because all art, poetry particularly, is concerned with form, and what the form encloses is always secondary, sometimes entirely negligible. A partial exception amongst these critics is Hugh Kenner, the Canadian critic, who is also the most readable of contemporary critics. He conducts his investigation rather like a combination of Sherlock Holmes, Maigret, and Hercule Poirot, and it's just as easy and fascinating to read as the chronicles of those illustrious detectives. If you get interested in the *Cantos,* don't neglect to read Kenner's books. But you don't *need* to. The sound alone will carry you through a great deal of the poem, and nearly all the matter, though it may seem obscure at first, clarifies itself bit by bit as the poem proceeds and as it takes up its relationship to all the other bits of matter in it.

However, Kenner has written very acutely about the first Canto as a programme for the whole.[14] I don't think he notices, or at any rate, brings out clearly, the fact that the second Canto is also part of this program with which he sets out. I'll tell you very briefly what these two Cantos seem to imply, and then I'll read them to you, and, if there's time afterwards, a bit from the middle of the poem, in which you won't understand the references, because they come in little by little as new themes are introduced; but you'll get some idea of the texture it produces.

The first Canto takes an episode from Homer's *Odyssey* which seems, on the face of it, to be Homer's refashioning of something very ancient indeed, the passage in which Odysseus visits the underworld to consult the dead seer Tiresias about his own future. They call this passage the Nekuia. To find out the future of course you must interrogate the past and that's what Odysseus is doing and this is part of what Pound intends to do in his poem. The ghosts that Odysseus meets can only talk when they have been fed with fresh blood from the sacrifice and this may be taken as a symbol of the severe labour and research. Odysseus has to drive away his own mother, Anticlea, to keep the blood of the sacrifices for Tiresias—as a poet must drive away his own intimate emotions to keep faithful to the form of his poem as a whole. And when Tiresias comes he says something that is not in Homer. He says, "A second time? why?" Odysseus only went to hell once.[15] The second visitor is Pound in the character of Odysseus. Now, to underline things still further, Pound shows that he is not translating direct from Homer, but from a Latin translation made by Andreas Divus in 1538, so that what we are getting is Pound's view of Divus' view of Homer's view of the pre-historic Nekuia, and that's the best that history can ever do for us. Hardly any of history's evidence is even second-hand. In the last two lines of the Canto Pound seems to identify Circe with Aphrodite. All this, except the last two lines, is done in a metre, or—'metre' is hardly the word—in a system which Pound first elaborated to reproduce what he felt to be, not the form, but the feeling of Old English verse, thus to ram home the notion that we are dealing with something very remote, archaic and fundamental. And so we are to interrogate the past.

But that's not all. We go on to the second Canto and he begins by complaining of Browning's romanticization of the Italian troubadour Sordello, about whom the real evidence is scanty and not very illuminating. 'The Sordellos come from Mantua' is the item which Pound uses for the purpose,[16] and a certain Chinese sage, So-shu, is discovered churning in the sea, as it might be Pound churning the inchoate mass of the past and its records. Now, if you churn milk, it turns into butter, so if you churn the sea, presumably it turns into dry land (that's what So-shu was busy with), with an identifiable shape, and if you churn history industriously enough, it too will take on a shape. A lot of people in the early part of this century expected to find laws of history like laws of nature — Spengler and Toynbee, for example.[17] But if you are going to get results of the kind they hoped for, you will need more than merely interrogating the dead and churning in the sea of facts.

There follows in the Canto a series of metamorphoses such as Ovid wrote about, that is, stories of how human beings were suddenly changed by the gods into trees, animals, all sorts of things, so that they became visible under a totally new aspect, just as by a sudden insight. Within the frame of reference set up by the first Canto, a metamorphosis can only mean the means by which we do suddenly see men and things under a new aspect — what are called moments of vision, whether we're talking about the abrupt formation of a new scientific hypothesis or the abrupt contact with God which mystics claim, or merely the insight that comes from a combination of study and natural sympathy.

The identification of Eleanor with Helen, by applying to her the famous Homeric tag, "destroyer of ships, destroyer of cities," and following with the words of the old men on the wall when they looked at Helen, is almost a metamorphosis in itself.

And then there are two sea-metamorphoses, divided by the main part of the Canto, which consists of a very free version of Ovid's story of how Acoetes warned King Pentheus against showing contempt for Dionysus, the god of wine, by telling about the ship and sailors which were trying to kidnap the young god, which he, when he discovered what they were up to, changed suddenly into rocks, vegetation and fishes. And, by the way, besides its function of showing the kind of thing that you are afterwards to expect in the poem — the sudden insight — this story had contemporary significance because it was elaborated at the moment when, against the will of Woodrow Wilson, Congress committed America to try Prohibition, a contempt for Dionysus which was, ultimately, thoroughly avenged.

Well, I'll read those first two Cantos, and hope that they will help you to see what goes on in the later ones.

Canto I

And then went down to the ship,
Set keel to breakers, forth on the godly sea, and
We set up mast and sail on that swart ship,
Bore sheep aboard her, and our bodies also
Heavy with weeping, so winds from sternward
Bore us out onward with bellying canvas,
Circe's this craft, the trim-coif'd goddess.
Then sat we amidships, wind jamming the tiller,
Thus with stretched sail, we went over sea till day's end.
Sun to his slumber, shadows o'er all the ocean,
Came we then to the bounds of deepest water,
To the Kimmerian lands, and peopled cities
Covered with close-webbed mist, unpiercèd ever
With glitter of sun-rays
Nor with stars stretched, nor looking back from heaven
Swartest night stretched over wretched men there.
The ocean flowing backward, came we then to the place
Aforesaid by Circe.
Here did they rites, Perimedes and Eurylochus,
And drawing sword from my hip
I dug the ell-square pitkin;
Poured we libations unto each the dead,
First mead and then sweet wine, water mixed with white flour.
Then prayed I many a prayer to the sickly death's-heads;
As set in Ithaca, sterile bulls of the best
For sacrifice, heaping the pyre with goods,
A sheep to Tiresias only, black and a bell-sheep.
Dark blood flowed in the fosse,
Souls out of Erebus, cadaverous dead, of brides,
Of youths and of the old who had borne much;
Souls stained with recent tears, girls tender,
Men many, mauled with bronze lance heads,

Battle spoil, bearing yet dreory arms,
These many crowded about me; with shouting,
Pallor upon me, cried to my men for more beasts;
Slaughtered the herds, sheep slain of bronze;
Poured ointment, cried to the gods,
To Pluto the strong, and praised Proserpine;
Unsheathed the narrow sword,
I sat to keep off the impetuous impotent dead,
Till I should hear Tiresias.
But first Elpenor came, our friend Elpenor,
Unburied, cast on the wide earth,
Limbs that we left in the house of Circe,
Unwept, unwrapped in sepulchre, since toils urged other.
Pitiful spirit. And I cried in hurried speech:
'Elpenor, how art thou come to this dark coast?
'Cam'st thou afoot, outstripping seamen?'
        And he in heavy speech:
'Ill fate and abundant wine. I slept in Circe's ingle.
'Going down the long ladder unguarded,
'I fell against the buttress,
'Shattered the nape-nerve, the soul sought Avernus.
'But thou, O King, I bid remember me, unwept, unburied,
'Heap up mine arms, be tomb by sea-bord, and inscribed:
'*A man of no fortune, and with a name to come.*
'And set my oar up, that I swung mid fellows.'

And Anticlea came, whom I beat off, and then Tiresias Theban,
Holding his golden wand, knew me, and spoke first:
'A second time? why? man of ill star,
'Facing the sunless dead and this joyless region?
'Stand from the fosse, leave me my bloody bever
'For soothsay.'
        And I stepped back,
And he strong with the blood, said then: 'Odysseus
'Shalt return through spiteful Neptune, over dark seas,
'Lose all companions.' Then Anticlea came.
Lie quiet Divus. I mean, that is Andreas Divus,
In officina Wecheli, 1538, out of Homer.
And he sailed, by Sirens and thence outward and away
And unto Circe.

Venerandam,
In the Cretan's phrase, with the golden crown, Aphrodite,
Cypri munimenta sortita est, mirthful, oricalchi, with golden
Girdles and breast bands, thou with dark eyelids
Bearing the golden bough of Argicida. So that:[18]

Canto II

Hang it all, Robert Browning,
      there can be but the one 'Sordello'.
But Sordello, and my Sordello?
Lo Sordels si fo di Mantovana.
So-shu churned in the sea.
Seal sports in the spray-whited circles of cliff-wash,
Sleek head, daughter of Lir,
      eyes of Picasso
Under black fur-hood, lithe daughter of Ocean;
And the wave runs in the beach-groove:
'Eleanor, ἐλέναυς and ἐλέπτολις!'
      And poor old Homer, blind, blind, as a bat,
Ear, ear for the sea-surge, murmur of old men's voices:
'Let her go back to the ships,
Back among Grecian faces, lest evil come on our own,
Evil, and further evil, and a curse cursed on our children,
Moves, yes she moves like a goddess
And has the face of a god
      and the voice of Schoeney's daughters,
And doom goes with her in walking,
Let her go back to the ships,
      back among Grecian voices.'
That by the beach-run, Tyro,
      Twisted arms of the sea-god,
Lithe sinews of water, gripping her, cross-hold,
And the blue-gray glass of the wave tents them,
Glare azure of water, cold-welter, close cover.
Quiet sun-tawny sand-stretch,
The gulls broad out their wings,
      nipping between the splay feathers;
Snipe come for their bath,
      bend out their wing-joints,

Spread wet wings to the sun-film,
And by Scios,
     to left of the Naxos passage,
Naviform rock overgrown,
     algae cling to its edge,
There is a wine-red glow in the shallows,
     a tin flash in the sun-dazzle.

The ship landed in Scios,
     men wanting spring-water,
And by the rock-pool a young boy loggy with vine-must,
     'To Naxos? Yes, we'll take you to Naxos,
Cum' along lad.' 'Not that way!'
'Aye, that way is Naxos.'
     And I said: 'It's a straight ship.'
And an ex-convict out of Italy
     knocked me into the fore-stays,
(He was wanted for manslaughter in Tuscany)
     And the whole twenty against me,
Mad for a little slave money.
     And they took her out of Scios
And off her course . . .
     And the boy came to, again, with the racket,
And looked out over the bows,
     and to eastward, and to the Naxos passage.
God-sleight then, god-sleight:
     Ship stock fast in sea-swirl,
Ivy upon the oars, King Pentheus,
     grapes with no seed but sea-foam,
Ivy in scupper-hole.
Aye, I, Acoetes, stood there,
     and the god stood by me,
Water cutting under the keel,
Sea-break from stern forrards,
     wake running off from the bow,
And where was gunwale, there now was vine-trunk,
And tenthril where cordage had been,
     grape-leaves on the rowlocks,
Heavy vine on the oarshafts,

And, out of nothing, a breathing,
>   hot breath on my ankles,
Beasts like shadows in glass,
>   a furred tail upon nothingness.
Lynx-purr, and heathery smell of beasts,
>   where tar smell had been,
Sniff and pad-foot of beasts,
>   eye-glitter out of black air.
The sky overshot, dry, with no tempest,
Sniff and pad-foot of beasts,
>   fur brushing my knee-skin,
Rustle of airy sheaths,
>   dry forms in the *aether*.
And the ship like a keel in ship-yard,
>   slung like an ox in smith's sling,
Ribs stuck fast in the ways,
>   grape-cluster over pin-rack,
>   void air taking pelt.
Lifeless air become sinewed,
>   feline leisure of panthers,
Leopards sniffing the grape shoots by scupper-hole,
Crouched panthers by fore-hatch,
And the sea blue-deep about us,
>   green-ruddy in shadows,
And Lyaeus: 'From now, Acoetes, my altars,
Fearing no bondage,
>   Fearing no cat of the wood,
Safe with my lynxes,
>   feeding grapes to my leopards,
Olibanum is my incense,
>   the vines grow in my homage.'
The back-swell now smooth in the rudder-chains,
Black snout of a porpoise
>   where Lycabs had been,
Fish-scales on the oarsmen.
>   And I worship.
I have seen what I have seen.
>   When they brought the boy I said:

'He has a god in him,
> though I do not know which god.'
And they kicked me into the fore-stays.
I have seen what I have seen:
> Medon's face like the face of a dory,
Arms shrunk into fins. And you, Pentheus,
Had as well listen to Tiresias, and to Cadmus,
> or your luck will go out of you.
Fish-scales over groin muscles,
> lynx-purr amid sea . . .
And of a later year,
> pale in the wine-red algae,
If you will lean over the rock,
> the coral face under wave-tinge,
Rose-paleness under water-shift,
> Ileuthyeria, fair Dafne of sea-bords,
The swimmer's arms turned to branches,
Who will say in what year,
> fleeing what band of tritons,
The smooth brows, seen, and half seen,
> now ivory stillness.
So-shu churned in the sea, So-shu also,
> using the long moon for a churn-stick . . .
Lithe turning of water,
> sinews of Poseidon,
Black azure and hyaline,
> glass wave over Tyro,
Close cover, unstillness,
> bright welter of wave-cords,
Then quiet water,
> quiet in the buff sands,
Sea-fowl stretching wing-joints,
> splashing in rock-hollows and sand-hollows
In the wave-runs by the half-dune;
Glass-glint of wave in the tide-rips against sunlight,
> pallor of Hesperus,
Grey peak of the wave,
> wave, colour of grape's pulp,

Olive grey in the near,
> far, smoke grey of the rock-slide,
Salmon-pink wings of the fish-hawk
> cast grey shadows in water,
The tower like a one-eyed great goose
> cranes up out of the olive-grove,

And we have heard the fauns chiding Proteus
> in the smell of hay under the olive-trees.
And the frogs singing against the fauns
> in the half-light.
And . . .[19]

By way of curiosity and to show you how carefully all the details are selected in this enormous mass of stuff, there is a name there, 'Ileuthyeria, fair Dafne of sea-bords', and in the heavy work of reference that has been concocted to tell you what's what all through the *Cantos,* they find no explanation {from} Ileuthyeria.[20] She's not in Ovid, she's not one of the usual metamorphoses about the place; but a few months ago I happened to read what I think is very rarely read except by professed classical scholars, the fragments of the Homeridae; and there in one of the followers of Homer, in a fragment saved by some dictionary maker, there's Ileuthyeria all right, doing just what Pound says she did.[21] He had read all these obscure things to make sure he got things right.

Well, I ought, I suppose, to try to read you a bit from later in the *Cantos,* which I must make no attempt to explain because all the various themes which recur again and again, and which are being made use of here, have been introduced in between the first and second Canto and the 72nd [i.e., 74th].[22] I'm not going to begin at the beginning of the 7[4th] Canto, because what I want you to feel is not the things there mentioned, but the way things are woven together.

The Canto as a whole is Pound's attempt, while he was living in the cage at Pisa, to come to terms with two very horrible deaths: one, the death of Mussolini, who as you know was first shot by the partisans and then hanged upside down in Milan; and the other, the hanging of a negro soldier called—what was his name again, I forget—we'll come to it soon, anyway—who was hanged for rape and murder in the camp at Pisa.[23]

In with this he weaves all manner of stuff: stories from Nigeria, reminiscences, thoughts about the early Popes—where he got those I don't know—and so on.[24] The shout which comes through and through all the time is part of the refrain of a Nigerian half-epic poem.[25]

> Lute of Gassir. Hooo Fasa
> came a lion-coloured pup bringing fleas
> and a bird with white markings, a stepper
> > > under *les six potences*
> Absouldre, que tous nous veuil absoudre
> lay there Barabbas and two thieves lay beside him
> infantile synthesis in Barabbas
> minus Hemingway, minus Antheil, ebullient
> and by name Thos. Wilson
> Mr K. said nothing foolish, the whole month nothing foolish:
> "if we weren't dumb, we wouldn't be here"
> > > and the Lane gang.
> Butterflies, mint and Lesbia's sparrows,
> the voiceless with bumm drum and banners,
> > > and the ideogram of the guard roosts
> el triste pensier si volge
> > ad Ussel. A Ventadour
> > > va il consire, el tempo rivolge
> and at Limoges the young salesman
> bowed with such french politeness "No, that is impossible."
> I have forgotten which city
> But the caverns are less enchanting to the unskilled explorer
> > than the Urochs as shown on the postals,
> we will see those old roads again, question,
> > > possibly
> but nothing appears much less likely,
> > > Mme Pujol,
> and there was a smell of mint under the tent flaps
> especially after the rain
> > > and a white ox on the road toward Pisa
> > > as if facing the tower,
> dark sheep in the drill field and on wet days were clouds
> in the mountain as if under the guard roosts.
> > A lizard upheld me
> > the wild birds wd not eat the white bread
> > from Mt Taishan to the sunset

From Carrara stone to the tower
   and this day the air was made open
     for Kuanon of all delights,
       Linus, Cletus, Clement
               whose prayers,
the great scarab is bowed at the altar
the green light gleams in his shell
plowed in the sacred field and unwound the silk worms early
              in tensile brightness
in the light of light is the *virtù*
      "sunt lumina" said Erigena Scotus
     as of Shun on Mt Taishan
and in the hall of the forebears
        as from the beginning of wonders
the paraclete that was present in Yao, the precision
in Shun the compassionate
in Yu the guider of waters

4 giants at the 4 corners
   three young men at the door
and they digged a ditch round about me
    lest the damp gnaw thru my bones
      to redeem Zion with justice
sd/Isaiah. Not out on interest said David rex
Light tensile immaculata
      the sun's cord unspotted
"sunt lumina" said the Oirishman to King Carolus,
     "OMNIA,
all things that are are lights"
and they dug him up out of sepulture
soi disantly looking for Manichaeans.
Les Albigeois, a problem of history,
and the fleet at Salamis made with money lent by the state to
              the shipwrights
     Tempus tacendi, tempus loquendi.
Never inside the country to raise the standard of living
but always abroad to increase the profits of usurers,
     dixit Lenin,
and gun sales lead to more gun sales

they do not clutter the market for gunnery
there is no saturation
Pisa, in the 23rd year of the effort in sight of the tower
and Till was hung yesterday
for murder and rape with trimmings   plus Cholkis
plus mythology, thought he was Zeus ram or another one
Hey Snag wots in the bibl'?
wot are the books ov the bible?
Name 'em, don't bullshit ME.

莫 $O\overset{\text{'}}{Y} TI\Sigma$

a man on whom the sun has gone down
the ewe, he said had such a pretty look in her eyes;
and the nymph of the Hagoromo came to me,
as a corona of angels
one day were clouds banked on Taishan
or in glory of sunset
and tovarish blessed without aim
wept in the rainditch at evening
Sunt lumina
that the drama is wholly subjective
stone knowing the form which the carver imparts it
the stone knows the form
sia Cythera, sia Ixotta, sia in Santa Maria dei Miracoli
where Pietro Romano has fashioned the bases
$O\overset{\text{'}}{Y} TI\Sigma$
a man on whom the sun has gone down
nor shall diamond die in the avalanche
be it torn from its setting
first must destroy himself ere others destroy him.
4 times was the city rebuilded, Hooo Fasa
Gassir, Hooo Fasa   dell' Italia tradita
now in the mind indestructible, Gassir, Hoooo Fasa,
With the four giants at the four corners
and four gates mid-wall Hooo Fasa
and a terrace the colour of stars
pale as the dawn cloud, la luna
thin as Demeter's hair
Hooo Fasa, and in a dance the renewal

> with two larks in contrappunto
> at sunset
> ch'intenerisce
> a sinistra la Torre
> seen through a pair of breeches.
> *Che sublia es laissa cader*
> between NEKUIA where are Alcmene and Tyro
> and the Charybdis of action
> to the solitude of Mt Taishan[26]

I'll leave it at that. I hope that that sample, taken not at random but fairly freely, would at least reassure you that if you will read the thing aloud it is a great pleasure, even when you don't know what the hell it's about; and bit by bit you will find out {what it's about}.

I WANTED to ask you about next week, those of you who propose to come next week. I might, if you like, try to say something about Zukofsky and other ways that modern poets have tried to deal with the suggestions of music. Or I might if you prefer it try to read you longer passages from the *Cantos*. It's up to you to say which pleases you best. {It'll} make no difference, for really the theme I've been lecturing on is more or less complete as it stands now; only footnotes to add to it.

[Audience: "Zukofsky."]

Zukofsky. Right. {I'll leave it at that.}

THIRTEEN

Zukofsky

Well, I shall have to begin, I'm afraid, with apologies; I've not got the lecture properly prepared this week. I made rough notes for about half of it, or a bit more, and then, unfortunately, before I could arrange the bits I wanted to read and so on, a man died, a man I had been going to visit next week. He was the oldest—the last remaining of the friends of my youth, and also the last except myself remaining on this side of the Atlantic of the generation of writers who between 1914 and 1930 made such very large changes in the notion of poetry in twentieth-century England.[1] Now I suppose that on the other side of the Atlantic I believe Hilda Doolittle is still alive though very very old,[2] and Louis Zukofsky is some four years younger than me, but there's only those three left in the world. And I'm going to have myself scheduled as an ancient monument, then I can charge sixpence for people to come and look at me.

Anyway, I apologise for not having the thing complete. I found the sudden feeling of complete isolation over here rather overwhelming.

I was going to talk about Louis Zukofsky. And he is unique in more ways than one. He's so singular, that it is for once worth while saying something about the man himself.[3] Because some of the unfamiliarity, and some of the genuine difficulty of his work, {that} often prevent people from getting as much enjoyment from it as they might, are a product of his singularity, and may be more easily assimilated if you bear that in mind.

To begin with, Zukofsky is the only considerable English poet that I can remember at present who did not have English as his mother tongue. The French are used to Americans and Irishmen and South Americans writing French poetry that is not negligible. And perhaps they trace the un-French terms in the language, but they don't allow that to prevent them from paying attention to a poet. But some of us have certainly allowed Zukofsky's angularities to turn us away from him.

He was born in New York of recent immigrants,[4] but the language he spoke until he went to school, and the only language in which he was ever able to talk to his parents, was Yiddish, and the Russian variety of Yiddish, rather than the better-known German variety. So he grew up bilingual. That is, he spoke Yiddish and American.

Now American began by being English such as the English speak, and only gradually became first a slightly old-fashioned English, as it was two centuries ago, and then, as the flood of immigrants began to flow last century—at the end of last century and the beginning of this—, American turned into a kind of Esperanto. The immigrants learned English words, and how to put them together in an English syntax. But the words did not bring with them all the hazy suggestions and cousinships that they have for English people. Nor does the syntax run as easily as we let it run. It's put together by rule. So little by little the immigrant English has coloured or discoloured the normal English of the United States. Words mean to an American, usually, what the dictionary says they mean, and no more.

An educated American, of course, enriches the meaning of his vocabulary by a more or less conscious effort of etymology, as well as by wide reading, where we seem to float in an unconscious soup of etymology, which we rarely make explicit and rarely perhaps are conscious of. The feel of the language which results is quite different.

Zukofsky is an educated American. Homonyms and puns in general seem to come to his mind more readily than the ancestral relations of words. They're a constant feature of his poetry, connecting things together; not only as jokes, {but as} a serious means of knitting together the poetry; as would be done, by an English poet, rather with the ancient cousinships of words which you hardly even notice.[5] Puns are much more prominent.

That is more natural to an American than to an Englishman because of the difference that has grown up between the two dialects because of the immigration.

For the same reason, that is that he is an educated American, conscious of using a language, rather than an Englishman talking (as most of us do) quite without any such reflection, Zukofsky's syntax, especially in his prose, is now and then harsh and awkward. Perhaps it's because of that that he gradually seems to have abandoned formal syntax almost completely in his verse. And his imitators have gone even further. If you read some of, oh, Duncan,[6] or more particularly some of—what do you call him, bless my soul—what do names go out of my head for—never mind: if you read some of his—the people who derived a good deal from Zukofsky—you'll find them using language with no syntax whatever, or none that you can discern.

Of course verse can usually manage without syntax. But we are used to finding a good deal of it, and not used to resolving the ambiguities that arise in its absence. Pound, likewise, often dispenses with syntax, but without causing much ambiguity, because he is simply naming or identifying one after another of his recurrent themes. We rarely have any similar help in understanding Zukofsky. But Pound and Eliot escaped most of the thinning-down of the implication of words which is the mark of all Esperantos. They were nearly twenty years older than Zukofsky, and would have had their education at a time before the immigrants had affected the language as widely as they have since, and in a class as remote from that of the immigrants as the English public school class is from the Jamaicans and Pakistanis of Peckham.[7] Their Americanism is a matter only of an occasional idiom, or a certain hospitality to slang. The same is true of Carlos Williams, but Zukofsky is altogether a twentieth-century American poet. His verse has to English ears always a somewhat foreign accent, which accounts for a part of the difficulty that some English people find in reading him.

Then again, Zukofsky is more completely a city poet than any I can think of for at least a century past. He has taught, for short periods, in universities outside New York,[8] and he has made three trips, I think, to Europe, very much in the regular American-tourist style, but almost all his life has been spent in New York. I doubt whether he has ever been happy for more than a few days out of reach of Washington Square.[9] Even suburban New York is strange and foreign territory to him. Moreover, he's never taken part in the social life of the city itself. He's closeted himself with his immediate family and a very few intimate friends. So almost all his observation has been concentrated into a very narrow field.

He has sharp eyes, and can produce very vivid details now and then. The ferries going backward and forward on New York harbour and so on have suggested much to him, and the gulls that are always haunting them. But you don't find in his poems much of that minute accuracy of observation that Carlos Williams gets into his, setting down what he sees and what he hears people say. Nor the sudden and quite frequent visual acuteness of Pound. Consequently, when Zukofsky is not dealing directly with his family, he is obliged to find his interests and his matter and his images, such as they are, either in books or in music. Or in contemplation of himself. Not in the unpleasant, narcissistic sort of pre-occupation of so many bad poets, but a very detached and objective and often amused view of himself.

Still, that is a narrow range from which to cull your images, and Zukofsky moves more readily than I like to see into abstractions.

Finally, he's a stubborn devil. When he starts something, he'll never say to himself, "Oh hell, this isn't working out," and throw it aside, he'll finish it, even though it be evidently dull or mistaken. Consequently his work contains poems and passages that are no recommendation to the rest of it. A reader who starts on one of those might be thoroughly put off before he has begun to discover Zukofsky's great merits.

Perhaps you were beginning to think that I wasn't going to allow him any merits. On the contrary he seems to me only less important than Pound to this century; as I hope to show.

For one thing, perhaps the chief thing, no other poet has stated and followed more clearly the notion of the closeness of poetry to music; even though he sometimes seems to forget it.

I think that Zukofsky knew, even at the very beginning of his career, how entirely he was going to give himself up to the notion of music in poetry, if I can judge by what he wrote. But later he married a pianist-composer, and their son turned out to be one of those astonishing infants who insist on fiddling like Heifetz almost before they can read.[10] So that Louis Zukofsky became more intimate with music and the technicalities of music than poets often have the chance to be. If he couldn't set his own songs, like Campion and perhaps Wyatt, his wife could and did set them, working with him.[11] And as with Wyatt and Campion, this has given his verse a clarity of sound that has steadily increased all his life. The later short poems show it particularly. It stays light in the mouth, where the rest of us, still using more or less the old Spenserian word-music, often go heavy. I don't mean that Zukofsky never uses the Spenserian stuff at all, but a large proportion of his work is quite clear of it. And this too makes it sound unfamiliar to people brought up on the anthologies we all have. It makes it sound as though he belonged to a different century.

What Whitman, and then Pound, borrowed from music, was chiefly the notion of modifying a theme, a rhythmic theme, especially, and—bit by bit—until it could be merged in a counter-theme or in some other way combined with it. Pound was fascinated by the idea of fugue, but found it necessary to change that notion fundamentally, and use images rather than rhythms to carry on a counterpoint in the reader's mind.[12]

Zukofsky makes use of both these methods, but also, very characteristically, of musical techniques that do not at first sight seem likely to work well in poetry. When he wanted to imitate a fugue, he determined that the actual sounds, not something more remotely analogous, should be the substance of it. And I think I ought to attempt to read you his well-known fugue from his long poem "*A*", about horses.

No doubt he had in mind Bach's fugues for unaccompanied violin, which are not quite true fugues, but something that sounds very like a fugue.[13]

The horses, about which this is, are peculiar. Zukofsky has always been fascinated by horses, perhaps because being younger than me he first saw horses when they were already obviously doomed as far as cities were concerned—going out—and he cannot have seen a live horse actually doing anything in New York for donkey's ages now. But there's a thing called a saw-horse, which you may be familiar with. Legs like that at one end and at the other end, and a piece across, on which you lay the wood that's to be sawn. And this is used—was more often used than now—by the men who open manholes, and dig holes in the street, and so on, to tell you to keep away, and not bust your car in their holes. And their name is 'horses', and it's these horses about which Zukofsky writes his fugue.[14]

You must take the fugue at a fairly steady pace, as you would if you were playing one of Bach's fugues.

"*A*"-7

Horses: who will do it? out of manes? Words
Will do it, out of manes, out of airs, but
They have no manes, so there are no airs, birds
Of words, from me to them no singing gut.
For they have no eyes, for their legs are wood,
For their stomachs are logs with print on them;
Blood red, red lamps hang from necks or where could
Be necks, two legs stand A, four together M.
"Street Closed" is what print says on their stomachs;
That cuts out everybody but the diggers;
You're cut out, and she's cut out, and the jiggers
Are cut out. No! we can't have such nor bucks

As won't, tho they're not here, pass thru a hoop
Strayed on a manhole—me? Am on a stoop.

Am on a stoop to sit here tho no one
Asked me, nor asked you because you're not here,
A sign creaks—LAUNDRY TO-LET
                 (creaks—wind—)—SUN—
(Nights?) the sun's, bro', what month's rent in arrear?
Aighuh—and no manes and horses' trot? butt, butt
Of earth, birds spreading harps, two manes a pair
Of birds, each bird a word, a streaming gut,
Trot, trot—? No horse is here, no horse is there?
Says you! Then I—fellow me, airs! we'll make
Wood horse, and recognize it with our words—
Not it—nine less two!—as many as take
To make a dead man purple in the face,
Full dress to rise and circle thru a pace
Trained horses—in latticed orchards, (switch!) birds.

Just what I said—Birds!—*See Him! Whom? The Son
Of Man,* grave-turf on taxi, taxi gone,
Who blabbed of orchards, strides one leg here, one
Leg there—wooden horses? give them manes!—(was on
A stoop, *He found them sleeping,* don't you see?)
See him! How? Against wood his body close,
Speaks: My face at where its forehead might be,
The plank's end 's a forehead waving a rose—

Birds—birds—nozzle of horse, washed plank in air . . .
For they had no manes we would give them manes,
For their wood was dead the wood would move—bare
But for the print on it—for diggers gone, trains'
    Run, light lights in air where the dead reposed—
    As many as take liveforever, "Street Closed".

"Closed"? then fellow me airs, We'll open ruts
For the wood-grain skin laundered to pass thru,
Switch is a whip which never has been, cuts
Winds for words—Turf streams words, airs untraced—New
The night, and orchards were here? Horses passed?
    There were no diggers, bro', no horses there,

But the graves were turfed and the horses grassed—
Two voices:—Airs? No birds. Taxi? No air—

Says one! Then I—Are logs?! Two legs stand "A"—
Pace them! in revolution are the same!
Switch! See! we can have such and bucks tho they
Are not here, nor were there, pass thru a hoop
(Tho their legs are wood and their necks 've no name)
Strayed on a manhole—See! Am on a stoop!

See! For me these jiggers, these dancing bucks:
Bum pump a-dumb, the pump is neither bum
Nor dumb, dumb pump uh! hum, bum pump o! shucks!
(Whose clavicembalo? bum? bum? te-hum . . .)
Not in the say but in the sound's—hey-hey—
The way to-day, Die, die, die, die, tap, slow,
Die, wake up, up! up! *O Saviour,* to-day!
Choose Jews' shoes or whose: anyway Choose! Go!

But they had no eyes, and their legs were wood!
But their stomachs were logs with print on them!
Blood red, red lamps hung from necks or where could
Be necks, two legs stood A, four together M—
    They had no manes so there were no airs, but—
    Butt . . . butt . . . from me to pit no singing gut!

Says you! Then I, Singing, It is not the sea
But what floats over: hang from necks or where could
Be necks, blood red, red lamps (Night), Launder me,
Mary! Sea of horses that once were wood,
Green and, and leaf on leaf, and dancing bucks,
Who take liveforever! Taken a pump
And shaped a flower. "Street Closed" on their stomachs.
But the street has moved; at each block a stump
That blossoms red, And I sat there, no one
Asked me, nor asked you. Whom? You were not there.
A sign creaked—LAUNDRY TO-LET—(creaked—
                    wind—)—SUN—
(Nights?) the sun's, bro', no months' rent in arrear—
    Bum pump a-dum, no one's cut out, pump a-
    Ricky, bro', Shimaunu-Sān, yours is the

Clavicembalo—Nine less two, Seven
Were the diggers, seven sang, danced, the paces
Seven, Seven Saviours went to heaven—
Their tongues, hands, feet, eyes, ears and hearts,

each face as

Of a Sea looking Outward (Rose the Glass
Broken), Each a reflection of the other.
Just for the fun of it. And 't came to pass

(Open, O fierce flaming pit!)

three said: "Bother,

Brother, we want a meal, different techniques."
Two ways, my two voices . . . Offal and what
The imagination . . . And the seven came
To horses seven (of wood—who will?—kissed

their stomachs)

Bent knees as these rose around them—trot—trot—
Spoke: words, words, we are words, horses, manes,

words.[15]

It's a very peculiar thing, but in fact the sound is much more than merely a joke reproduction of a fugue; it has very much of the quality of sound of a fugue. Bach has always been a passion with Zukofsky; he studied the whole range of inversions and reversals, canon and what have you, used by Bach and exemplified in Bach's *Art of Fugue,* and the similar manipulations used by Schoenberg and his pupils on their tone-rows, and he's tried them out, often very effectively, in rows of words. I'll try to find one of those, presently, in this maze of book-marks.

Such feats as he performs with them treat words as musical elements more uncompromisingly than anyone else has done. The words are often robbed almost entirely of their meaning.

This leads on easily enough to the idea that translation as we practise it is quite wrong. To try and reproduce the meaning of a foreign poem in English loses, as Zukofsky would say, all the poetry, since the poetry is in the sound, not in the meaning, which is at best secondary and quite often trivial. That is true. Then Zukofsky goes on to try and reproduce the foreign sounds by means of English words, neglecting the meaning, whenever it is at all inconvenient to make use of it. I'm going to read you a passage from the *Book of Job,* which he has included in his long poem

"*A*", in which the Hebrew sounds are imitated with hardly any reference whatever to the meaning of words.[16] But it makes an impressive noise.

> He neigh ha lie low h'who y'he gall mood
> So roar cruel hire
> Lo to achieve an eye leer rot off
> Mass th'lo low o loam echo
> How deal me many coeval yammer
> Naked on the face of white rock—sea.
> *Then* I said: Liveforever my nest
> Is arable   hymn
> Shore she   root to water
> Dew anew to branch.
>
> Wind: Yahweh at Iyyob
> Mien His roar 'Why yammer
> Measly make short hates oh
> By milling bleat doubt?
> Eye sore gnaw   key heaver haul its core
> Weigh as I lug where hide any?
> If you—had you towed beside the roots?
> How goad Him—you'd do it by now—
> My sum My made day a key to daw?
> O Me not there allheal—a cave.
>
> All mouth deny hot bough?
> O Me you're raw—Heaven pinned Dawn stars
> Brine I heard choir and weigh by care—
> Why your ear would call by now Elohim:
> Where was soak—bid lot tie in hum—
> How would you have known to hum
> How would you all oats rose snow lay
> Assáy how'd a rock light rollick ore
> Had the rush in you curb, ah bay,
> Bay the shophar yammer *heigh horse'*
>
> Wind: Yahweh at Iyyob 'Why yammer,'
> Wind: Iyyob at Yahweh, 'Why yammer
> How cold the mouth achieved echo.'
> Wind: Yahweh at Iyyob 'Why yammer
> Ha neigh now behēmoth and share I see see your make

Giddy pair—stones—whose rages go
Weigh raw all gay where how spill lay who'
Wind: Iyyob
'Rain without sun hated? *hurt no one*
In two we shadow, how hide any.'[17]

The extraordinary thing is, I once got another—an English—orthodox—Jew to read me that bit of *Job* in Hebrew, and if you allow for the
fact that Hebrew has several sounds that don't exist in any of the Western languages—simply omit those—the rest of it does sound *extremely*
like the original. A very very clever piece of work.

I found that sound interesting, and even fascinating; a bit disturbing. Clearly it is just as much a translation as the words in the English
Bible. But also just as little a translation. The one misses out the meaning, the other misses out the sound. I'm not familiar with the sound
of Hebrew. Zukofsky's translation cannot be quite accurate, because the
English doesn't possess some of the sounds which are in all the Semitic
languages. One of them is described in my Arabic grammar, for you to
imitate if you can, as the noise made by a baby camel being sick. On
the other hand, when I am familiar with the original sounds, as I am
with those of Catullus, in Latin, I'm not at all satisfied with Zukofsky's
rendering of them through English words.[18] Perhaps a reader with no
Latin would get more pleasure from his translation of Catullus than I
can. But it's also clear that Zukofsky has not only failed to reproduce
the Latin sounds convincingly, but to get as much of them as he does
get, he has not only neglected and distorted the meaning, he has completely changed the whole tone of Catullus. Whether Catullus is being
ornamental or direct, he uses invariably the most straightforward Latin
syntax, the language of a man talking. But Zukofsky uses a contorted
syntax, and a diction as far from colloquial as it well could get. The experiment fails, I think, as of course most experiments always fail. That
doesn't mean that they're not worth the making. We have at least the advantage of knowing that even the most skilful manipulator of words of
our day cannot make much of this particular process, so that we need
not waste our time repeating the experiment. It shows some of the limits
that exist to the identification of poetry and music. They're twins, but
they're not identical twins.

Another notable thing about Zukofsky's verse is the extreme condensation he has always insisted on. Pound called constantly for condensation, but he did not always follow his own dogma. Zukofsky always does, except where he modifies it for musical purposes.

That's probably the best-known thing about his verse, the thing that has had the greatest influence on American poets, particularly. People can learn to imitate it, at least with a little prompting at first—that is to say, the condensation. The most outstanding of Zukofsky's pupils in this matter was certainly of course William Carlos Williams; not at any time a diffuse poet, but who learned in a series of consultations with Zukofsky in the 1920s how to make his poetry much tighter—to leave out what didn't matter, what the reader could supply for himself, what merely repeated or served only for elegant variation.[19] But people who like a clear voice and a minimum of words will find another of Zukofsky's pupils, Lorine Niedecker, a poet of great power and continual pleasure.[20]

However, there are several possible ways of condensing a poem, and a poet may not manage to use all of them simultaneously. I think Pound, and Zukofsky too, though less, was surer of himself when he was condensing syntax, by leaving out useless connecting words or stripping away needless adjectives, than when it was a matter of leaving out chunks of argument, evidence and so forth, that were in fact obvious or repetitive, or that merely confirmed or expanded evidence already given.[21] I could lose quite a lot of pages from Pound's *Cantos*, with satisfaction, and quite a lot of pages from Zukofsky's *"A"*. Nevertheless I think that, for the moment, Zukofsky is best known as the poet who boiled everything down, and some of his many imitators in this respect are over-enthusiastic. They go on boiling down until the poetry has evaporated.

Well, it's time, or we'll lose the time altogether, that I showed you a sample of Zukofsky's mature work, in which all these virtues—the condensation, the singing voice, the musical expertise, the patient, obstinate work on very difficult forms—are put into the service of strong emotion.

I'll read this, and then I'll read you some of his short pieces, if time serves.

This is a poem for his wife and son.[22]

"A"-11

River that must turn full after I stop dying
Song, my song, raise grief to music
Light as my loves' thought, the few sick

So sick of wrangling: thus weeping,
Sounds of light, stay in her keeping
And my son's face—this much for honor.

Freed by their praises who make honor dearer
Whose losses show them rich and you no poorer
Take care, song, that what stars' imprint you mirror
Grazes their tears; draw speech from their nature or
Love in you—faced to your outer stars—purer
Gold than tongues make without feeling
Art new, hurt old: revealing
The slackened bow as the stinging
Animal dies, thread gold stringing
The fingerboard pressed in my honor.

Honor, song, sang the blest is delight knowing
We overcome ills by love. Hurt, song, nourish
Eyes, think most of whom you hurt. For the flowing
River 's poison where what rod blossoms. Flourish
By love's sweet lights and sing *in them I flourish.*
No, song, not any one power
May recall or forget, our
Love to see your love flows into
Us. If Venus lights, your words spin, to
Live our desires lead us to honor.

Graced, your heart in nothing less than in death, go—
I, dust—raise the great hem of the extended
World that nothing can leave; having had breath go
Face my son, say: 'If your father offended
You with mute wisdom, my words have not ended
His second paradise where
His love was in her eyes where
They turn, quick for you two—sick
Or gone cannot make music
You set less than all. Honor

His voice in me, the river's turn that finds the
Grace in you, four notes first too full for talk, leaf
Lighting stem, stems bound to the branch that binds the
Tree, and then as from the same root we talk, leaf

After leaf of your mind's music, page, walk leaf
Over leaf of his thought, sounding
His happiness: song sounding
The grace that comes from knowing
Things, her love our own showing
Her love in all her honor.' [23]

Well, the songs of course are much simpler things than these, and yet,
I think, mostly not very easy. Here is—oh yes, let's try {you with this one}.

Send regards to Ida the bitch
whose hate's unforgiving,
why not send regards?
There are trees' roots, branchtops
      —as is
one who can take his own life
      and be quit
except he might hurt—as
      he imagines
here he's gone—
a person, two; if not the sun.[24]

The green leaf that will outlast the winter
    because sheltered in the open:
the wall, transverse, and diagonal ribs
    of the privet that pocket air
      around the leaf inside them
and cover but with walls of wind:
it happens wind colors like glass shelter,
    as the light's aire from a vault
    which has a knob of sun.[25]

Ah, here's Zukofsky enjoying himself.

Belly Locks Shnooks Oakie
When he awoke, he
Scared all the spooks. He
Was some oak, he
    Was.[26]

Drive, fast kisses,
no need to see
hands or eyelashes
a mouth at her ear
trees or leaves
night or the days.[27]

{There should be one I wanted to read here.}

The rains, the rains
Toward spring pour thru
The winter night
And freeze to hail.

Seasoned armies
Tested in defeat
Retreating now
In that order

They cannot yield,
No more than weather
Of their hemisphere:
The rain that turns

To hail before
The thunderstorms,
The rains, the rains
Of spring call out.[28]

This is one I was looking for much earlier on, where he {proclaims} the idea of music:

The lines of this new song are nothing
But a tune making the nothing full
Stonelike become more hard than silent
The tune's image holding in the line.[29]

When the crickets
sound like fifty water-taps
forsaken at once

the inclemency
of the inhuman noises
is the earth's

with its roadways
over cabins in the forests

the sheets smell
of sweet milk

all the waters
of the world

we are going
to sleep to sleep [30]

I walked out, before
"Break of day"
And saw
Four cabins in the hay.

Blue sealed glasses
Of preserves—four—
In the window-sash
In the yard on the bay.

Further:
The waters
At the ramp
Running away. [31]

I remember this one, the way we enjoyed it about the streets of Brooklyn in 1928 or so: [32]

There's naw—thing
    lak po—ee try
it's a delicacy
    for   a horse:

Dere's na—thing
    lak pea-   nut-brittle
it's a delicacy
    for   the molars. [33]

Passing tall
Who walk upon the green
So light they are not heard
If never seen; —

Willow above in spring haze,
Green sprig and pendulous; —
Wind, white lightning
In branches over us;

Sun;
All weathering changing loves,
In the high grass (kiss!)
Will not uncover us.[34]

Ah yes.

These are not my sentiments,
Only sometimes does one feel that intimate.

God, LL.D.,

I want to resign
You can have what's mine
And what ain't mine,

I want to resign
What's mine ain't mine
What ain't mine is
                    Thine,

SOS

P.S. I *want* to resign.[35]

How sweet is the sun, is the sun
How sweet is the sun
With the birds, with the summer months
                    the notes of a run
How sweet, sweet is the sun.

You ask what I can do—
My name is Jackie

I am Jack-of-all-trades:
Homer—the carpenter—
Did you write that book?
Is your fir squared
        and its end true?

How sweet is the sun, is the sun
How sweet is the sun
With the birds, with the summer months
            the notes of a run
How sweet, sweet is the sun.[36]

Footprint and eye fringe
Shake off snow—
All wise
Flinging.

Pupil and fingers
Draw the bow—
All wise
Singing.

Heartbeat and feathers
Sow birds so—
All wise
Ringing.[37]

Here is a peculiar feat of merely changing punctuation again and again:

Hear, her
Clear
Mirror,
His error.
In her
Care
Is clear.

Hear her
(Clear mirror)
Care.

His error.
In her care—
Is clear.

Hear, her
Clear
Mirror,
Care
His error.
In her,
Care
Is clear.

Hear her
Clear mirror
Care his error
In her care
Is clear

Hear
Her
Clear
Mirror
Care
His
Error in
Her
Care
Is clear

Hear
Her
Clear,
Mirror,
Care
His
Error in
Her—
Care
Is
Clear.[38]

{ } That's a trick of the sort I said he learned from people like Schoenberg.

> Marry or don't
> (If you wish)

> Weigh the way in May
> Given to brighter green
> > Than that seen
> Thru white curtain.

> Love, weigh the way
> Green, coat this May's green.
> > No wish seen
> Is uncertain.

> Kiss the child's hard cheek.
> Draw from a light green
> > Away, seen
> Thru white curtain.

> It is the way the cheek
> Shocks a bright green
> > Makes it seen
> Who is certain.[39]

And, if you can spare another minute, I'll read you a little bit from his very earliest beginnings, to show you that before he had thought out what he wanted to do with poetry, he already had great skill {at} words. He must have been about nineteen when he wrote these.[40]

> Horses that pass through inappreciable woodland,
> Leaves in their manes tangled, mist, autumn green,
> Lord, why not give these bright brutes—your good land—
> Turf for their feet always, years for their mien.
> See how each peer lifts his head, others follow,
> Mate paired with mate, flanks coming full they crowd,
> Reared in your sun, Lord, escaping each hollow
> Where life-struck we stand, utter their praise aloud.
> Very much Chance, Lord, as when you first made us,
> You might forget them, Lord, preferring what
> Being less lovely where sadly we fuss?

> Weed out these horses as tho they were not?
> Never alive in brute delicate trembling
> Song to your sun, against autumn assembling.[41]

And one I enjoyed very greatly from the first time I saw it:

> How hard the cat-world.
> On the stream Vicissitude
> Our milk flows lewd.
>
> We'll cry, we'll cry,
> We'll cry the more
> And wet the floor,
>
> Megrow, megrow,
> Around around,
> The only sound
>
> The prowl, our prowl,
> Of gentlemen cats
> With paws like spats
>
> Who weep the nights
> Till the nights are gone—
> —And r-r-run—the Sun![42]

That, I'm afraid, is the best I can do for you today; I'm sorry.

Well, there are no more of these lectures till some future term, or year, or {goodness knows when}. I've more or less, I think, illustrated the point through all eight of them[43] of the fact that music and poetry are very very closely intertwined, and that as soon as you begin to part them things begin to go wrong.

Notes

Introduction

1. The reader should treat the historical detail in these lectures with caution; its value is sometimes more mythic than factual.

2. *Finnsburh Fragment* 7 (*scyld scefte oncwyth*), 5–6 (*fugelas singath, / gylleth graeghama, guthwudu hlynneth*); *Beowulf* 322–23 (*hringiren scir / song in searwum*); cf. Bunting, *Briggflatts* I: "harness mutter to shaft," *The Spoils:* "Tide sang. Guns sang."

3. To Louis Zukofsky, 16 May 1951, HRC.

4. "La rapsode foraine et le pardon de Saint-Anne."

5. To Zukofsky, 9 May 1943, HRC (in which Bunting remembers it as "Syrte"); from *Odes* 1.22.

6. William Warren Vernon, *Readings on the Paradiso of Dante,* 2 vols. (London: Macmillan, 1900).

7. Bunting, "The Use of Poetry," ed. Peter Quartermain, *Writing* 12 (Summer 1985): 41.

8. To Zukofsky, 19 Apr. 1951, HRC.

9. To Zukofsky, 13 Mar. 1951, HRC.

10. Pound, Canto XCVIII; a more pristine version of the interview is quoted in Charles Norman, *Ezra Pound,* rev. ed. (London: Macdonald, 1969), 312.

11. "The title to consideration of Dante, Dryden, Pope, is the same as that of Shakespeare, Wordsworth, Baudelaire, Walt Whitman or any other poet, regular or irregular, namely, their fidelity to Nature and to the sublime, their faculty of distilling the essence of life in words." Basil Bunting, "Music of the Month: On Playing It Backwards," *Town Crier* 84 (Apr. 1928): 142.

12. Bunting acknowledges this change in his opinions in A. McAllister and S. Figgis, "Basil Bunting: The Last Interview," *Bête noire* 2/3 (1987): 32; there he says he came to clarify his own views in this area by arguing with Pound.

13. Cf. esp. ibid., passim; also Dale Reagan, "An Interview with Basil Bunting," *Montemora* 3 (Spring 1977): 78.

14. Paul Johnstone, "Basil Bunting: Taken from Two Interviews, Recorded by Paul Johnstone in April 1974 and April 1975," *meantime* 1 (Apr.

1977): 75. The tremendous difficulty of this truth is renewed from generation to generation: the concerns of new poems (the liberation of the masses in Auden's 1930s; the brutality of the father in Plath's 1970s) seem eternally so urgent as to make coherence unimportant.

If "temporally" here is a correct transcription, it reflects Bunting's repeated suggestion in his late years that poetry and works of art in general ought to be made in the same spirit as once they were made, that is, in praise of God: see *B:SV,* 208, n. 61.

15. See below, chap. 10, where the argument is that "the precepts of Pater" are aligned with the practice of Mallarmé, who "never lost sight of the idea that poetry is essentially the same as music." See also McAllister and Figgis, "Last Interview," 26.

16. Walter Pater, *The Renaissance: Studies in Art and Poetry,* ed. Donald L. Hill (Berkeley: U of California P, 1980) 108–9 ("The School of Giorgione").

17. Cf. *B:SV,* 157. Note also how Bunting proposes a balance between plot elements (Cuthbert and Alexander). Ibid., 152, 180.

18. To Zukofsky, 3 Nov. 1948, HRC.

19. Cf. *B:SV,* 118.

20. Hence, I think, his strong defense of the sea terms in *The Spoils,* "compared, lets say, with TSE and his garboard-strakes etc" (i.e., in *Four Quartets*). To Zukofsky, 25 June 1951, HRC.

21. See Johnstone, "Bunting," 74.

22. See below, chap. 11.

23. Present-day Mallarméans such as John Ashbery do not much share Bunting's concern with sound-form.

24. To George Oppen, 6 Feb. 1973, Buffalo.

25. To Gael Turnbull, 13 Jan. 1965, private collection.

26. On Williams's advantage in this, cf. Johnstone, "Bunting," 76.

27. McAllister and Figgis, "Last Interview," 22–23: "I think that there is a sense in which 'Objectivist' is not too bad a term for Louis . . . ; the idea being a noble one: one, the poem is an object . . . ; and secondly, the proper matter for poetry is objects, things about the place. . . . Zukofsky wanted to look at the things about him and to put them down as things."

28. See Johnstone, "Bunting," 70.

29. Hugh Kenner, *The Poetry of Ezra Pound* (London: Faber, 1951), 76–105; Peter Makin, *Pound's Cantos* (reprint, Baltimore: Johns Hopkins UP, 1992), 34–36, 63–77.

30. These are the main points of Bunting's very harsh initial reaction to the *Pisan Cantos* in a letter to Zukofsky, 17 June 1949, HRC. When Zukofsky (it seems) expressed shock at this letter, Bunting reiterated his great respect for the master, but in rather general terms (6 Aug. 1949, HRC). It is evident from the present lectures that Bunting's view of the *Pisan Cantos* had changed greatly by the seventies.

31. See below, chap. 13, n. 9.

32. "I . . . take that side of myself out in playing chess, it's the same sort of thing.' McAllister and Figgis, "Last Interview," 29.

33. Ibid., 22; and "a poem regarded as a commentary on the life around you as it alters day by day is a trap anyway. No poet is wise enough or witty enough to keep it going." To Tom Pickard, 19 Mar. 1983, Buffalo.

34. Johnstone, "Bunting," 70: "He thought, certainly his disciples go into raptures over it, that it was an absolutely new discovery that the length of a line of poetry was determined by the breath." To Tom Pickard, 19 Mar. 1983, Buffalo: "As to Olson, he never really tried to have a structure, and his poem degenerated into library notes and became a proper bore."

35. For the drive against the language of logical classes and toward the language of the whole event, cf. Charles Olson, *Selected Writings,* ed. Robert Creeley (New York: New Directions, 1966), 54, 59, with Basil Bunting, "Some Limitations of English," *The Lion and the Crown* 1/1 (1932): 26–33, reprinted in Bunting, *Three Essays,* ed. Richard Caddel (Durham: Basil Bunting Poetry Centre, 1994), 21–26. For the drive toward the active verb, cf. Olson, *Selected Writings,* 21, with Bunting, "The Lion and the Lizard" (essay sent to Zukofsky in 1935), in Bunting, *Three Essays,* 27–31, esp. 29. For Irving Kaplan's contribution to this thinking, see *B:SV,* 290 ff. (There I wrongly attribute Kaplan's essay beginning "The written record" to Bunting, as Andrew Crozier has pointed out: see his "Paper Bunting," *Sagetrieb* 14/3 [1995].) For Olson's indebtedness to Fenollosa, see e.g., Charles Olson and Robert Creeley, *The Complete Correspondence,* vol. 7, ed. George F. Butterick (Santa Rosa: Black Sparrow, 1987), 211–12, and also 208; for Bunting on Fenollosa, see "The Lion and the Lizard," 29.

36. See esp. to Zukofsky, 2 Oct. 1932, HRC, including "OPEN LETTER to Louis Zukofsky," the English original of his "Lettera aperta a Louis Zukofsky," published in Rapallo in the same year. See also *B:SV,* 40–42.

37. Olson, *Selected Writings,* 50.

38. In the famous "Projective Verse" essay, Olson wants "obedience of the ear to the syllable" to play a leading part in writing, and there is much rhetoric about the exacting labor this imposes. But he nowhere says what feature of the syllable he refers to. If it is stress, an English syllable has no inherent stress: its relative stress is conferred on it by lexis and by syntax; the ear should therefore be listening for the contour of stresses provided by these two. Conceivably Olson means syllable length, but in English this is subject (as Bunting points out) to violent modification by stress, with the same consequence. What degree of inherent length there is in English syllables comes from their varying inner construction from consonants and vowels; but when Olson gives a handful of examples of quantity in his essay "Quantity in Verse," they demonstrate an ignorance for which one would have to go back to the age of Puttenham to find parallels.

Having said nothing concrete about the syllable in the "Projective Verse" essay, Olson then proceeds to argue that "together, these two, the syllable *and* the line" (emphasis in original) are the key to a poem. If this is so, these two entities ought presumably to interact. Yet in English, line and syllable cannot interact except through intermediaries such as stress, word boundary, and syntax—unless the writer falls back on the perfectly arbitrary device of making his line by counting syllables without regard to the nature of the utterance. It becomes apparent that Olson has chosen these particular features of language to foreground in his theory because first, he is able to associate each of them with the metaphysics of the self (via "breath"), and second, each of them is related to orality. For there is no evident reason why the "field of composition" should place orality (rather than semantics, for example) at its center, and Olson's gestures at technical observation of these sound-features give the appearance of providing such a reason.

39. Reagan, "Interview with Bunting," 78.

40. Olson, *Selected Writings,* 20. "Treacherously": is a conception that has existed somewhere in the poet for two years before he puts pen to paper, thereby "from outside the poem"? At what point does the present self begin?

41. "An Interview with Peter Bell," *The Recordings of Basil Bunting: Northumberland, 1981, 1982,* ed. Richard Swigg (cassette tape) (Keele: Keele University, 1995).

42. To George Oppen, 6 Feb. 1973, Buffalo.

43. This would also explain why Bunting placed Charles Reznikoff's postwar *Testimony* higher than anything by Rakosi, Oppen, or any of the other collaborators (except Zukofsky himself) in the Objectivist movement; and similarly why he was more interested in the work of Gary Snyder than in that of other Beats.

44. See below, chap. 10.

45. See below, chap. 5; italics here mine.

46. Bunting, "Carlos Williams's Recent Poetry," *Westminster Magazine* 23/2 (1934): 150.

47. Hendrick van der Werf, *The Chansons of the Troubadours and Trouvères* (Utrecht: Oosthoek, 1972), 37–38, gives a useful sketch of the late classical and medieval tradition of treatises "On Music." These were not centrally about music but were "speculative discussions of numerical laws . . . which were supposed to govern all movements and functions of the universe." The term *Musica* referred to these laws. In the treatises, music and meter are discussed because they offer "the only readily measurable element, in the entire realm of Musica." But even those authors who set out to describe music "insist upon taking it for granted that music has all the properties of Musica and that therefore music must be measurable in all aspects, regardless of whether they can discern this measure." For a similar circularity see the third-century

treatise of Aristides Quintilianus, *On Music: In Three Books,* trans. Thomas J. Mathiesen (New Haven: Yale UP, 1983), 41. The world structure and the place of music in it remain remarkably unchanged between Aristides and the age of Castiglione and Sidney: see a convenient summary of Aristides' views in M. L. West, *Ancient Greek Music* (Oxford: Clarendon Press, 1992), 252.

Prosody had an important place in this, and St. Augustine, *De Musica* 6, gives a typical example. He takes as a building block in his celebration of the divine unities the basic fact of classical metrics: the distinction between short and long syllables, which (he declares) is in the perfect proportion 1:2. This is observationally not true, as some ancient rhythmicians knew: cf. M. L. West, *Greek Metre* (Oxford: Clarendon Press, 1982), 20. But such observation was current in a tradition of study that the theoreticians of meter and music did not care to take note of; their concerns were fundamentally metaphysical.

48. Cf. Edmund Horace Fellowes, *The English Madrigal Composers,* 2d ed. (London: Oxford UP, 1948), 138–39; and, on the eighteenth- and nineteenth-century practice of editing these "irregularities" out of the scores, Fellowes, *The English Madrigal* (1925; reprint, Salem, N.H.: Ayer, 1972), 53, 60.

49. See Richard Caddel and Anthony Flowers, *Basil Bunting: A Northern Life* (Newcastle: Newcastle Libraries & Information Service; Durham: Basil Bunting Poetry Centre, 1997), 29.

50. Frank Howes, *William Byrd* (London: K. Paul, Trench, Trubner, 1928), 92; see also W. Gillies Whittaker, "Byrd's Great Service," *Musical Quarterly* 27 (1941): 477–78.

51. Cf. Jonathan Williams, *Descant on Rawthey's Madrigal: Conversations with Basil Bunting* (Lexington, Ky.: Gnomon Press, 1968), [6]; and Eric Mottram, "Conversation with Basil Bunting on the Occasion of His Seventy-fifth Birthday, 1975," *Poetry Information* 19 (Autumn 1978): 7.

52. Bunting to Pound, 4 Mar. 1936, Beinecke.

53. See Fellowes, *English Madrigal Composers,* 124–25, emphasis in original.

54. See also Paul Fussell, *Theory of Prosody in Eighteenth-Century England* (Archon Books, 1966), 3, 9–10.

55. Bunting, "All the cants they peddle," 125.

56. Below, chap. 5.

57. Bunting says, in effect, that if we understand the verse to be "iambic pentameter," this means we think the writer expected us to deliver a swat on every second syllable:

My <u>liege</u>, I <u>did</u> de<u>ny</u> no <u>prisoners</u> . . .

Yet even in the tradition of academic prosody, few have believed that. As for performance, it would seem that at most periods, most actors have done as they now do: they have delivered the natural phonology of the words with a very slight optional "tilting" toward the alternation of the meter. This is what Bunting himself does when he reads "pentameters"—even Wyatt's.

Indeed, Bunting in practice accepts that a hinting at such alternation is built into the words and that it is the framework of the verse, even in his most acute remarks about rhythm in these lectures: those concerning Wyatt's verse. He relates the rhythms of Wyatt's verse to those of the Tudor musicians. As those musicians were fond of syncopating, of "beginning a note just before where we now place the bar, and carrying it on over the bar," so in this line—

> With naked foot stalking in my chamber

—Wyatt "intends the first syllable of 'stalking' to carry on over the bar." Tape (1974) *incipit* "We get more." But if we follow Bunting's claim that it does not matter how many weak syllables there are—and he says so in a number of different ways—it has no meaning to say, with reference to Wyatt, "The effect is to displace a stress, or lose it altogether" (ibid.; see also below, chap. 4). If the bar divisions simply note where the strong stress is, and if we are taking no note of the number or presence of weak stresses, then the proper bar marking in this case must be:

> / naked / foot / stalking / in my

And then nothing is displaced: the first syllable of *stalking* is in its rightful position in the bar, for the bar is the "measure" from strong stress to strong stress, with no count of weaks in between (and a strong stress, in the modern musical practice Bunting is speaking of, is by definition the beginning of the bar).

Bunting is in fact acknowledging the demands of the "grammarians," presumably because the environment inescapably hints at an alternation, wherein a single stressed is more often than not preceded by an unstressed. Thus if a stressed appears conjacent to another stressed, when neither seems to be filling a weak position, then the ear will make some kind of adjustment; and I think Bunting's is the right one. (The weak positions are occupied: Bunting acknowledges this when he concedes the presence of an ongoing "frame-beat" by saying that Wyatt turns the line upside down in the middle.)

58. On the baselessness of attempts to describe the poets' practice, at least up to Jespersen, see esp. Paul Kiparsky, "Stress, Syntax, and Meter," *Language* 51/3 (1975): 576–78; Kiparsky, "The Rhythmic Structure of English Verse," *Linguistic Inquiry* 8/2 (1977): 245. On the actual basis of the "roughness" of Donne and its contrast with Pope see, e.g., Kiparsky, "Stress, Syntax, and Meter," 605. On the failure even of the linguistic explanations of Halle, Keyser, and Kiparsky to work with complete consistency, see esp.

Gilbert Youmans, "Iambic Pentameter: Statistics or Generative Grammar?" *Language and Style* 19/4 (1986): 398–99.

59. See Donald Davie, "A Demurral" (review of *The Collected Poems of William Carlos Williams*, vol. 1, 1909–1939), *New Republic*, Apr. 1987, 35.

60. There seems no reason to suppose in advance that prosodists of a given age understood the prosody that contemporary poetries were using. The persistent tendency to do so seems the result only of a misplaced dread of being anachronistic in criticism. John Thompson, *The Founding of English Metre* (reprint, New York: Columbia University Press, 1989), 69 ff., finds a crucial step forward in Gascoigne's view that the abstract pattern of the meter must always be realized, absolutely, in performance, even if the words of the line fail to offer any hint whatever of the values the pattern requires. This, Thompson thinks, at last recognizes the independent existence of the meter. Since it denies absolutely the existence of anything else, I see no way forward from it to a metric of tension. Gascoigne in 1575 is as anachronistic as Puttenham in 1589; he has learned nothing even from the Wyatt that Tottel printed in 1557:

> May chance thee lie witherd and olde,
> In winter nightes that are so colde,
> Playning in vaine vnto the mone:
> Thy wishes then dare not be tolde.
> Care then who list, for I haue done.

Tottel's Miscellany (1557–1587), ed. Hyder Edward Rollins, rev. ed. (Cambridge: Harvard UP, 1965), 1:63. The verse writers who followed Gascoigne and Puttenham clearly did not learn from them: they learned from *The Shepheardes Calender* and from *Tamburlaine*. One may point out that, similarly, prosody took no note of the existence of accentual verse in Latin until Bede, some three centuries after its creation: see Dag Norberg, "La Récitation du vers latin," *Neuphilologische Mitteilungen* 66 (1965): 503–5.

61. See below, chap. 4.

62. See, for example, the way in which Puttenham turns Wyatt's opening line "Farewell love . . ." into regular trochees: George Puttenham, *The Arte of English Poesie*, ed. Gladys Doidge Willcock and Alice Walker (reprint, Cambridge: Cambridge UP, 1970), 132. Long syllables are to be discovered by following the "orthography," that is, in fact, the so-called rules of position in Latin, as in "Let no nobilitie" (two dactyls, 127). But when the same method would produce an inconvenient, that is, an irregular result, Puttenham sets it aside: "Morne, noone, and eue in age and eke in eld" (123–24) is iambic throughout. For the general confusion as to what is long and what accented, see, e.g., 120–21.

63. See Roger Fowler, *The Languages of Literature: Some Linguistic Contri-*

butions to Criticism (London: Routledge & Kegan Paul, 1971), 194–96 (I take the term *misbracketing* from Kiparsky).

64. S = strong metrical position; underline = accented syllable (both these categories marked selectively); A = adjective, N = noun, V = verb.

65. George T. Wright, *Shakespeare's Metrical Art* (Berkeley: U of California P, 1988), 54.

66. See e.g., *The Tempest* 4.1.146, "You do look, my son, in a mov'd sort," which Hanmer fixes by adding "Why," at the front. Pope had sorted it out by dropping "do."

67. Wright's "scannings" always involve a weighting of stress toward that required by the metrical scheme, but they override the language in varying ways. Sometimes they misconstrue the vocabulary (thus 99, "Still climbing after knowledge infinite" [*Tamburlaine* pt. 1, 2.7.24], where *still* means "always"); sometimes they make a semantic choice that the context rules out (thus 55, "Four lagging winters and four wanton springs" [*Richard II* 1.3.214]).

Wright appears to be only intermittently conscious of this. He sets out to give a description of the arrangements of natural language that can be accepted as giving rise to a sense of iambic pentameter: these amount, he thinks (8), to "the uniform recurrence of a *relative* superiority of stress in every second syllable (or in most of them) over the one it follows." He comes to "When in disgrace with fortune and men's eyes," scans *-tune and* as a pyrrhic, and remarks: "the line is less divergent than it appears. For one thing, the so-called pyrrhic and spondaic feet do not run counter to the basic iambic requirement that the second syllable in the foot be pronounced [*sic*] more strongly than the first. It is only that the differences here seem minimal, that '-tune and' seem almost equal in value, though both are lightly stressed." This clearly sets out to be a description of natural stressings, yet as clearly ignores the fact that the inequality, if any, is not in favor of the iambic pattern but against it. Cf. the scansion

"withered"

on the previous page, and (10),

"the first thing that,"

which is explicitly offered as a "natural reading."

These tilted-readings-as-scansions are really performance suggestions, set at a level which is neither (say) that of Gascoigne or Bentley, nor that of Gielgud, but at some arbitrarily chosen aesthetic or historical point in between.

Sometimes Wright in effect acknowledges that he believes that, as long as the material is to be described as verse, its natural phonology cannot usefully be considered without first reading into it the meter. To the question, "Here is the abstract pattern: but what kinds of syllable can go into it?"

he must then answer: "The syllables that the educated reader will naturally tilt to fit its positions." Either this means "Any natural-language syllable" (so that the poet's choices merely add water to thin soup), or it evades the consequent question: "Which syllables in the language can be thus tilted, and which can't?" (See esp. Kiparsky's remarks in "Stress, Syntax, and Meter," 586–87.) But a confusion of meter with rhythm has been endemic to the tradition, as Kiparsky notes.

68. For a brilliant exposition of Bunting's idea and its implications, see Hugh Kenner, *A Sinking Island: The Modern English Writers* (New York: Knopf, 1988), 92–93; also 38, 63, 67–68, 216–17, 219.

69. See below, chap. 5. Though the influence is there ascribed to Spenser, and though its mechanisms in Spenser are there listed, the Spenser verse that Bunting goes on to read (from the *Calender*) is explicitly not an example of these mechanisms, being an early, relatively restrained work.

70. See esp. Bunting, "Carlos Williams's Recent Poetry" (1934), 150; Bunting, "The Lion and the Lizard" (1935), passim.

71. Here (*Beowulf*, ll. 736–37) the "shorts" are normal, in the sense that they are allowed by the meter (as an example of resolution). But this does not mean they do not have effect as a variant. A similar point should be made where Bunting says that Dante allows himself enormous variation with his syllable count. Though the variations in syllable count, despite Bunting, are easily accounted for by rules governing elision, they still stand as variations, chosen by the poet for their difference.

72. Louis Zukofsky, *Prepositions: The Collected Critical Essays* (London: Rapp & Carroll, 1967), 133, 135.

73. In this prosodic notation, as in all others, it is by intention that I do not mark any patterned linguistic feature exhaustively, still less try to mark all patterned features in the given words.

In the prosodies of many poets there are certain features that are systematically and exhaustively patterned: as, for example, syllable length throughout Horace, or syllable count in *Paradise Lost*. (There are no such features in Bunting's *Briggflatts*.) But in all poets there are also transient patternings of various features, which may become affective. Whether they are foregrounded enough to do so depends on their interaction with the environment of other features. (Thus in Whitman, relations with local syntax determine whether a given stress sequence group is noticed as such by the reader.) In any given location, such interactions make patternings of certain features very prominent, others less so, and others scarcely at all.

For prosodic purposes, there is no point whatever in marking patterns where they do not seem to rise to affective prominence; though, necessarily, there is no objective way of setting a standard for such prominence. Further, where a poet knits his patterns as thickly as does Spenser, it would be self-defeating even to mark exhaustively all those that do so rise to prominence, since the markings would merely bury each other. The best one can do is to mark important instances, and leave the rest for the reader to seek out.

For an outline of this approach to prosody, see the discussion of cadence and, in particular, *constantes rhythmiques,* in "Whitman: Editor's Explanatory Note," below, chap. 8.

74. See below, chap. 6, and nn. 5, 6.

75. Bunting, "The Lion and the Lizard," 31.

76. Pound, "Portrait d'une Femme" (1912). This is Pound's go at "Full fathom five," which became almost as popular a test piece with the moderns as the famous loud-sounding sea in Homer (*Od.* 13.220); cf. the "Death by Water" passage in *The Waste Land,* and Bunting, *Briggflatts* "Fells forget him. . . ."

77. Its influence among novelists seems as strong now as in 1916, and it is sad to see a writer such as Toni Morrison sacrificing as industriously on this altar as on the altar of the brilliant metaphor.

78. Bunting, "The Lion and the Lizard," 30–31; cf. Bunting, "Carlos Williams's Recent Poetry," 150.

79. Peter Craven and Michael Heyward, "An Interview with Basil Bunting," *Scripsi* 1/3–4 (1982): 30.

80. "Take the plainest words and dodge them into the right shape." Bunting quoted by Brent MacKay, "Bunting as Teacher," *Conjunctions* 8 (1985): 181.

81. "I am agog for foam" (1926).

82. See below, chap. 13. He probably considered Lorine Niedecker and Tom Pickard as worthy successors to Zukofsky. On Niedecker see Bunting to Tom Pickard, 28 Aug. 1967, Buffalo: "Very delicate; many implications, none obvious." On Pickard see Bunting's preface to Pickard, *High on the Walls* (London: Fulcrum, 1967).

83. See below, chap. 2, n. 1.

CHAPTER 1. THE CODEX

1. A melodrama; first known performance, 1840.

2. Sir J. C. Squire (1884–1958), poet, critic, parodist, Fabian, literary editor of the *New Statesman.*

3. MS: 'Robert Bridges and other poets'

4. "Certain grammarians in Alexandria," to Bunting, carries a point (see Tape [1974] *incipit* "Well, I see"): these prosodists' description of the hexameter postdates by half a millennium the making of Homer's verse.

5. See Canto XLVI (first published 1936). The anecdote came from Marmaduke Pickthall, English novelist and sometime resident in the Near East: see Carroll F. Terrell, ed., *A Companion to the Cantos of Ezra Pound* (Berkeley: U of California P, 1980), 1: 181.

6. Bunting was on his way to take up a post at the British embassy in Teheran; he described the incident soon after it happened in a letter to Dorothy Pound dated 1 May 1947, Indiana.

7. British Library Cotton MS Nero D. IV (the Lindisfarne Gospels), datable late 7th to early 8th century; quite probably made for the translation (in 698) of the relics of St. Cuthbert from Farne Island to the monastery at Holy Island (Lindisfarne).

8. T. D. Kendrick et al., *Evangeliorum Quattuor Codex Lindisfarnensis*, 2 vols. (Lausanne: Urs Graf, 1956–60).

9. The Echternach Gospels, now in Paris (BN MS lat. 9389), were formerly in the monastery at Echternach, Luxembourg.

10. There is a core of three books (the Lindisfarne Gospels; the Echternach Gospels; and the book whose extant fragments are BL Cotton Otho C.V and Cambridge Corpus 197B), which, there can be no doubt, come from a milieu where Irish and Northumbrian cultures were closely twined. It is fiercely disputed which culture dominated in that immediate milieu; my view is that it was more Northumbrian than Irish. The Book of Durrow and (much later) the Book of Kells seem to me a different matter altogether: I take them to be much more Irish. (Bunting said of the Book of Kells: "It sacrifices color for the effects of gold. It is vulgar in comparison." Brian Swann, "Basil Bunting of Northumberland," *St Andrews Review* 4/2 [1977]: 40.) See *B:SV*, 334–36; and, for a recent pro-Irish view, William O'Sullivan, "The Lindisfarne Scriptorium: For and Against," *Peritia* 8 (1994): 80–94.

11. Bunting here offers two alternative pronunciations of the name: "Edfrith" and "Ee-adfrith." In what follows he uses the latter.

12. MS: "If you would like to see what his work can teach a poet, look at the gospel of St Matthew, Chapter i verse 18."

13 MS: "Beneath this extremely rich work of art, and combined with it . . . is another, no less striking, though quite different in character, and almost austere beside it."

14. It is not clear which of the five other initial pages Bunting is referring to here, or to which of the five cross-carpet pages he refers in what follows. For an example of the latter, see fig. 5; reproductions of the rest are readily available in Janet Backhouse, *The Lindisfarne Gospels* (Ithaca, N.Y.: Cornell UP, 1981).

15. MS: "glorious pages."

16.   Winter wrings pigment
     from petal and slough
     but thin light lays
     white next red on sea-crow wing,
     gruff sole cormorant
     whose grief turns carnival.
             Briggflatts, 60.

17. Some have claimed that it is not a cormorant: but see Janet Backhouse, "Birds, Beasts and Initials in Lindisfarne's Gospel Books," in Gerald Bonner et al., *St Cuthbert, His Cult and His Community to AD 1200* (Woodbridge, Suffolk: Boydell, 1989), 167–69.

18. MS: "He leaves him to find it, to discover for himself that what holds the page together and gives it meaning is the cross half-concealed in it. Less delicate artists have mostly shown less restraint, but there are examples to show that Eadfrith's example was not altogether lost on Northumberland."

19. Between the north transept aisle and the choir aisle in Hexham Priory Church (also known as Hexham Abbey). King Aelfwald (or Aelfwold) of Northumbria reigned 778–88 and was buried in Hexham. To my teacher William Scobie I owe the comment that the main design of the tomb cover is of a vine representing Christ's life on earth, rather than the "tree of life" properly so called (an Eastern motif), and that the work is probably to be dated c. 1100–1200.

20. *Sir Gawain* is usually said to be in a dialect of the Northwest Midlands, though E. V. Gordon extended the dialect area as far as upper Ribblesdale. Bunting believed that its dialect was that of Teesdale and that the places named in the poem reflected an actual journey between more northerly points than those usually proposed. See also chap. 4.

21. For some indications of this period in Northumbria, see *B:SV*, 177–78, 196, 199–200.

22. MS: "with their own notions of art." On these cross-flows in the visual arts, see also *B:SV* 220–21 and app. 4.

23. See esp. Peter Quartermain, *Basil Bunting: Poet of the North* (Durham: Basil Bunting Poetry Archive, 1990), 5–7 and refs.

24. MS: "now built into." At the church of St. Andrew, Bywell, there are 25 of these cross slabs; the best examples have now been removed from the outside wall and placed inside the church. See fig. 8.

25. In *Presidential Addresses: An Artist's View on Regional Arts Patronage* (Newcastle: Northern Arts, 1976), 1–2, Bunting writes on the same theme of the essence of Northumbrian culture, and there he also includes the Acca crosses as examples.

26. It is evident from the example of the Lindisfarne cormorant that though Bunting here seems to mean formalization (a movement away from representation and toward establishing a system of forms independent of any origin), he is yet insisting that these forms reflect and recall natural features by summarizing them.

CHAPTER 2. THUMPS

1. See the numerous translations from Manuchehri (d. about 1040) in Bunting's *Complete Poems*. Bunting remarked on his admiration for "the

makers of something not altogether drawn from the life: the enamelled
flora, alcoholic crescendo, goldleaved erudition, with which Manuchehri
surrounds simplicities and gives them overwhelming power. (There are fitful glimpses of the kind of thing in Catullus and Villon)" (to Ezra Pound,
c. Apr. 1954, Beinecke).

2. See, e.g., Franz Boas, *Primitive Art* (Cambridge: Harvard UP, 1928),
299–348 and refs.; C. M. Bowra, *Primitive Song* (London: Weidenfeld &
Nicolson, 1962).

3. Here and again below, Bunting has deleted "Chippewa" and inserted
"Menominee." The songs of these two neighboring tribes are closely re-
lated: see Frances Densmore, *Menominee Music* (Washington, D.C.: U.S. Govt.
Printing Office, 1932), v. The Menominee reservation is in Wisconsin, and
Bunting seems to have visited his in-laws at Eau Claire, Wisconsin, in 1930;
but it is also possible that he first heard of the Menominee songs from Louis
Zukofsky, who worked for a while in Wisconsin, or, via Zukofsky, from Lorine
Niedecker, who lived in Wisconsin and studied its Indian history. (On Nie-
decker see also chap. 13, n. 20.)

4. Ezra Pound, *Culture* (New York: New Directions, 1938; published in
the U.K. as *Guide to Kulchur* [London: Faber & Faber, 1938]), 211–13.

5. *The Poems of Sir Walter Ralegh,* ed. Agnes M. C. Latham (London: Routledge & Kegan Paul, 1951), 45–47.

6. It seems to be true that writers in a given language do not develop
verse forms out of the features that are not phonemic in their language (and
Roman Jakobson would appear to have been the discoverer of the fact).
Thus while regular syllable-tone patterns have been obligatory in New Style
poetry in Chinese, beginning in the T'ang era, such a framework for verse
would be inconceivable in English. That is true, important, and sufficient for
Bunting's argument.

But it is not true that poets in a language must pattern all its distinctive
(phonemic) features. They could not; the verse would die of its encrustation.
Accordingly, in many genres of Chinese verse, it seems, there is no expected
pattern of tones. In Ancient Greek, the best opinion would seem to be that
pitch was not used for metrical purposes.

Still less is it true that melody composers have to take account of all the
sound-features of the words that are distinctive, or even of all those that are
distinctive *and* made into verse patterns. It seems to depend on the relative
phonemic importance of the feature in question. In the case of Greek pitch,
apparently the melody was related to the linguistic pitch-contours in some
kinds of song but not in others. Pitch was obviously less important than
length in the Ancient Greek language, and (it seems) not important at all in
verse forms. The song form can thus ignore some linguistic features of the
verse, whether these have been developed into elements of versification or
not, without necessarily either making the words unintelligible or destroy-

ing the sense of verse form—which can be based firmly enough on other features.

The *relative* importance of the distinctive features in the given language, then, seems to be what matters. Bunting's main target in what follows is syllable count in English; and the proper claim would seem to be not that it has no value as a basis for a system of English versification, but that its value is less than that of strong-accent-pattern.

For the relevant points concerning Greek verse, see esp. A. M. Dale, *Collected Papers* (Cambridge: Cambridge UP, 1969), 162, 236; M. L. West, *Greek Metre* (Oxford: Clarendon Press, 1982), 162; West, *Ancient Greek Music* (Oxford: Clarendon Press, 1992), 208–9.

7. I.e., Thomas Campion, the subject of a later lecture by Bunting: see Tape (1974) *incipit* "Well, I see," Bunting Archive.

8. On the Elizabethan quantitative movement, see Derek Attridge, *Well-weighed Syllables* (Cambridge: Cambridge UP, 1974), which demonstrates at great length that the poets did not know what they were doing. From this it seems to follow, with the usual logic of criticism, that their poetic results are without value; for Attridge devotes no more than a few borrowed adjectives to the point. Seth Weiner has since shown that the demonstration was less conclusive than it seemed: see his "Spenser's Study of English Syllables and Its Completion by Thomas Campion," *Spenser Studies* 3 (1982): 3–56.

9. Edmund Spenser, *The Minor Poems*, vol. 2, ed. Charles Grosvenor Osgood and Henry Gibbons Lotspeich, vol. 8 of *The Works of Edmund Spenser* (Baltimore: Johns Hopkins Press, 1943), 267.

10. Bunting, "Dear be still," 87 (dated there to 1929).

11. Catullus 51, "Ille mi par esse deo videtur," an imitation of Sappho, "Phainetai moi kenos isos theoisin," and imitated in turn by Bunting in his "O, it is godlike to sit selfpossessed," 123; this poem dated by Bunting to 1965.

12. "In the general fabrication of his lines he is perhaps superior to any other writer of blank verse; his flow is smooth, and his pauses are musical; but the concatenation of his verses is commonly too long continued, and the full close does not recur with sufficient frequency. The sense is carried on through a long intertexture of complicated clauses, and as nothing is distinguished, nothing is remembered." "Akenside," in Johnson's *Lives of the English Poets* (1779–81).

13. *Y Gododdin*, in its original form, may have been composed by the bard Aneirin (Aneurin) in about A.D. 600.

14. The *Cantar de mio Cid* (*Poema de mio Cid, Poema del Cid*) (c. 1140).

15. MS: "There are many languages [added: and they have poetry,] in which stress plays no part worth mentioning, and [deleted: many whose literature] would show no trace of a four-stress pattern."

16. On the tradition of the four-stress line, Bunting seems indebted, di-

rectly or not, to the influential essay of Northrop Frye: two of his three quoted examples coincide with Frye's. See Frye, *Anatomy of Criticism: Four Essays* (Princeton: Princeton UP, 1957), 251–52.

17. "(to break the pentameter, that was the first heave)." Canto LXXXI, 553.

18. See also below, chap. 6.

CHAPTER 3. EARS

1. "From a phonological point of view, it is actually surprising that quantity has not played a more important role in English metrics. . . . Syllable length is deeply implicated . . . in English phonology, being the main determinant of such core processes as word stress (Chomsky and Halle 1968; Hayes 1982). Hence it would not go against the grain of English for syllable length to interact with stress in its metrics too." Paul Kiparsky, "Sprung Rhythm," 338, in Kiparsky and Gilbert Youmans, eds., *Phonetics and Phonology*, vol. 1, *Rhythm and Meter* (San Diego: Academic Press, 1989), 305–38. This adds some weight to Bunting's remark: "Like Pound, I decided in the end (much later than he did) to let quantitative patterns alone, but to keep my ear open for quantity in anything I wrote." To Peter Makin, 22 Sept. 1977.

2. Bunting probably refers to the mysticism that Westerners have delighted to find in Persian poets. Of Manuchehri he remarked, "There is not one trace of Neo-Platonic Mysticism, all that bloody stuff that European Orientalists are always looking for"; and of Hafez, "There are lots of translations made by people who think he was expounding good Sufi doctrine. I don't believe it a minute." Jonathan Williams, "An Interview with Basil Bunting," *Conjunctions* 5 (1983): 82.

3. *Jongleur:* see below, n. 4.

4. Not every troubadour had a *jongleur* (Old Provençal *joglar*) in his service, but Bunting's description of the *jongleur*'s function is generally accurate: see William Paden, Jr., "The Role of the Joglar in Troubadour Lyric Poetry," in Peter S. Noble and Linda M. Paterson, eds., *Chrétien de Troyes and the Troubadours: Essays in memory of the Late Leslie Topsfield* (Cambridge: St. Catherine's College, 1984), 90–111. There is no contemporary evidence that troubadours or *jongleurs* accompanied themselves on any instrument; see Elizabeth Aubrey, *The Music of the Troubadours* (Bloomington: Indiana UP, 1996), 254 ff.

5. It seems certain that Anne Boleyn played the lute: Edward E. Lowinsky, "A Music Book for Anne Boleyn," in John G. Rowe and William H. Stockdale, eds., *Florilegium Historiale: Essays Presented to Wallace K. Ferguson* (Toronto: U of Toronto P, 1971), 186–88. Henry played several instruments and was a passionate amateur of music, at least in his young days; see Peter Holman, "Music at the Court of Henry VIII," in David Starkey, ed., *Henry VIII: Royal Meridian: A European Court in England* (London: Collins & Brown, in asso-

ciation with the National Maritime Museum, 1991), 104–5. Wyatt, intimate friend of both of these, might have looked foolish in so eloquently addressing his lute in his poems had he played no such instrument. But John Stevens's influential *Music and Poetry in the Early Tudor Court* (1961; reprint, Cambridge: Cambridge UP, 1979), esp. 134–35, argues otherwise.

6. There is a confusion of persons here, but it does not affect Bunting's point that Anne received the best education available in Europe. Margaret of Austria was regent in the Low Countries; Eric Ives calls her the doyenne of the Franco-Flemish culture which then dominated Europe north of the Alps (*Anne Boleyn* [Oxford: Blackwell, 1986], 28). Anne was brought up at her court. But Anne was probably never a member of the household of Marguerite of Navarre, authoress of the *Heptaméron*, though she seems to have known her. See, in general, ibid., 22–43.

7. At about the age of 19; see ibid., 21, 43.

8. It is not known what Tudor songs Bunting had his assistant play on the phonograph in this lecture, but it is clear that they were those of the Elizabethans, among whom he most frequently mentioned Byrd and Dowland. In 1934 he was suggesting that Dowland's music might help in poetic composition: "Dance and sing something and try to find out what the proper words ought to be. Jazz is just as good as anything else for the purpose. But if you can get John Dowland's songbooks . . . it might be a more sympathetic study" (to George Marion O'Donnell, 18 Apr. 1934, Washington). Where Bunting proposes a theory that Yeats's and Pound's rhythms were influenced by the Elizabethan song-books edited by Keel, he refers to the same rhythmic effects as those he finds, in the following lecture, in Wyatt.

9. For an example of such syncopation in music see the passage from Bach's Two-Part Invention no. 6 cited in *New Grove's* s.v. "Syncopation."

In a lecture in the 1974 series (Tape [1974] *incipit* "We get more," Bunting Archive), Bunting remarks on the practice of syncopation among the Tudor composers: "The effect is to displace a stress, or to lose it altogether." He observes that in the line "With naked foot stalking in my chamber," "Wyat intends the first syllable of 'stalking' to carry over the bar." We may therefore notate it thus:

With/*na-* ked/*foot* sta-/*alk-* ing/*in* my/*cham-* ber/

We should bear in mind, however, that this is merely (as Bunting says in the present lecture) "where a modern writer would have drawn a bar," for the modern convention is that a bar begins with a beat. Bunting by no means intends to claim that the line is essentially trochaic.

Bunting restated the idea in various ways. In chap. 11, below, he writes: "These Elizabethan song writers were the heirs of Wyat. Like him they often carried on the sound of a syllable over the beat." In his preface to Joseph Skipsey's *Selected Poems,* ed. Bunting (Sunderland: Ceolfrith Press, 1976), 13, he says Skipsey failed to notice "how one syllable drawn out beyond the metrical limit can keep the swing of the rhythm yet introduce an expressive change of pace." See also below, chap. 4.

10. Sir Thomas Wyatt died in 1542. In 1549 appeared his *Penitential Psalms,* heavily re-edited (apparently by Nicholas Grimald), and in 1557 the first edition of Tottel's *Miscellany,* containing 97 poems attributed to Wyatt, again with heavy "improvement."

11. Sir Arthur Quiller-Couch, ed., *The Oxford Book of English Verse* (Oxford: Oxford UP, 1900; new eds. and reprs. at least to 1953) leaves largely unscathed the poems that have more orthodox rhythms; but for "They flee from me," he offers, with no indication that he is doing so, Tottel's rewriting. Bunting, however, seems unaware of the edition by Nott (1816), which did not "improve" the text.

12. See also below, chap. 11.

13. Cf. Whitman, "Out of the Cradle" (above, p. 86). From this point in the manuscript a new pagination begins ("Ear + 1," "Ear + 2," and so on), so that the remainder of the lecture forms an addendum.

14. Dolmetsch began restoring early instruments and (with his wife, daughter, and pupils) performing on them, in the early 1890s. "Yeats had known him since he played before the Rhymers Club in 1891-2. . . . Dolmetsch became interested in Yeats's methods of chanting and employed them in training the chorus for the Elizabethan Stage Society's production of *Samson Agonistes* in April 1900. Following the success of the chorus in that momentous performance Dolmetsch had become increasingly important to Yeats, not only to the theory of his lyric art but to the furtherance of his slowly surfacing dramatic movement." Dolmetsch developed a psaltery to be used by Florence Farr in the "chanting" method of speech Yeats prescribed. See Ronald Schuchard, "W. B. Yeats and the London Theatre Societies, 1901–1904," *Review of English Studies* 19/116 (1978): 422-23. For Pound's interest in Dolmetsch, see Pound, *Literary Essays,* ed. T. S. Eliot (London: Faber, 1960), 431-40.

15. This was in 1911-12; the troubadour and trouvère songs that Pound and Rummel edited together were published as *Walter Morse Rummel . . . Hesternae Rosae: Serta II* in March 1913.

16. Frederick Keel, *Elizabethan Love-Songs: Edited and Arranged, with Pianoforte Accompaniments Composed, or Adapted from the Lute Tablature,* sets 1 and 2 (London: Boosey, 1909, 1913). The two sets contain thirty songs each; the composers are Dowland, Ford, Corkine, Campion, Rosseter, Morley, and others. Keel, a professor of the teaching of singing at the Royal Academy of Music and sometime editor of the Folk-song Society's *Journal,* seems to have edited no other collections of Elizabethan songs. The dates therefore may create a difficulty for Bunting's suggestion about Keel's influence on Pound and Yeats.

17. Edmund Fellowes' immensely influential editions of Tudor music began with the 36 volumes of *The English Madrigal School* (1913–24).

18. Ferrabosco set only one of Donne's songs, "So, so, leave off" (see John Duffy, *The Songs and Motets of Alfonso Ferrabosco, the Younger (1575–1628)* [Ann Arbor, Mich.: UMI Research Press, 1980], 295); but Coperario, Corkine, Dowland, Hilton, Lawes, and anonymous contemporaries also set songs by or ascribed to Donne.

19. This was an important *exemplum* to Bunting, but one radically improved by Memory, which he once referred to as "a persistent liar." Malherbe "wrote always and definitely to be sung," he writes to Pound in 1934 (?), Beinecke. In 1977 he clarifies this view: "Even very formal verse was usually written with a lute in hand. Malherbe never learnt to 'finger' it and felt handicapped, but seeing he knew what was lacking he, by taking infinite pains, remedied the defects of his musical education" (Bunting to Makin, 22 Sept. 1977). In 1974 (Tape [1974] *incipit* "Well, I see"), there are yet further details. Saying that Malherbe "died . . . complaining" of the same lifelong handicap, Bunting suggests that Malherbe had naturally wanted to compose poetry with a tune in mind, but, since his parents had never taught him how to play the lute, he "always had to get somebody else to do it for him when he composed." Yet in 1951 the main datum of the situation is reversed. Malherbe was so much a player of the lute that without it his poetry was stuck: "Malherbe complaining he was handicapped by rheumatism, so that he couldnt finger his lute: couldnt compose odes any other way" (to Louis Zukofsky, 14 Mar. 1951, HRC).

In most of these cases, Bunting refers explicitly to the *Vie de Monsieur de Malherbe* drafted by Malherbe's disciple Racan about twenty years after the poet's death in 1628. But Malherbe's alleged lament does not appear in Racan; nor does any sign of any interest, on Malherbe's part, in possible relations between verse and music.

In the *Vie,* Racan says that he himself "jouoit un peu du luth et aymoit la musique" and attributes certain of his own insights about stanza forms to his experience with singing. (Bunting seems to take up this point in notes on Malherbe recorded c. 1935 by Zukofsky [HRC]: and Bunting was always interested in the relation between line length and breath.) But according to Racan, Malherbe manifested no interest in the musical origins of Racan's insights, which merely (to Malherbe) confirmed a point about stanza forms that Malherbe had already accepted, apparently on nonmusical grounds, from another disciple. Meanwhile, it is Racan's experience with singing that sets him against certain other of Malherbe's views on stanza forms, and it seems to Racan that Malherbe remains unconverted because he has no clue to, or interest in, singing. See Honorat de Bueil, Seigneur de Racan, *Vie de Monsieur de Malherbe,* ed. Marie-Françoise Quignard (Paris: Gallimard, 1991), 52–54.

These data perhaps correspond with Bunting's early version of the *exem-*

plum in a letter of 1934: "As late as 1630 Racan was lamenting that his old pal Malherbe had been seriously handicapped in composition by his inability to finger the lute" (to George Marion O'Donnell, 18 Apr. 1934, Washington). No doubt Bunting's warm feeling for Malherbe on other grounds—his craftsmanship, his independence and his *robustezza*—made him later transfer the consciousness of music's importance from Racan to his master.

20. *Fioriture* (It.), "ornamental passages" (sing. *fioritura*).

CHAPTER 4. WYAT

1. In the TS draft of Bunting's verse anthology (Bunting Archive), with the exception of "The Wife of Bath," the section entitled "Narrative" consists solely of Wordsworth.

2. On the *Gawain* author see also above, chap. 1, n. 20.

3. John Barbour, d. 1395, author of *The Bruce*; Blind Hary, d. c. 1495, author of *Wallace*.

4. William Dunbar wrote the "Lament for the Makaris" in about 1508; Gavin Douglas's version of the *Aeneid* was printed in 1553.

5. The musicologist Winifred Maynard concludes that at least six of Wyatt's lyrics were meant for specific tunes that survive in the song-book known as Henry VIII's (BM Add. MS 31922); and her study of Wyatt's lyrics in which the lute is mentioned indicates that each was intended as a song. But as for the single setting by Cornish of a Wyatt poem ("A, robyn"), "Wyatt is just as probably recasting older words as Cornysh is reworking a popular tune." See Maynard, "The Lyrics of Wyatt: Poems or Songs?" pts. 1 and 2, *Review of English Studies* 16 (1965): 1–13, 246–57.

6. See above, chap. 3 and n. 9.

7. *Collected Poems of Sir Thomas Wyatt*, ed. Kenneth Muir (London: Routledge & Kegan Paul, 1949), 142–43. Since Bunting's aim here is to illustrate rhythmic and stanzaic forms, I have shortened some of the poems. Further citations appear in the text.

8. Music in lute tablature for this lyric has been found in a manuscript dating from about 1551: see Maynard, "Lyrics of Wyatt," 252 n; and Edward Doughtie, *English Renaissance Song* (Boston: Twayne, 1986), 35–36.

9. Paraphrased from the quotation in Wyatt, *Collected Poems*, xlvi. For concrete evidence of Wyatt's ability to count syllables when he wanted to, see Joost Daalder, "Wyatt's Prosody Revisited," *Language and Style* 10 (1977): 10.

10. How small is the proportion of cases in which a "Romance accentuation" would affect a disputed cadence in Wyatt can be seen from the sample in Daalder, "Wyatt's Prosody Revisited," 11–12.

11. Wyatt died in 1542; George Puttenham's *Arte of English Poesie*, apparently begun in the late 1560s, was published in 1589. (George Gascoigne's *Certayne Notes of Instruction* had appeared in 1575.)

12. Kenneth Muir, in Wyatt, *Collected Poems*, xix–xxi.

13. "All these strict forms were made to be sung. . . . Hence the pause between octet and sestet in sonnets. An octet was a good lungful, and the singer had to have time to get his puff before he went on to the sestet" (to George Marion O'Donnell, 18 Apr. 1934, Washington).

14. Wyatt, *Collected Poems*, 84, a reproduction of Egerton MS 2711, fol. 69v ("What rage is this?").

15. From Petrarch's "Amor, che nel penser mio vive e regna" (*Rime,* cxl).

16. On Easter Sunday 1341.

CHAPTER 5. SPENSER

1. Thomas Sackville (Sackvile) was the author of contributions to *A Mirror for Magistrates* in the enlarged edition of 1563.

2. *The Shepheards* [or *Shepheardes*] *Calender,* 1579.

3. Ibid., "December," l. 14.

4. See esp. "May"; and "October," ll. 45–48 with the Spenser-authorized gloss by E.K.

5. As well as "Sestina: Altaforte" (pub. 1909), Pound wrote "Sestina for Ysolt" (pub. 1909) and the Pico della Mirandola version "The Golden Sestina" (pub. 1911). Spenser's in *The Shepheards Calender,* "August," ll. 151–89, is apparently the first English sestina.

6. Ben Jonson, *Timber: Or, Discoveries,* 1640: "*Spencer,* in affecting the Ancients, writ no Language: Yet I would have him read for his matter; but as *Virgil* read *Ennius.*"

Bunting wrote to Pound in April 1954 (Beinecke) about the hostile reception of the assorted dialects and archaisms in his translation (1953–54) of Sophocles' *Women of Trachis.*

7. Elsewhere, Bunting suggested the problem had been that the world was changing too fast, in Spenser's age as in Pound's: Paul Johnstone, "Basil Bunting: Taken from Two Interviews, Recorded by Paul Johnstone in April 1974 and April 1975," *meantime* 1 (Apr. 1977): 67–68, etc. Bunting clearly considered that one of the merits of his own design in *Briggflatts* was that the length of it precluded this problem: see A. McAllister and S. Figgis, "Basil Bunting: The Last Interview," *Bête noire,* 2/3 (1987): 27, etc.

8. Spenser, *Fowre Hymnes,* 1596; "Epithalamion," 1595; *Prothalamion,* 1596.

9. Spenser, *Prosopopoia: or Mother Hubberds Tale,* 1591.

10. The passage from Spenser that Bunting reads in this lecture is explicitly *not* offered as an example of this decoration; nor does Bunting give other examples. For suggested examples, see the introduction to this book.

11. "Fear adjectives; they bleed nouns." Bunting, "I Suggest," reprint, Durham: Basil Bunting Poetry Archive, 1990.

12. The text given here (*The Poetical Works of Edmund Spenser in Three Vol-*

umes, vol. 1, *Spenser's Minor Poems*, ed. Ernest de Selincourt [Oxford: Clarendon Press, 1910], 107–11) is that of the photocopies (now in the Bunting Archive) prepared for Bunting's tape-recorded verse anthology (Newcastle University). In these photocopies, the Dirge for Dido (ll. 53–202 of "November") begins on p. 107, which fits with the page number given here in the lecture text; and in the taped verse anthology, Bunting's reading of "November" consists of the whole Dirge only.

CHAPTER 6. AFTER SPENSER

    1. *Macbeth* 2.2.61; cf. Ezra Pound, *ABC of Reading* (London: Faber, 1961), 71. Bunting read this work when it appeared in 1934 and commented on it to Pound.

    2. MS., in margin: "at least if you omit Ibsen."

    3. Bunting here no doubt plays with Ralegh's name; in his time he was also Rawely, Rawley, Rawleigh, Raley, etc.

    4. "The Phoenix and Turtle" (pub. 1601) appears in Bunting's TS verse anthology (Bunting Archive).

    5. *The Tempest* 1.2.399–407; appears in Bunting's TS and taped verse anthologies (Bunting Archive and Newcastle Univ.).

    6. Goethe's poem entitled *Ein Gleiches*, i.e., to have the same title as the *Wandrers Nachtlied*, which precedes it; written in 1780, published in 1815.

> Über allen Gipfeln
> Ist Ruh,
> In allen Wipfeln
> Spürest du
> Kaum einen Hauch;
> Die Vögelein schweigen im Walde.
> Warte nur, balde
> Ruhest du auch.

("Over all the hill-tops it is still; in all the tree-tops you can hardly feel a breath stirring. The little birds are silent in the forest. Wait! soon you too will be still." Goethe, *Selected Verse*, ed. David Luke [London: Penguin, 1986], 50.)

Horace's "O fons Bandusiae" is *Odes* 3.13:

> O Fons Bandusiae, splendidior vitro,
> dulci digne mero non sine floribus,
>   cras donaberis haedo.
>
> . . . .
>
> Fies nobilium tu quoque fontium
> me dicente cavis inpositam ilicem
>   saxis, unde loquaces
>   lymphae desiliunt tuae.

("O Fount Bandusia, brighter than crystal, worthy of sweet wine and flowers, to-morrow shalt thou be honoured with a firstling of the flock. . . . Thou, too, shalt be numbered among the far-famed fountains, through the song I sing of the oak planted o'er the grotto whence thy babbling waters leap." Loeb.) Bunting spoke of the "matchless onomatopoeia" of this poem (Peter Craven and Michael Heyward, "An Interview with Basil Bunting," *Scripsi* 1/3– 4 [1982]: 30). His "Stones trip Coquet burn" (written 1970) is in part an imitation of it.

"Hafez, . . . about 1300. He depends entirely on sound, there is little else. In the famous second poem of his *Divan,* in about 14 or 15 couplets, he is merely telling you that he won't be able to come to dinner. Tears come to one's eyes over such beauty." Jonathan Williams, "An Interview with Basil Bunting," *Conjunctions* 5 (1983): 82.

7. *The Poetical Works of John Milton,* ed. David Masson (London: Macmillan, 1874), 2: 119, 109–10, 104–5 (*Samson Agonistes,* ll. 606–32; 293–99; 118–34). Since the page numbers correspond (with one slight discrepancy) with those given by Bunting, this was presumably his text.

8. Bunting, *Briggflatts* I.

9. *Arden of Feversham* was published in 1592; the three parts of Shakespeare's *Henry VI* had been performed by September of that year.

10. *Arden of Feversham,* 5.6, in Ashley Thorndike, ed., *The Minor Elizabethan Drama, vol. 1, Pre-Shakespearean Tragedies* (London: J. M. Dent, 1910), 123–24. This was probably Bunting's text; it is the text used for this passage in Bunting's TS verse anthology (Bunting Archive), and the same volume contains Peele's *David and Bethsabe,* which Bunting later drew from: see Tape (1974) *incipit* "Well, I see," Bunting Archive.

11. If we look at the context here and compare the remarks about *Arden* in Tape (1974) *incipit* "Pointed out that" (Bunting Archive), it becomes clear that this remark concerns *end-stopped* blank verse *only.*

On 18 Oct. 1929 (Buffalo) Bunting wrote to Louise Theiss of his friend J. J. Adams: "He found in 'Arden of Feversham' the same sort of hints on prosody that Eliot got from the less excellent Webster & co."

12. "Cooper's Hill," ll. 161–92, from *The Poetical Works of Sir John Denham* (Edinburgh: Apollo Press, 1779), 29–30 (Bunting's text in the TS verse anthology, Bunting Archive). The poem was first published in 1642, but Bunting's text is based on the much revised 1655 edition, where the lines for which Denham is famous first appear.

13. In the margin are the words "as suddenly ubiquitous as an Irish rebellion." Bunting echoes Waller's remark about Denham's tragic melodrama in blank verse, *The Sophy* (perf. 1641), which "took extremely much, and was admired by all ingenious men, particularly by Edm. Waller of Beaconsfield, who then said of the author, that he broke out like the Irish Rebellion, threescore thousand strong, when no body was aware, or in the least suspected

it." Anthony Wood, *Athenae Oxonienses*, 1721, 2: 423, quoted in Theodore Howard Banks, ed., *The Poetical Works of Sir John Denham*, 2d ed. (Hamden, Conn.: Archon Books, 1969), 6.

14. See refs. and discussion in ibid., 29–31.

15. MS., in margin: "1643 – 25 yrs before Boileau". But Corneille is usually said to have perfected the alexandrine; the fifth act of his *Horace* (1640) was translated by Denham.

16. In Pope, *An Essay on Criticism*.

17. "For *Spencer* and *Fairfax* both flourish'd in the Reign of Queen *Elizabeth*: Great Masters in our Language; and who saw much farther into the Beauties of our Numbers, than those who immediately followed them. *Milton* was the Poetical Son of *Spencer*, and Mr. *Waller* of *Fairfax*; for we have our Lineal Descents and Clans, as well as other Families: *Spencer* more than once insinuates, that the Soul of *Chaucer* was transfus'd into his Body; and that he was begotten by him Two hundred years after his Decease. *Milton* has acknowledg'd to me, that *Spencer* was his Original; and many besides my self have heard our famous *Waller* own, that he deriv'd the Harmony of his Numbers from the *Godfrey of Bulloign*, which was turn'd into *English* by Mr. *Fairfax*." Dryden, preface to *Fables Ancient and Modern* (1700). Edward Fairfax's *Godfrey of Bulloigne*, a translation of Tasso's *Gerusalemme liberata*, was published in 1600.

18. MS., in margin: "(It was worse in France)".

19. Allan Ramsay, poet, editor of *A New Miscellany of Scots Song* (1727), author of *The Gentle Shepherd: A Scots Pastoral Comedy* (pub. 1725). Robert Blair published in 1743 *The Grave*, a moral meditation in blank verse. Robert Burns plowed; William Blake engraved.

CHAPTER 7. REALISM

1. From "When daisies pied and violets blue" (*Love's Labour's Lost* 5.2.884–912), presumably taken by Bunting as a parody of the "spring opening" to the courtly love lyric, or of pastoral in general. Bunting's text not determined.

2. I have not found this poem among Butler's works. The text I give is from Jonathan Williams, "An Interview with Basil Bunting," *Conjunctions* 5 (1983): 77, where Williams describes it as "Basil's six-liner attributed to Samuel Butler, from 'A Satire on the Players.'" In Bunting's TS draft for his projected verse anthology (Bunting Archive), the lines appear as "Satire on the stage"; the only significant variant is "delve" (for "dive") in the last line. The passage had been in Bunting's mind for a long time. In a letter to Zukofsky dated 28 Oct. 1935 (HRC), he refers to "Butler's 'smock-faced boys'" as an equivalent to Horace, *Odes* 2.5.24, *ambiguoque voltu*, which Loeb translates as "and [with] his girl-boy face." (Cf. Bunting's own version in "That

filly couldnt carry a rider.") The Butler-Horace comparison is part of his explication to Zukofsky of the draft of *The Well of Lycopolis* (1935), where he uses the Horace phrase.

3. *Lazarillo de Tormes,* a picaresque novel of unknown authorship; 1st ed. (now lost) probably printed c. 1552–53.

4. Michelangelo Buonarotti "the younger," b. Florence 1568, d. there 1642; collaborator on the *Vocabolario* of the Accademia della Crusca, host of a noted literary salon, and author of *Tancia* (1612), a rustic comedy, and *Fiera* (1618), a comedy of manners. In a letter dated 17 June 1930 (Beinecke), Bunting reports to Pound that he has read "the enormous twentyfive act play of Michelangelo junior."

5. "The Jolly Beggars": "Love and Liberty—A Cantata," possibly written in 1786, was first published posthumously in 1799 as *The Jolly Beggars; Or Tatterdemallions. A Cantata.*

6. After *The News-paper* (1785), Crabbe was silent until 1807.

7. Chiefly for *An Essay on Man* (1733–34).

8. I.e., *The Prelude* (first drafts composed 1798–99; much revised, notably in 1804–5, 1816–19, and 1832; pub. 1850). *The Excursion* (1814) was intended as the "dramatic" (i.e., narrative) section of *The Recluse,* but Wordsworth was never able to write the philosophical section of this poem.

9. See Mary Moorman, *William Wordsworth: A Biography: The Early Years: 1770–1803* (Oxford: Clarendon Press, 1957), 346–49.

10. This clause is a later insertion by Bunting.

11. Wordsworth was born in 1770; the first (much shorter) *Salisbury Plain* was composed 1793–94.

12. But Wordsworth's remission of the gibbeting can apparently be dated to 1841 (he had rediscovered the *Salisbury Plain* material in 1839); Coleridge had died in 1834 and does not seem ever to have commented adversely on the ending of the poem. See Stephen Gill, *William Wordsworth: A Life* (Oxford: Clarendon Press, 1989), 99, 191, 404–5; and *The Salisbury Plain Poems of William Wordsworth,* ed. Stephen Gill (Ithaca, N.Y.: Cornell UP, 1975), 3–14, 280–83.

13. See also below, chap. 13.

CHAPTER 8. WORDSWORTH AND WHITMAN

1. It is not clear whether the present elements of this lecture were originally together; the original lecture may have been cannibalized for another occasion or occasions. Some parts repeat (or are repeated by) other lectures to a degree Bunting could hardly have wanted in one lecture series; yet the following lecture refers back to the reading of "The Brothers" specified in this script. As it stands, the present lecture has no title. It consists of five handwritten pages (paginated 1–5), two pages in typescript (paginated [1]–

2), and finally, under the heading "Whitman," six pages of extremely compressed scribbled notes (paginated 5–11). The scrawled diagonal note at the head, "BBC, with Brothers," relates to the fact that the first four pages were used for Bunting's BBC broadcast on Wordsworth (7 Apr. 1970), and were immediately followed on that broadcast by a complete reading of Wordsworth's poem "The Brothers." I have therefore inserted the poem here. But on the tape of that reading, nothing more follows the poem.

2. Thomas Parnell died in 1718; "The Hermit" was first published by Pope, in effect his literary executor, in 1722. The most famous of Crabbe's narratives, *The Village*, appeared in 1783.

3. The characters of "The Brothers," like Wordsworth himself, are people of Cumberland. Bunting, born just outside Newcastle, described himself as a speaker of Northumbrian (but not "Geordie"), though the parts of his childhood spent among Cumberland people never left him (see *Briggflatts* I, and *B:SV*, 129–59). The poet Norman Nicholson (1914–87) spent his entire life in the small industrial town of Millom in Cumberland.

4. Wordsworth talked with "a strong tincture of the northern *burr*, like the crust on wine." Hazlitt, "My First Acquaintance with Poets."

5. See above, n. 1. Bunting's reading accords with the text of *The Poetical Works of Wordsworth*, ed. Thomas Hutchinson (London: Oxford UP, 1928), 95–102, with the following variants (possibly slips): l. 192, "many a strange"; l. 237, "you're among your own kindred!"; l. 290, "is still left." Bunting used Hutchinson's edition for the next lecture (chap. 9).

6. This paragraph and the next (separate pages in the MS) are typewritten and are preserved in reverse order in the MS.

7. From here the MS is handwritten; in this section I have not regularized punctuation (the marks for which are sometimes ambiguous) or layout.

8. "Sea-Drift" was first published as a group in the 1881 edition of *Leaves of Grass*. It contains "Out of the Cradle Endlessly Rocking," which Bunting cites below and whenever he wishes to illustrate Whitman's method and influence, as well as other poems whose content Bunting seems to draw on (cf. *B:SV*, 12–14).

9. "One root," i.e., of Whitman's new kind of verse. " 'Free verse' is a French 19th century term, at first a mere slackening of the very strict conventions of their alexandrines, which has gradually degenerated into bad prose chopped up. That gets confused with verse that is derived from Walt Whitman (mainly by Pound and me) which is constructed by modifications of the musical phrase, in the manner of music, which seems 'free' to people who don't have ear enough to detect the principle." Peter Craven and Michael Heyward, "An Interview with Basil Bunting," *Scripsi* 1/3–4 (1982): 28.

10. See Willi Apel, *Gregorian Chant* (Bloomington: Indiana UP, 1958), esp. 262–63. For Bunting's conception of cadence, see "Explanatory Note" at the end of this chapter.

11. Hebrew parallelism is the verse form used in all the poetry of the Bible. In one of the 1974 Newcastle lectures (Tape *incipit* "Well, I see," Bunting Archive), Bunting lists the following Old Testament verse passages: Deut. 32.1–43; Judg. 5; the Psalms; the Song of Songs, "much of the Book of Job, and many messages in the Prophets." Hebrew parallelism was first described in modern times by Bishop Lowth in 1753, and Bunting seems to follow Lowth's view in some respects. A useful recent description of the form is Robert Alter, "The Characteristics of Ancient Hebrew Poetry," in Alter and Frank Kermode, eds., *Literary Guide to the Bible* (Cambridge: Belknap Press, Harvard UP, 1987), 611–24.

Miles Coverdale's was the first English-language translation of the Psalms, being printed with his complete Bible in 1535. His 1539 version of them (with some further revisions by him) was taken almost without exception into the Book of Common Prayer (1549). This, and not the 1611 Authorised Version's Psalms, stayed in the Book of Common Prayer and was thus used in all services until the 1970s.

Though Bunting from childhood was saturated with the Bible, naturally it was the Authorized Version's Job and Song of Songs that he absorbed (Jonathan Williams, *Descant on Rawthey's Madrigal: Conversations with Basil Bunting* [Lexington, Ky.: Gnomon, 1968], [4–5]); and in the recordings for his taped verse anthology (Newcastle University) it was the Authorized Version's Song of Songs (2.7–4.7) that he used, not Coverdale's. But Coverdale more than any other created the rhythms that went into the Authorized Version.

12. Thomas Cranmer is generally considered to have been the main author of the 1549 Book of Common Prayer: that is, to have had the chief hand in writing the Litany, canticles, and collects in it, in choosing the versions of the Psalms and other scriptural readings, and in arranging the whole. For his typescript verse anthology (Bunting Archive), Bunting listed "Cranmer's Psalms" (i.e., Coverdale's), but the Cranmer materials ultimately included *in extenso* were:

1. "The Prayer and Saying of Thomas Cranmer, a little before his death . . . ," written shortly before his burning at the stake, 21 Mar. 1556, from Thomas Cranmer, *Miscellaneous Writings and Letters,* ed. John Edmund Cox (London: Parker Society, 1846) (vol. 2 of Cranmer, *Works*), 565, "O Father of heaven. . . . Thy kingdom come, &c.";
2. "Man that is born of a woman . . . subdue all things to himself," from the Order for the Burial of the Dead in the Book of Common Prayer;
3. The Litany, in the text of 1544, from William Keatinge Clay, ed., *Private Prayers, Put Forth by Authority During the Reign of Queen Elizabeth* (London: Parker Society, 1851), 570–76.

13. Hugh Latimer, a prolific preacher, eventually became Bishop of Worcester; he was burned at the stake, 16 Oct. 1555. His most famous sermon is the "Sermon of the Plough," of 1548. I have found no specific selections by Bunting from his works.

14. This is a sideswipe at T. S. Eliot, to whose essay in *For Lancelot Andrewes* (1928) Andrewes owes his place in current guides to English literature. (Bunting's marked copy of Eliot's book is now in the Bunting Archive.)

15. I have not found any specific selections by Bunting from Burton, Browne, or Macpherson. On Macpherson's "crudity" see also Explanatory Note.

For the typescript verse anthology (Bunting Archive), under the heading "The Growing Stem," Bunting included *in extenso* a passage from Smart's *Jubilate Agno,* beginning "Let Nepheg rejoice" and ending "For I am ready to die for his sake . . .," with the "Let" verses arranged to match their "For" verses. *Jubilate Agno,* unpublished till 1939, is thought to have been written between c. 1758 and 1773, therefore entirely or almost entirely while Smart was in the madhouse. Its most immediate models are the Benedicite and perhaps the Magnificat in the Book of Common Prayer.

The *Tale of a Tub* (written c. 1696, pub. 1704) was cited very frequently by Bunting, though always, to my knowledge, as a model for command of syntax: he would prescribe a diet of it for his more crabbed correspondents.

16. See below, "Whitman: Editor's Explanatory Note," and esp. chaps. 12, 13; see also *B:SV,* 258–59, 341–43.

17. It was most probably at this point that Bunting asked his hearers to re-read Whitman's "Out of the Cradle Endlessly Rocking": see the closing remarks in chap. 11.

The text of "Out of the Cradle" given here is transcribed from the photocopy in the Bunting Archive of Bunting's marked text prepared for his reading on tape.

Most of Bunting's markings concern intonational phrase breaks. There seems to be a distinction between minor pauses, marked with a short raised slash (here transcribed arbitrarily as ^), and major pauses, marked with a full slash (here given as /). Unfortunately, in the Bunting Archive's copies, these marks, and the distinction between them, are not always clear.

Apart from these pauses, Bunting obviously took it for granted that Whitman's commas showed intonational breaks; in only one case (doubtless an oversight) did he add a slash to Whitman's comma. It is also very clear that he by no means intended to mark all phrase breaks. It seems to follow that he wanted to indicate only those phrase breaks that marked off stress groups raised (by semantic importance, and/or by their echo of a similar stress group in the neighbourhood) to the level of a rhythmic motif.

All underlines in the transcription reproduce Bunting's.

18. Edward Carpenter (1844–1929), mystic Socialist, disciple of Whitman, author of the long poem *Towards Democracy* (completed ed. pub. 1905). Bunting tells us that when in his schooldays, in 1916, he wrote an essay on Whitman that won a prize and was published in a Quaker journal, Carpenter cycled from Sheffield to (apparently) Ackworth School to congratulate him. See Eric Mottram, "Conversation with Basil Bunting on the Occasion of His Seventy-fifth Birthday, 1975," *Poetry Information* 19 (Autumn 1978): 6.

19. Note, however, that Newcastle's literati had discovered Whitman before anyone in the United States except Emerson (*B:SV,* 8–10) and that Whitman was much admired by Swinburne and Hopkins. Pound left an unpublished essay dated 1 Feb. 1909, in which he acknowledged an influence from Whitman on his rhythms: see Ezra Pound, *Selected Prose, 1909–1965,* ed. William Cookson (New York: New Directions, 1973), 145–46. Pound's poem "A Pact" (i.e., with Whitman) was published in 1913.

20. "One or two poets before and after 1920 who had understood the notion of modifying and combining rhythmic themes in the way Whitman had sometimes done and Pound did in his *Propertius* . . . , and who found that a satisfactory way of conducting the verse from line to line or over a few pages, began to wonder whether music could furnish them with an overall shape as well as with a tissue or texture." See below, chap. 12.

21. Bunting used the Authorized Version text there: see above, n. 11.

22. Tape (1974) *incipit* "Well, I see," Bunting Archive.

23. See also n. 31.

24. "It's a matter of making the rhythms develop and shift around themselves chiefly. . . . The thing seems to have happened, whether consciously or not, first with Walt Whitman. . . . Whitman's best pieces are very much like what Liszt was writing at the time—as far as form goes." Jonathan Williams and Tom Meyer, "A Conversation with Basil Bunting," *Poetry Information* 19 (Autumn 1978): 38. See also David Holloway, "A Live Tradition: Pound's *Personae* and *The Pisan Cantos,*" *Paideuma* 8/3 (1979): 563–64: "the metrical themes of . . . 'Out of the Cradle . . . ' and . . . the way in which Whitman (like Liszt and Berlioz) allowed themes to transform themselves as the piece developed" (Bunting's reported remarks at a Pound conference); and below, chap. 12.

25. In *Fingal* (1765 version), Macpherson develops a ∕ × × ∕ motif, but foregrounds no other rhythmic pattern, so that this motif becomes drearily insistent: "said the maid of the tearful eye. Is he fallen on his echoing heath; the youth with the breast of snow? he that was first in the chace of the hill."

26. See *B:SV,* 264, 341–43.

27. It is essential to this view of rhythmic motifs that they are made *relatively* prominent, by semantic and syntactic means, so that there are necessarily many ambiguities (see, below, the views of Duhamel and Vildrac).

28. Duhamel and Vildrac's *Notes sur la technique poétique* was boomed by

Pound in the famous manifesto "A Few Don'ts," of 1913, a work that Bunting later recommended to at least one disciple (to George Marion O'Donnell, 18 Apr. 1934, Washington). If Bunting read the book, he would certainly have known enough to use its germ-ideas while discounting the factors that apply to French but not to English.

29. Georges Duhamel and Charles Vildrac, *Notes sur la technique poétique* (Paris: Champion, 1925), 14–15.

30. Ibid., 16, 36–37.

31. The fundamental reason for saying so is that rhythmic motifs would not even come to "exist," affectively, without the effects of semantics and syntax. Without those factors to distinguish and foreground it, there is no reason for finding the motif / × × / in the words "where the child leaving his bed" rather than, for instance, the motif × / / ×: "the child leaving / his bed wandered." The sequences of stress produced in fifteen-or-more-syllable lines like many of Whitman's:

$$\times / \times / \times \times \times / \times / \times \times / / \times \times / \times / \times \times /$$

are arithmetically capable of enough kinds of grouping to satisfy whatever "scansion" the prosodist cares to dream up—in the absence of semantics and syntax to mark groups off and to bring some of them to prominence. (The same of course is true of blank verse: without semantics and syntax, the lines do not exist.) Now this prominence is relative; and if these factors bring particular groups to relative prominence, they will leave others unnoticed.

This is an ambiguous kind of demarcation: like species in biology, not like storage tanks in a gas station. There will always be subfamilies threatening to bud off the main rhythmic branches. The question is not whether these families can be said to exist at all; nor even whether they would conflict with others that are more prominent (such conflict is a component in musical interest, as basic to it as the conflict between bar division and melodic contour in Scarlatti); but whether they are strong enough to nudge us for some degree of residual attention; or whether, rather, they are so trivial as to be part of a kind of background noise.

It follows naturally that some passages in Whitman's prose are rhythmically more patterned than some passages in his verse: that they are, according to Bunting's definition ("poetry is a sound"), verse where the "verse" is not. Meanwhile the method of analyzing all parts of every line into sequences of rhythmic groups betrays its arbitrariness when it is applied just as easily to third-rate verse like Amy Lowell's, and to parts of Whitman where the poet has manifestly not yet got into rhythmic gear. Clive Scott thus applies it in *French Verse-Art: A Study* (Cambridge: Cambridge UP, 1980), 189; and Scott, *Vers Libre: The Emergence of Free Verse in France, 1886–1914* (Oxford: Clarendon Press, 1990), 101.

32. D. W. Harding, "The Rhythmical Intention in Wyatt's Poetry," *Scrutiny*

14 (1946): 90–102; James G. Southworth, *Verses of Cadence: An Introduction to the Prosody of Chaucer and His Followers* (Oxford: Blackwell, 1954); and Southworth, *The Prosody of Chaucer and His Followers: Supplementary Chapters to "Verses of Cadence"* (Oxford: Blackwell & Mott, 1962).

33. Bunting, "The Use of Poetry," ed. Peter Quartermain, *Writing* 12 (Summer 1985): 41–42.

34. See below, chap. 12. It is possible that structuring by rhythmic motif requires a much more compact form, since rhythmic contrasts may be harder to sustain in the memory than are denotative contrasts.

35. See below, chap. 12 and n. 3.

CHAPTER 9. WORDSWORTH AND THE XIX CENTURY

1. See *The Letters of W. B. Yeats,* ed. Allan Wade (London: Rupert Hart-Davis, 1954), 710: "The over childish or over pretty or feminine element in some good Wordsworth . . . comes from the lack of natural momentum in the syntax. This momentum underlies almost every Elizabethan and Jacobean lyric and is far more important than simplicity of vocabulary. If Wordsworth had found it he could have carried any amount of elaborate English." See also Yeats, *Essays and Introductions* (New York: Macmillan, 1961), 521–22.

2. *The Poetical Works of Wordsworth,* ed. Thomas Hutchinson (London: Oxford UP, 1928), 119; poem written in 1802.

3. MS *sic;* perhaps "hardiness" was intended.

4. See above, chap. 7, n. 8.

5. In light of the fact that elsewhere mysticism, far from being dismissed by Bunting, is the only form of religion he approves of (*B:SV,* 202–10), these remarks should be construed with care. They do not mean that Wordsworth was not—or was—a mystic; or that mysticism is bunk; but only that the *criticism* that tries to show he was a mystic, on the basis of his poems, is a waste of time, for all texts are equally convertible to that use. On the other hand, Bunting does wish to say that insofar as Wordsworth thought he had a philosophy, he was deluded.

6. Hutchinson, ed., *Poetical Works of Wordsworth,* 190.

7. See also Bunting's remarks in an interview dated 1968: "My father was very fond of Wordsworth, and he used to read Wordsworth to us when we were very small children, and at some exceedingly early age I discovered that there was nothing else that could move me so much as the best of Wordsworth. There is for instance the poem—I forget its name—about the forty feeding like one, the spring on the mountains, which uses only the very simplest words, and I cannot have been more than eight or nine years old when it was borne in on me that the use of very simple words would get you a great deal further than trying out fancy ones. Very very many people imagine poetry to be a matter of education but it's not. . . . You read Spenser's

'Epithalamion' to someone who can't understand more than two lines of it, they will still enjoy it: the noise is a very beautiful noise." "Release: Basil Bunting," BBC TV program, 23 Nov. 1968.

This is therefore a key poem in a number of ways: (a) Wordsworth uses ordinary words and thus demonstrates that (b) the poem can be made a self-sustaining object not by profound content but primarily by means of sound pattern; (c) the demonstration lies fallow until Pound does it again with "Alba," in 1918, which is the beginning of another revolutionary career. (See below, chap. 11.)

Further, (d), the remark "There hadnt been anything like that in English since the Elizabethans" may be a specific rather than a general comparison: it refers most probably to the rhythmic effects of the madrigalists, and of Wyatt, their predecessor. A Wyatt-like play with tension can be heard in Bunting's reading, for example, of line 5 here, where the dactyl is not treated merely as an "allowable substitution," and therefore temporally identical: it forces a *ritardando*. See above, chap. 3 and n. 9.

8. Cf. above, chap. 8, n. 4.

9. In "Yarrow Unvisited" and "Yarrow Revisited," Wordsworth picks up from an older ballad the rhyme of "Yarrow" (the river) with "marrow" ("companion"). For the pronunciation Bunting speaks of, see, e.g., Tom Pickard's poem "The Devil's Destroying Angel Exploded" (1971): "he said you wore a workers cap / called everybody marra / but the word I heard was slave." Jarrow is on the Tyne, downriver from Newcastle.

10. I.e., no doubt, *The Lay of the Last Minstrel,* by Sir Walter Scott, published in 1805.

11. In his early teens, Bunting "came across Rossetti's translations of the early Italian poets. As soon as I could I learned Italian and read Dante." (Raymond Gardner, "Put Out More Flags," *Guardian,* 27 June 1973). Rossetti's *Early Italian Poets . . . Together with Dante's Vita Nuova* was first published in 1861.

12. For the following, see also above, chap. 8.

13. The MS here has "p 184-5-6" in the left margin, vertically, beside the first three lines of the paragraph: clearly this refers to a Whitman passage, and if it was not some example of Whitman's worst, it may have been "Out of the Cradle."

CHAPTER 10. PRECURSORS

1. On "persona," see below, chap. 11; and esp. chap. 12 and n. 1.

2. *The Idylls of the King,* published between 1857 and 1885.

3. Hopkins's mature writing began in 1875; few and unnoticed poems appeared before Bridges' posthumous edition of 1918.

4. Doughty broke his pentameters with back-to-back spondees, end-of-line reversed feet, and excess syllables:

> An hundred on their beasts'
> Bare chines sit, Almain riders, by their guise,
> Such as were wont to vex, with oft inroads,
> The lands of neighbour Gauls. In days of peace,
> Is this most honour of their warlike youth.
> Contemners of the cold, the wind, and the rain;
> Short pilches clothe them, broached with brazen pin,
> Or thorn, at the large breast; and long rough braies.
> Come mingled with them runners, fleet of foot,
> And all are armed with javelins and broad shields.
>   Now those, which passed in hazardry have and feast
>
> . . . .
> Much night . . .

He had studied (as Bunting thought a poet should) Old and Middle English, trying to get free of the unconcreteness of Latin-based English words. But his fanciful-archaic syntax and word order leak the energy of the thought into a crossword puzzle, which makes his six-volume epic of the marriage of Christianity with Celtic vigor (pub. 1906–7) more labor than light. For Yeats's interest in it, see Pound, Canto LXXXIII, 570.

5. The MS has "at any rate . . . industry." added in handwriting at the foot of the page, apparently for insertion here.

6. Ford's mother, at any rate, was a daughter of Ford Madox Brown, and Kipling's mother's sister the wife of Sir Edward Burne-Jones; both men grew up in subsections of the Pre-Raphaelite clan.

7. *The Rubáiyát of Omar Khayyám,* trans. Edward Fitzgerald (first pub. 1859), st. xxvii: "Myself when young did eagerly frequent / Doctor and Saint, and heard great Argument / About it and about; but evermore / Came out by the same Door as in I went."

8. Rudyard Kipling, *Complete Verse: Definitive Edition* (New York: Doubleday, 1989), 81. Further citations appear in the text. I have not been able to determine Bunting's text.

9. Bunting writes to Pound, apparently in April 1954 (Beinecke), that Eliot's "smokescreens such as religion" distracted his attention from the poetry, so that "his perception of poetical technique diminished. Anyway, he's still using the same genus of coarse (though catchy) rhythms that made it possible for Prufrock to compete with Vachel Lindsay or Kipling. The pattern is altered, but not the texture."

10. On Bunting's period as Ford's subeditor at the *Transatlantic Review* (Paris, 1923), see esp. Alan Judd, *Ford Madox Ford* (London: Collins, 1990), 345, 350–51.

11. This aligns Ford with both Wordsworth and Fenollosa: see below, chap. 12; and *B:SV,* 269–73.

12. "Ford and Conrad talked too much about Flaubert but did not waste time playing hide-and-seek with the precise word. They surrounded their meaning with successive approximations instead, and so repeated in the texture of prose the pattern by which their narrative captured their theme. It is a circuitous technique, prodigal of paper. For sure, Flaubert would not have recognized it: yet nebulosities and imprecisions are much of our landscape without or within, and worth reproducing. . . . There are explorations that can never end in discovery, only in willingness to rest content with an unsure glimpse through mists, an uncertain sound of becks we shall never taste: approximations. To this Ford's rhythm and diction in these poems tend steadily; to this their matter is organized with great skill." Ford Madox Ford, *Selected Poems,* ed. Basil Bunting (Cambridge, Mass.: Pym-Randall, 1971), vii–viii.

13. Ford Madox Hueffer [Ford Madox Ford], *Collected Poems* (London: Max Goschen, 1914), 33–35.

From here the lecture is handwritten.

14. See above, chap. 9 and n. 1.

15. W. B. Yeats, *The Collected Poems* (London: Macmillan, 1950), 23. I have not determined Bunting's text.

16. No doubt those in "The School of Giorgione," in Walter Pater, *The Renaissance: Studies in Art and Poetry* (London: Macmillan, 1924), 139–45. See also A. McAllister and S. Figgis, "Basil Bunting: The Last Interview," *Bête noire* 2/3 (1987): 26.

17. Yeats, *Collected Poems,* 48–49.

18. Ibid., 86.

19. Victor Plarr (1863–1929), lyricist, member of the Rhymers Club, close friend of Ernest Dowson; Pound sat at his feet in 1909 to gather tales of the ancestors, and he appears as "Monsieur Verog" in Pound's *Hugh Selwyn Mauberley.*

CHAPTER 11. 1910–20

1. Edgar Jepson (1863–1938), novelist, associate of Pound, Ford, Aldington, and Lewis in the restaurants of Soho and Regent Street during World War I; see also Pound, Canto LXXXIV, 459.

Selwyn Image (1849–1930), painter of stained glass, sometime editor of the journal of the "Century Guild" of artists, member of the Rhymers Club, shared a house with Lionel Johnson; one of the literary elders whom Pound sought out, c. 1909, for instruction.

Concerning Victor Plarr, see above, chap. 10, n. 19.

2. F. T. Marinetti (1876–1944), Italian poet and leader (from 1909) of the Futurists.

3. *The Complete Poetical Works of T. E. Hulme,* in Ezra Pound, *Personae: The Collected Shorter Poems* (New York: New Directions, 1949), 252–53.

4. In "A Lecture on Modern Poetry," probably presented to the Poets' Club in 1908, and first published posthumously in 1938, Hulme wrote: "This new verse resembles sculpture rather than music; it appeals to the eye rather than to the ear. It has to mould images, a kind of spiritual clay, into definite shapes. This material, the ὕλη of Aristotle, is image and not sound. It builds up a plastic image which it hands over to the reader, whereas the old art endeavoured to influence him physically by the hypnotic effect of rhythm."

5. The Notebooks of Butler (1835–1902) began to appear in the *New Quarterly Review* from 1907 and were published in book form in 1912. Four of the six poems Hulme published in his lifetime came out in 1909 and the other two in 1912.

6. Georges Sorel (1847–1922), revolutionary syndicalist; Hulme translated his *Réflexions sur la violence*.

7. Edward Clark contributed to the BBC's programs from 1924 to 1936: "a Gateshead man," as Bunting described him (Jonathan Williams, *Descant on Rawthey's Madrigal: Conversations with Basil Bunting* [Lexington, Ky.: Gnomon Press, 1968], 10), therefore a Northerner. He "should have a leading place in any history of twentieth-century British music. He knew everything that was going on in the world of contemporary music—particularly in Europe—and everybody who was engaged in it. Through him the BBC was involved from the 1920s onward in the hazardous enterprise of introducing to the British listener Schönberg and Webern as well as Bartok and Stravinsky." Asa Briggs, *The Golden Age of Wireless,* 2d ed. (Oxford: Oxford UP, 1995), 160. Contrast also the general lack of interest in the London premiere of Schönberg's *Gurrelieder,* noted by Briggs, with Bunting's much moved review of it in "Gurrelieder," *Outlook* 61/1566 (1928): 140.

8. Dame Clara Butt (1872–1936), a patriotic and powerful contralto. "Someone remarked that the Albert Hall must have been built in intelligent anticipation of Butt's advent." *New Grove's.*

9. For all this, see also Bunting's articles in 1927–29 as music critic for the *Outlook* and the *Town Crier.*

10. See above, chap. 3, n. 14.

11. The significance of the date may be that in 1926 Bunting moved to London; his close acquaintance with the London music scene would date from that year.

12. See above, chap. 3, n. 17, and the introduction.

13. See above, chap. 3, nn. 15, 16.

14. Bunting's "Well of Lycopolis" (1935) contains reflections on literary Bloomsbury, thus presumably on the circle of Lady Ottoline Morrell.

15. Nancy Cunard (1896–1965), avant-garde poet, publisher, patron of the arts, political activist.

16. Olivia Shakespear (1863–1938), novelist, beauty; hostess of a literary and artistic salon in Brunswick Gardens, Kensington, from c. 1909 onward;

sat for Wyndham Lewis, purchased his works; Yeats's mistress (the "Diana Vernon" of his *Memoirs*).

17. See also above, chap. 3 and n. 8.

18. *The Oxford Book of English Verse*, ed., Sir Arthur Quiller-Couch (Oxford: Oxford UP, 1900; new eds. and reprs. at least to 1953). But see above, chap. 3, n. 11.

19. See above, chap. 10, n. 3.

20. W. B. Yeats, *The Collected Poems* (London: Macmillan, 1950), 124, 135–36. I have not determined Bunting's text.

21. Pound, Canto LXXXI, 553.

22. Pound, *Personae*, 64–65 (poem abridged here).

23. Ibid., 74.

24. Ibid., 117.

25. Part of "From the *Hippolytus* of Euripides," *Collected Poems of HD* (New York: Liveright Publishing, 1925), 127–29.

26. HD was not at the University of Pennsylvania but at Bryn Mawr; she, Pound, and Williams (who were both at the university) made up a group from about 1905.

27. In Eliot's introduction to Pound's 1928 *Selected Poems;* Bunting is no doubt conscious of Eliot's point in using the word *inventor.*

28. Ernest Fenollosa's notebooks were Pound's source for his versions in *Cathay.*

29. Pound, *Personae*, 133.

30. As Bunting's remarks suggest, *Quia Pauper Amavi* bore no date; it was in fact published after the war, in October, 1919. And Bunting dates to that year his first encounter with the book: "It was at that stage, when I was 19, that Nina Hamnett first showed me Eliot's early work and Pound's 'Propertius.' You can imagine my excitement. . . . Ezra was using a rhythmical ease and freedom which put much within reach that had seemed out of reach before." Bunting, "The Use of Poetry," ed. Peter Quartermain, *Writing* 12 (Summer 1985): 41.

Here, as elsewhere, Bunting gives the page references for the *Personae* volume (1926 and many reprints); but it is clear that he is thinking of the original *Quia Pauper Amavi*, which he must once have owned. The title *Quia Pauper Amavi* does not survive in *Personae;* nor, of course, do the "Three Cantos" that had been in the earlier volume.

31. Pound, *Personae*, 171.

32. Bunting probably refers here to "Written in March, While Resting . . ." ("The Cock is crowing"): see above, chap. 9 and n. 7.

33. Though Pound dated the work to 1917, it was probably not finished before the middle of 1918; parts of it began to appear in March 1919.

34. On "persona," see above, chap. 10; and below, chap. 12 and n. 1.

35. Pound, *Personae*, 214–15, 218–19.

36. See above, chap. 8.

37. See also James Laughlin, *Pound As Wuz* (London: Peter Owen, 1989), 97.

38. The MS—and so also the 1969 lecture series—ends thus (but the text reaches the foot of the page: further pages may once have followed). It is clear that the *Sextus Propertius* was the ultimate target of the whole series' trajectory, for Bunting many times restated his view of its significance for this age, and its connection with Whitman. Thus a letter to Massimo Bacigalupo, 20 Mar. 1985, Bunting Archive: "So far as modern American poetry is concerned, that poem is (though the poets rarely recognise the fact) the foundation document. In your translation I even imagine I can catch the flavour of Whitman's 'Sea Drift,' which is where Ezra caught the hint of it." ("Out of the Cradle" appears in *Sea-Drift;* I have not found mention by Bunting of other poems in that collection, but see *B:SV,* 13–14 for some possible reminiscences of it in his work.)

CHAPTER 12. POUND'S CANTOS

1. On "persona," see also above, chap. 10; and later in this lecture. Bunting remarks to Pound, in a letter of the mid-thirties (Beinecke), that to Browning should be attributed the "revival" of what he (Bunting) calls the persona: he may have been thinking of Burns's "Holy Willie's Prayer" (see chap. 7) as an earlier example. What Bunting has to say really applies not particularly to the use of "personae" but to dramatic monologue in general: any poem in which a character is made to speak alone, in the thick of some implied situation, and to manifest his character solely by the discrepancies and juxtapositions in his uttered reactions to that situation. By *persona* (Pound's term: see *OED,* 2d ed.), Pound intended a character created by the poet as a mask for himself: thus the Bertran de Born and the Villon who speak in Pound's poems. The mask would project certain aspects of the poet, and the successive creating and superseding of these masks would constitute a self-analysis by the poet. The McAndrew and the Blougram who speak in Kipling's and Browning's poems cannot usefully be read as projections of their authors.

2. The speaker in Kipling's "McAndrew's Hymn" (see above, chap. 10).

3. See esp. above, chap. 9, "Whitman: Editor's Explanatory Note," and chap. 11.

In what follows, Bunting makes clear the approach to major musical form that Pound used in the *Cantos:* namely, to organize the *ideational material* in the same sort of way that *sounds* are organized in musical form. He emphasizes that this is not musical form itself but an analogy with it: for musical form is a structuring of sounds, but this is a form not of the sounds of the words but rather of other things (images, ideas). Pound indeed *textured* his word-sounds as Whitman had, by the play of rhythmic motifs; but this was not his method of making main form.

These distinctions are present in Bunting's mind because he was conscious that the other path—structuring a longish poem by the sounds of the words themselves—was available and that it was the path he himself had attempted to follow. When he says "One or two poets . . . began to wonder whether music could furnish them with an overall shape," the only candidate for the reference, apart from Pound and Zukofsky, seems to be Bunting himself.

Bunting always said his formal model was the sonata. And he told Hugh Kenner: "Music is organised in various ways, and one of the inventions—[an] eighteenth-century invention, for which I think the chief responsibilities lie with Domenico Scarlatti and John Christian Bach—[was] the notion of a sonata, where two themes which at first appear quite separate, and all the better if they're strongly contrasted . . . gradually alter and weave together until at the end of your movement you've forgotten they are two themes, it's all one. And that struck me when I was very young, as a form that poetry could and should exploit. And I've tried to do it" (Basil Bunting, "The Sound of Poetry," interview by Hugh Kenner, National Public Radio, Feb. 1980). Bunting's letter to Sister V. M. Forde of 23 May 1972 (Victoria Forde, *The Poetry of Basil Bunting* [Newcastle-upon-Tyne: Bloodaxe Books, 1991], 242) shows a wonderful example of the developing in his mind of theme and "anti-theme," and the effort to work out their transformation. Elsewhere he remarked, "I thought that to be able to marry themes, perhaps a little in between what Scarlatti did and what was being done sixty or seventy years later . . . might give a chance to make shapes." Dale Reagan, "An Interview with Basil Bunting," *Montemora* 3 (Spring 1977): 74.

Now, when Bunting gives examples of such themes and their transformations, they are to my knowledge always ideational themes. Yet he insists that when he builds a sonata he is thinking of rhythm-shapes first: "It's a matter of making the rhythms develop and shift around themselves chiefly, partly having something to adapt in the way of matter to that" (Jonathan Williams and Tom Meyer, "A Conversation with Basil Bunting," *Poetry Information* 19 [Autumn 1978]: 38). Whitman provided the mechanism for the handling of rhythms, as is apparent from the final lecture in this volume: "What Whitman, and then Pound, borrowed from music, was chiefly the notion of modifying a theme, a rhythmic theme, especially, . . . bit by bit, until it could be merged in a counter-theme or in some way combined with it." All that Bunting had to do was to plan such contrasts, modifications, and mergings of rhythms so that their organization constituted not merely the texture but the main structuring of the whole.

For all this see also *B:SV*, 258 ff., 341–43.

4. "I pointed out to [Eliot]—he hadn't noticed it himself—in 1922 or 1923, that the form "The Wasteland" took, if you omitted the short fourth

movement, is exactly that of a classical sonata. This seems to have stuck in his mind, so that when he wrote the 'Four Quartets,' each of them an exact copy of the shape of 'The Wasteland,' he calls them quartets—quartets being normally a sonata form" (Williams and Meyer, "Conversation with Bunting," 38). "We know now that that form was the almost accidental result of the cuts Pound made in Eliot's poem, but it didn't seem accidental to me then." (Bunting, "The Use of Poetry," ed. Peter Quartermain, *Writing* 12 (Summer 1985): 42).

5. Bunting refers to the sonatas for unaccompanied violin, BWV 1001, 1003, 1005, whose second movements are marked "Fuga."

6. Bunting and Goacher read Canto LXXIV in a tribute to Pound at the Institute of Contemporary Arts in London, 27 June 1973; see below, n. 22.

7. See also above, chap. 8; and below, chap. 13.

8. "The Chinese Written Character as a Medium for Poetry" was edited (somewhat creatively) by Pound from Fenollosa's notes and first published in 1919. Bunting's exposition here, though it owes points to Hugh Kenner, is perhaps the best extant.

9. This common opinion stems mainly from a wild attack by George Kennedy of Yale; but Fenollosa's main philological point was that the origins of the Chinese character were to a considerable extent in metaphor, which remains valid. See Peter Makin, "Kennedy, Fenollosa, Pound and the Chinese Character," *Agenda* 17/3–4, and 18/1 (1979–80): 220–37.

10. See esp. the passage in Hugh Kenner, *The Poetry of Ezra Pound* (London: Faber, 1951), 76 ff., beginning "Ideogram, at least as a poetic principle, is not a Sinophile fad. It inheres in Aristotle on metaphor."

11. For Eleanor see Canto II (read by Bunting below), Canto VI, etc. To make this link with Helen, Canto VI uses her apocryphal affair with Saladin and the wrath aroused in Louis VII of France when she left him for Henry Plantagenet, taking her patrimony of Aquitaine with her. See Peter Makin, *Provence and Pound* (Berkeley: U of California P, 1978), 76–77, 308–10, 261–65, and, for Eleanor's life, 120–33.

The "President's wife" presumably refers to Peggy Eaton (see Cantos XXXIV, XXXVII), wife of Andrew Jackson's secretary of war. The other cabinet wives considered her too low to associate with, and Eaton was eventually forced to resign.

12. The connection in Bunting's mind is made clear in a magnificent letter to Sister Victoria Marie Forde, dated 23 May 1972, about experiences to be incorporated into a new long poem: "Then one night I saw the new moon, the very first new moon, emerging from the old moon as Helen, Selanna, the new moon, must have emerged from Leda's egg" (Forde, *Poetry of Bunting*, 243). Pound, to my recollection, mentions a "Selena" only in Canto CVI (pub. 1959), where no connection with Helen seems to suggest itself. The

Aeolic form *selanna,* the moon, is used by Sappho; its Attic form is *selene,* not *Helene.* The reference books take Helen to be the mythic survival of a vegetation goddess, not a goddess of the moon or childbirth. They seem to follow Plato, *Cratylus,* in deriving Selene's name from *selas,* "brightness"; while the origin of *Helen* is generally deemed obscure (one scholar has related it to the Latin *Venus:* cf. Hjalmar Frisk, *Griechisches Etymologisches Wörterbuch* [Heidelberg: Carl Winter, 1973], 489).

13. Peire Vidal's lady: see Canto IV. Pound's version of the story is given as a headnote to his "Piere [*sic*] Vidal Old": "he ran mad, as a wolf, because of his love for Loba of Penautier, and . . . men hunted him with dogs through the mountains of Cabaret and brought him for dead to the dwelling of his Loba (she-wolf) of Penautier." Ezra Pound, *Personae: The Collected Shorter Poems* (New York: New Directions, 1949), 30.

14. See esp. Hugh Kenner, *The Pound Era* (Berkeley: U of California P, 1971), 349 ff.

15. It is likely that Pound had not noticed this discrepancy. The Greek text used by Andreas Divus presumably read, as ours do, "Tipt' aut' . . . ?"; and here *aute,* as Heubeck and Hoekstra say, has "almost the force of a sympathetic reproach," so that modern translators render the whole with phrases such as "what now? Why . . . ?" "pourquoi donc?" But Divus took *aute* in its primary sense of "again," and rendered it in Latin as "Cur iterum . . . / Venisti . . . ?" (see Pound, *Literary Essays,* ed. T. S. Eliot [London: Faber, 1960], 262). This can quite normally be translated, as Pound translates *i* (264), "why come a second time . . . ?" and, in Canto I, "A second time?"

16. "Lo Sordels si fo di Mantovana" in fact means "Sordello was from Mantua region"; but Bunting is here following *Annotated Index to the Can[ ] Ezra Pound,* ed. John Hamilton Edwards and William W. Vasse (Berkel[ ] of California P, 1957), 130.

17. Oswald Spengler's *Untergang des Abendlandes* (1918–22), publi[ ] English as *The Decline of the West* (1926–28) was a theory that civi[ ] must all pass through a predictable life cycle; Arnold Toynbee's *St[ ] tory* (1934–59) was similarly a theory of universal historical cycle[ ] had strongly recommended Toynbee to his friend Zukofsky (19[ ] HRC); he even feared in 1941 that his own lectures on history[ ] "a vulgarisation of a part of Toynbee," though they were writ[ ] had read the historian (to Zukofsky, 15 Dec. 1941, HRC). Bu[ ] Spengler certainly, and perhaps Toynbee also, had become[ ] amples of the pervasive Western urge to draw up geometr[ ] to impose them willy-nilly on reality. See Basil Bunting, *A[ ]* ed. Richard Caddel (Durham: Basil Bunting Poetry Arch[ ]

18. Pound, Canto I, 7–9. Bunting's photocopies from[ ] tos I, II, and LXXIV, prepared for the recording of his t[ ]

(Newcastle University), are in the Bunting Archive. In l. 66, Bunting reads "Shall return . . .": presumably a slip.

19. Pound, Canto II, 10–14. Bunting's changes to the text are presumably slips: l. 80, "fur brushing against"; l. 94, " 'From now on, . . .' "; l. 101, "now in the rudder-chains."

20. Edwards and Vasse, eds. *Annotated Index.*

21. It seems likely that Bunting refers here to Eilithyia as she appears in the *Homeric Hymn to [Delian] Apollo,* ll. 97 ff. (The Homeric Hymns were traditionally ascribed to the Homeridae, the "sons of Homer," who had the job of reciting the Homeric epics at festivals. Bunting had presumably been reading the hymns in search of data about Selene [see above, n. 12], to whom one of them is addressed.) In the *Hymn to Apollo,* Eilithyia is assisting (as goddess of childbirth) at the birth of Apollo. This is not exactly "doing just what Pound says she did"; but in the canto her function has puzzled many readers. The line in question, "Ileuthyeria, fair Dafne of sea-bords," must mean "Ileuthyeria [is] a Daphne of the seacoasts: one who, fleeing the would-be lover, turned, not into a laurel-bush, but into coral": see the slightly obscure comment by Pound recorded by Mary de Rachewiltz in *Ezra Pound, Father and Teacher: Discretions* (New York: New Directions, 1975), 159, where Pound also makes it clear that here he is inventing his own myth. The name Ileuthyeria itself does not appear in the texts, and Bunting's suggestion as to its source seems as likely as any. (His remark about Ovid is mistaken: see *Met.* 9.283.)

22. Canto LXXIV is the first of the *Pisan Cantos.* See also an important letter to Denis Goacher, dated 14 May 1973 (Bunting Archive), concerning the tribute to Pound (above, n. 6): "I'm more and more attracted by the notion of doing 74 entire, and letting that be the whole programme. . . . it is the first canto in which the notion of interweaving themes making one whole works *freely* (he was away from his books, couldnt get snagged on details, and yet didnt ride away on a detachable lyric); it deals in one way or another with almost everything the cantos are concerned with; it has many splendid passages, but all dependant on each other; 'the rose in the steel dust'—EP must have known he'd really done it at last. Other Pisans, each fine, many wonderful, are yet less fully representative. Same goes for Thrones, where also the themes crowd too tight for a reader who hasnt read the rest thoroughly to get them clearly. But 74 is quite easy to follow if you dont demand logic and prose qualities." Bunting included this canto in his tape-recorded verse anthology (Newcastle University), and the photocopied materials gathered in reparation for this (Bunting Archive) include Canto LXXIV, heavily annotated in Bunting's hand with factual points about the data the canto refers to.

23. Louis Till was hanged on 24 July 1945, apparently within sight of the re in which Pound was detained, and was one starting point for a long litation on the flame and its extinction:

> black that die in captivity
>   night green of his pupil, as grape flesh and sea wave
> undying luminous and translucent
>
>   Est consummatum, Ite;
>
>   surrounded by herds and by cohorts looked on Mt Taishan

Canto LXXIV, 458; cf. esp. 456.

24. I.e., "Linus, Cletus, Clement / whose prayers" (Canto LXXIV, 455), from the Roman Mass.

25. "The shout": "Hooo Fasa."

26. From Canto LXXIV, 454–57. Where the text on 455 has the Chinese ideogram *ming,* Bunting instead reads "brightness." On 457 he reads "fire must destroy himself" (presumably a slip).

CHAPTER 13. ZUKOFSKY

1. Possibly David Jones (d. 28 Oct. 1974).

2. In fact H.D. had died on 28 Sept. 1961.

3. In what follows, Bunting, holding always that the structures and hence proper evaluations of poems have nothing to do with gossip, omits what another might have considered his main qualification for holding opinions about Zukofsky. Their relationship had begun with a postcard in July 1930 ("Ezra Pound says I ought to look you up. May I? I liked the 'Henry Adams.' Yrs Basil Bunting" [HRC]), that is, only two years after Zukofsky's launch as a poet in Pound's magazine *Exile.* And from that beginning till at least 1964, Bunting and Zukofsky had been principal midwives to each others' works: each habitually submitted drafts to the other and heeded the other's detailed criticisms. Also, Bunting forcefully attacked Zukofsky's views on art as they revealed themselves; Zukofsky, as far as one can surmise, forcefully replied.

Our knowledge of the relationship is lopsided because Bunting, on principle, destroyed letters he received, and Zukofsky did not keep carbons. But it is clear there were fundamentals they shared (see above, introduction), allowing them to disagree so sharply that at times the spectator may feel they should have had nothing left to discuss.

In their sense of the integrity and ideational uniqueness of languages, both poets certainly drew on their mutual discussions and on ideas fed in by Zukofsky's friend Irving Kaplan. (See Andrew Crozier, "Paper Bunting," *Sagetrieb* 14/3 (1995): 45–74, correcting my *B:SV,* 290 ff., where I mistakenly attribute Kaplan's essay beginning "The written record" to Bunting).

The sharpest dispute between Bunting and Zukofsky was over what Bunting called "abstraction." Zukofsky was very willing to use the generalizing terms of philosophy, a discipline he revered; Bunting (to Zukofsky, 27 Apr. 1934, Beinecke) considered them a sin against reality (which was "above all, opaque and complex"), hence against communication and hence even against political well-being. This concern produced an open letter from Bunting against Zukofsky's quasi manifesto for the "Objectivists," in 1932, and in 1934 a violent letter (copied to Pound!) against Zukofsky's *Le Style Apollinaire.* In both cases the attack was to some degree public. But Bunting told Pound ("end of May," c. 1934, Beinecke) that the fundamental ambiguity imported by abstractions, rampant in Zukofsky's prose, was absent from his verse: whether because of greater concreteness there, or because verbal music helped to define perception and emotion, he did not say.

4. Zukofsky's father, Pinchos, and mother, Chana, were born in the early 1860s in what is now Lithuania; Pinchos came to the United States in 1898, and by 1903 had earned enough to send for his family. Louis was born in 1904 and died in 1978.

5. Bunting might have considered his "Painful lark, labouring to rise!" (in *Briggflatts*) an apt example: the sense of *painful* is infected with older and French senses, as in "taking pains" and *homme de peine.*

6. Robert Duncan, 1919–88.

7. Peckham, in southeast London.

8. University of Wisconsin, Madison, from Sept. 1930 to June 1931; poet in residence for a summer in California (1958); guest professor at a graduate school in Connecticut after his retirement.

9. Pound to Zukofsky, July 1933, trying to browbeat him into prolonging his very brief first stay in Paris: "of course a persistent & cultivated refusal of experience is bound to leave (ultimately) traces on a guy's style" (*Pound/Zukofsky: Selected Letters of Ezra Pound and Louis Zukofsky,* ed. Barry Ahearn [London: Faber, 1987], 153). Zukofsky, defiantly, in an interview (1933) translated by Pound: "In America we have grown out of this interest in Europe" (Charles Norman, *Ezra Pound,* rev. ed. [London: Macdonald, 1969], 318). Bunting to Zukofsky, 5 Mar. 1949, doubtfully offering to enquire about a job for him in Iran: "Anyway, you wouldnt stay here if you did come. You'd get homesick for Brooklyn" (HRC).

10. Celia Thaew Zukofsky, 1913–80; Louis and Celia married in 1939. Paul Zukofsky, violinist and conductor, born 1943, made his debut at Carnegie Hall in 1956; Jascha Heifetz, violinist, born 1901, had made his in Berlin in 1912.

11. She composed the music for Zukofsky's *Autobiography* poems; for *Pericles,* the second volume of his *Bottom: On Shakespeare;* and (using the music of Handel) she arranged the "Masque" used by Zukofsky for *"A"*-24.

12. See above, chaps. 8 and 12.

13. See above, chap. 12.

14. For a discussion see Hugh Kenner, "Of Notes and Horses," in Carroll F. Terrell, ed., *Louis Zukofsky: Man and Poet* (Orono, Maine: National Poetry Foundation, 1979), 187–94.

15. Louis Zukofsky, *"A" 1–12* (London: Jonathan Cape, 1966), 45–48. Bunting uses this movement of *"A,"* together with movements 11 and 15 (see below), for his taped verse anthology (Newcastle University); the photocopies (Bunting Archive) of the three movements prepared for this recording correspond typographically with the Cape 1966 and 1969 editions of *"A"* (see below, n. 17).

16. Cf. Kenner, "Of Notes and Horses," 188.

17. Louis Zukofsky, *"A" 13–21* (London: Jonathan Cape, 1969), 106–7 (from *"A"*-15).

18. The point here is that Zukofsky "translated" Catullus, for the most part, in the same way as he rendered *Job* in *"A"*-15, in which (as Bunting noted) "the Hebrew sounds are imitated with hardly any reference whatever to the meaning of words." This is the opening of Catullus 45:

> Acmen Septimius suos amores
> tenens in gremio 'mea' inquit 'Acme,
> ni te perdite amo atque amare porro
> omnes sum assidue paratus annos,
> quantum qui pote plurimum perire,
> solus in Libya Indiaque tosta
> caesio veniam obvius leoni.'

("Septimius, holding in his arms his darling Acme, says, 'My Acme, if I do not love thee to desperation, and if I am not ready to go on loving thee continually through all my years as much and as distractedly as the most distracted of lovers, may I in Libya or sunburnt India meet a green-eyed lion alone.'" Loeb.) It is rendered by Zukofsky:

> Acme, Septimius sighs so amorous,
> tenoned, sighing agree, "my" and quiet "Acme
> knee too pretty to mar, what qualm, I pore oh
> on my sum I see due, and if years part us
> a wan tomb cool my pluck, may it perish
> solus in Libya or India, tossed a
> case of—went and met with a blue-eyed lion."

Catullus (Gai Valeri Catulli Veronensis Liber), trans. Celia and Louis Zukofsky (London: Cape Goliard, 1969), n.p. Celia Zukofsky described their procedure: "I wrote out the Latin line and over it, indicated the quantity of every vowel and every syllable, that is long or short; then indicated the accented syllable. Below the Latin line I wrote the literal meaning or meanings of every word indicating gender, number, case and the order or sentence structure. . . . Louis then used my material to write poetry—*good poetry.*" Quoted by Burton Hatlen, "Zukofsky as Translator" 347, in Terrell, *Zukofsky,* 345–64.

19. Their contact dates from 1928 (when Zukofsky was 24, Williams 45). Zukofsky's suggestions for the trimming of Williams's poems seem to have been at their most detailed and brilliant in the MS for *The Wedge,* sent and returned in 1943. See Neil Baldwin, "Zukofsky, Williams, and *The Wedge: Toward a Dynamic Convergence,*" in Terrell, *Zukofsky,* 129–42.

20. This relationship is charted in Jenny Penberthy, *Niedecker and the Correspondence with Zukofsky, 1931–1970* (Cambridge: Cambridge UP, 1993). Zukofsky wrote to Niedecker about Bunting at least from the late '30s, and no doubt to Bunting about Niedecker from a similar date. Niedecker and Bunting at last met in July 1967. For their comments on each other, see Jenny Penberthy, " 'Brief Words are Hard to Find': Basil Bunting and Lorine Niedecker," *Conjunctions* 8 (1985): 159–64; and esp. Bunting's "To abate what swells," 182, originally published in *Epitaphs for Lorine,* ed. Jonathan Williams (Penland, N.C.: Jargon Society, 1973), n.p.

21. See above, chap. 7.

22. The dedication of "*A*"-11 reads "for Celia and Paul."

23. Zukofsky, "*A*" *1–12,* 130–31. The form of this passage is indebted to Cavalcanti's "Perch' io no spero": see Barry Ahearn, *Zukofsky's "A": An Introduction* (Berkeley: U of California P, 1983), 118–21.

24. "Barely and widely," # 6, in Louis Zukofsky, *ALL the collected short poems 1923–1958* (London: Jonathan Cape, 1966), 121. The text of the photocopies of Zukofsky's short poems (in the Bunting Archive) prepared for Bunting's taped verse anthology (Newcastle University) corresponds typographically with the Cape, 1966 and (see below, n. 35) 1967 editions.

25. "Barely and widely" # 3, in ibid., 119.

26. "Anew" # 38, in ibid., 107.

27. "Anew" # 33, in ibid., 105.

28. "Anew" # 28, in ibid., 102.

29. "Anew" # 20, in ibid., 97.

30. "Anew" # 7, in ibid., 88.

31. "Anew" # 1, in ibid., 85. Bunting skips the epigraph, "che di lor suona su nella tua vita," from Dante, *Inferno* 4.77.

32. Bunting was based mainly at 62 Montague Street in Brooklyn during his stay in the United States from mid-1930 to early 1931; during that period he met Williams, Zukofsky, and René Taupin and married Marian Culver.

33. "29 Songs" # 5, in Zukofsky, *Short Poems 1923–58,* 48. Bunting skips the epigraph, "It's a gay li - ife."

34. "29 Poems" # 10, in ibid., 30.

35. "Light" # 4, Louis Zukofsky, in *ALL the collected short poems 1956–1964* (London: Jonathan Cape, 1967), 18; see above, n. 24.

36. "Chloride of Lime and Charcoal" # 3, in ibid., 26–27.

37. " 'All Wise,' " in ibid., 39.

38. "Songs of Degrees" # 1, 2, in ibid., 45–47. Bunting skips the two epigraphs, "With/ a Valentine/ (the 12 February)" and "With a Valentine/ (the 14 February)."

39. "Que j'ay dit devant" # 2, in ibid., 15–16.

40. Both of the following pieces are parts of Zukofsky's "Poem beginning 'The' " (in *Short Poems 1923–58*, 11–22), whose writing is dated by Celia Zukofsky to 1926 ("Year by Year Bibliography of Louis Zukofsky," 385, in Terrell, *Zukofsky*). Both appeared in Ezra Pound's magazine *Exile* 3 (Spring 1928), as well as in his anthologies *Profile* (Milan: Scheiwiller, 1932), and *Active Anthology* (London: Faber, 1933).

41. From "Fifth Movement: Autobiography" of "Poem beginning 'The,' " in Zukofsky, *Short Poems 1923–58*, 19.

42. From "Third Movement: In Cat Minor" of "Poem beginning 'The,' " in ibid., 17. In this edition, as in the early printings listed in n. 40 above, the first line reads "Hard, hard the cat-world."

43. I.e., of the 1974 series: see "A Note on Texts," above.

Bibliography

Ahearn, Barry. *Zukofsky's "A": An Introduction*. Berkeley: U of California P, 1983.

Alter, Robert. "The Characteristics of Ancient Hebrew Poetry." In *Literary Guide to the Bible*, edited by Robert Alter and Frank Kermode. Cambridge: Belknap Press, Harvard UP, 1987.

Apel, Willi. *Gregorian Chant*. Bloomington: Indiana UP, 1958.

Aristides Quintilianus. *On Music: In Three Books*. Translated by Thomas J. Mathiesen. New Haven: Yale UP, 1983.

Attridge, Derek. *Well-weighed Syllables*. Cambridge: Cambridge UP, 1974.

Aubrey, Elizabeth. *The Music of the Troubadours*. Bloomington: Indiana UP, 1996.

Backhouse, Janet. "Birds, Beasts and Initials in Lindisfarne's Gospel Books." In *St Cuthbert, His Cult and His Community to AD 1200*, edited by Gerald Bonner et al. Woodbridge, Suffolk: Boydell, 1989.

——. *The Lindisfarne Gospels*. Ithaca, N.Y.: Cornell UP, 1981.

Baldwin, Neil. "Zukofsky, Williams, and *The Wedge:* Toward a Dynamic Convergence." In *Louis Zukofsky: Man and Poet*, 129–42, edited by Carroll F. Terrell. Orono, Maine: National Poetry Foundation, 1979.

Boas, Franz. *Primitive Art*. Cambridge: Harvard UP, 1928.

Bowra, C. M. *Primitive Song*. London: Weidenfeld & Nicolson, 1962.

Briggs, Asa. *The Golden Age of Wireless*. 2d ed. Oxford: Oxford UP, 1995.

Bunting, Basil. "Carlos Williams's Recent Poetry." *Westminster Magazine* 23/2 (1934): 149–54.

——. *Collected Poems*. London: Fulcrum, 1968.

——. *The Complete Poems*. Edited by Richard Caddel. Oxford: Oxford UP, 1994.

——. "An Interview with Peter Bell." In *The Recordings of Basil Bunting: Northumberland 1981, 1982* (cassette tape), edited by Richard Swigg. Keele: Keele University, 1995.

——. "I Suggest." Hand-printed postcard of suggestions for poets. Reprint, Durham: Basil Bunting Poetry Archive, 1990.

——. "The Lion and the Lizard." In Bunting, *Three Essays,* 27–31, edited by Richard Caddel. Durham: Basil Bunting Poetry Centre, 1994.

——. "Music of the Month: On Playing It Backwards." *Town Crier* 84 (Apr. 1928): 142.

———. *A Note on Briggflatts.* Edited by Richard Caddel. Durham: Basil Bunting Poetry Archive, 1989.

———. Preface to Tom Pickard, *High on the Walls,* 7. London: Fulcrum, 1967.

———. Preface to Joseph Skipsey, *Selected Poems,* 7–14, edited by Bunting. Sunderland: Ceolfrith Press, 1976.

———. *Presidential Addresses: An Artist's View on Regional Arts Patronage.* Newcastle: Northern Arts, 1976.

———. "Release: Basil Bunting." BBC TV program, 23 Nov. 1968.

———. "Some Limitations of English." *The Lion and the Crown* 1/1 (1932): 26–33. Reprinted in Bunting, *Three Essays,* 21–26, edited by Richard Caddel. Durham: Basil Bunting Poetry Centre, 1994.

———. "The Sound of Poetry." Interview by Hugh Kenner. National Public Radio, Feb. 1980.

———. "The Use of Poetry." Edited by Peter Quartermain. *Writing* 12 (Summer 1985): 36–43.

Caddel, Richard, and Anthony Flowers. *Basil Bunting: A Northern Life.* Newcastle: Newcastle Libraries & Information Service; Durham: Basil Bunting Poetry Centre, 1997.

Clay, William Keatinge, ed. *Private Prayers, Put Forth by Authority During the Reign of Queen Elizabeth.* London: Parker Society, 1851.

Cranmer, Thomas. *Miscellaneous Writings and Letters.* Edited by John Edmund Cox. Vol. 2 of Cranmer, *Works.* London: Parker Society, 1846.

Craven, Peter, and Michael Heyward. "An Interview with Basil Bunting." *Scripsi* 1/3–4 (1982): 27–31.

Crozier, Andrew. "Paper Bunting." *Sagetrieb* 14/3 (1995): 45–74.

Daalder, Joost. "Wyatt's Prosody Revisited." *Language and Style* 10 (1977): 3–15.

Dale, A. M. *Collected Papers.* Cambridge: Cambridge UP, 1969.

Davie, Donald. "A Demurral." Review of *The Collected Poems of William Carlos Williams,* vol. 1: *1909–1939. New Republic,* Apr. 1987, 34–39.

Denham, Sir John. *The Poetical Works.* Edinburgh: Apollo Press, 1779.

———. *The Poetical Works.* 2d ed. Edited by Theodore Howard Banks. Hamden, Conn.: Archon Books, 1969.

Densmore, Frances. *Menominee Music.* Washington, D.C.: U.S. Govt. Printing Office, 1932.

Doolittle, Hilda. See *H.D.*

Doughtie, Edward. *English Renaissance Song.* Boston: Twayne, 1986.

Duffy, John. *The Songs and Motets of Alfonso Ferrabosco, the Younger (1575–1628).* Ann Arbor, Mich.: UMI Research Press, 1980.

Duhamel, Georges, and Charles Vildrac. *Notes sur la technique poétique.* Paris: Champion, 1925.

Edwards, John Hamilton, and William W. Vasse, eds. *Annotated Index to the Cantos of Ezra Pound.* Berkeley: U of California P, 1957.

Fellowes, Edmund Horace. *The English Madrigal.* 1925. Reprint, Salem, N.H.: Ayer, 1972.

———. *The English Madrigal Composers.* 2d ed. Oxford: Oxford UP, 1948.

Ford, Ford Madox. *Selected Poems.* Edited by Basil Bunting. Cambridge, Mass.: Pym-Randall, 1971.

Forde, Victoria. *The Poetry of Basil Bunting.* Newcastle-upon-Tyne: Bloodaxe Books, 1991.

Fowler, Roger. *The Languages of Literature: Some Linguistic Contributions to Criticism.* London: Routledge & Kegan Paul, 1971.

Frisk, Hjalmar. *Griechisches Etymologisches Wörterbuch.* Heidelberg: Carl Winter, 1973.

Frye, Northrop. *Anatomy of Criticism: Four Essays.* Princeton: Princeton UP, 1957.

Fussell, Paul. *Theory of Prosody in Eighteenth-Century England.* N.p.: Archon Books, 1966.

Gardner, Raymond. "Put Out More Flags." *Guardian,* 27 June 1973.

Gill, Stephen. *William Wordsworth: A Life.* Oxford: Clarendon Press, 1989.

Goethe, Johann Wolfgang von. *Selected Verse.* Edited by David Luke. London: Penguin, 1986.

Harding, D. W. "The Rhythmical Intention in Wyatt's Poetry." *Scrutiny* 14 (1946): 90–102.

Hatlen, Burton. "Zukofsky as Translator." In *Louis Zukofsky: Man and Poet,* 345–64, edited by Carroll F. Terrell. Orono, Maine: National Poetry Foundation, 1979.

HD (Hilda Doolittle). *Collected Poems of HD.* New York: Liveright Publishing, 1925.

Holloway, David. "A Live Tradition: Pound's *Personae* and *The Pisan Cantos.*" *Paideuma* 8/3 (1979): 563–70.

Howes, Frank. *William Byrd.* London: K. Paul, Trench, Trubner, 1928.

Hueffer, Ford Madox [Ford Madox Ford]. *Collected Poems.* London: Max Goschen, 1914.

Ives, Eric. *Anne Boleyn.* Oxford: Blackwell, 1986.

Johnstone, Paul. "Basil Bunting: Taken from Two Interviews, Recorded by Paul Johnstone in April 1974 and April 1975," *meantime* 1 (Apr. 1977): 67–80.

Judd, Alan. *Ford Madox Ford.* London: Collins, 1990.

Keel, Frederick. *Elizabethan Love-Songs: Edited and Arranged, with Pianoforte Accompaniments Composed, or Adapted from the Lute Tablature.* Sets 1 and 2. London: Boosey, 1909, 1913.

Kendrick, T. D., et al. *Evangeliorum Quattuor Codex Lindisfarnensis.* 2 vols. Lausanne: Urs Graf, 1956–60.

Kenner, Hugh. "Of Notes and Horses." In *Louis Zukofsky: Man and Poet,* 187–94, edited by Carroll F. Terrell. Orono, Maine: National Poetry Foundation, 1979.

———. *The Poetry of Ezra Pound.* London: Faber, 1951.

———. *The Pound Era.* Berkeley: U of California P, 1971.

———. *A Sinking Island: The Modern English Writers.* New York: Knopf, 1988.

Kiparsky, Paul. "The Rhythmic Structure of English Verse." *Linguistic Inquiry* 8/2 (1977): 189–247.

———. "Sprung Rhythm." In *Phonetics and Phonology,* vol. 1, *Rhythm and Meter,* 305–38. Edited by Kiparsky and Gilbert Youmans. San Diego: Academic Press, 1989.

———. "Stress, Syntax, and Meter." *Language* 51/3 (1975): 576–616.

Kipling, Rudyard. *Complete Verse: Definitive Edition.* New York: Doubleday, 1989.

Laughlin, James. *Pound As Wuz.* London: Peter Owen, 1989.

MacKay, Brent. "Bunting as Teacher." *Conjunctions* 8 (1985): 181.

Makin, Peter. *Bunting: The Shaping of His Verse.* Oxford: Clarendon Press, 1992.

———. "Kennedy, Fenollosa, Pound and the Chinese Character." *Agenda* 17/3–4, and 18/1 (1979–80): 220–37.

———. *Pound's Cantos.* Reprint, Baltimore: Johns Hopkins UP, 1992.

———. *Provence and Pound.* Berkeley: U of California P, 1978.

Maynard, Winifred. "The Lyrics of Wyatt: Poems or Songs?" pts. 1 and 2, *Review of English Studies* 16 (1965): 1–3, 246–57.

McAllister, A., and S. Figgis. "Basil Bunting: The Last Interview." *Bête noire* 2/3 (1987): 22–50.

Milton, John. *The Poetical Works.* Vol. 2. Edited by David Masson. London: Macmillan, 1874.

Moorman, Mary. *William Wordsworth: A Biography: The Early Years: 1770–1803.* Oxford: Clarendon Press, 1957.

Mottram, Eric. "Conversation with Basil Bunting on the Occasion of His Seventy-Fifth Birthday, 1975." *Poetry Information* 19 (Autumn 1978): 3–10.

Norberg, Dag. "La récitation du vers latin." *Neuphilologische Mitteilungen* 66 (1965): 496–508.

Norman, Charles. *Ezra Pound.* Rev. ed. London: Macdonald, 1969.

Olson, Charles. *Selected Writings.* Edited by Robert Creeley. New York: New Directions, 1966.

Olson, Charles, and Robert Creeley. *The Complete Correspondence.* Vol. 7. Edited by George F. Butterick. Santa Rosa: Black Sparrow, 1987.

O'Sullivan, William. "The Lindisfarne Scriptorium: For and Against." *Peritia* 8 (1994): 80–94.

Paden, William, Jr. "The Role of the Joglar in Troubadour Lyric Poetry." In *Chrétien de Troyes and the Troubadours: Essays in Memory of the Late Leslie Topsfield.* Edited by Peter S. Noble and Linda M. Paterson. Cambridge: St. Catherine's College, 1984.

Pater, Walter. *The Renaissance: Studies in Art and Poetry.* London: Macmillan, 1924.

———. *The Renaissance: Studies in Art and Poetry.* Edited by Donald L. Hill. Berkeley: U of California P, 1980.

Penberthy, Jenny. "'Brief Words are Hard to Find': Basil Bunting and Lorine Niedecker." *Conjunctions* 8 (1985): 159–64.

————. *Niedecker and the Correspondence with Zukofsky, 1931–1970.* Cambridge: Cambridge UP, 1993.

Pound, Ezra. *ABC of Reading.* London: Faber, 1961.

————. *The Cantos.* London: Faber, 1964.

————. *Culture.* New York: New Directions, 1938.

————. *Literary Essays.* Edited by T. S. Eliot. London: Faber, 1960.

————. *Personae: The Collected Shorter Poems.* New York: New Directions, 1949.

————. *Selected Prose, 1909–1965.* Edited by William Cookson. New York: New Directions, 1973.

————. ed. *Active Anthology.* London: Faber, 1933.

————. ed. *Profile.* Milan: Scheiwiller, 1932.

Pound, Ezra, and Louis Zukofsky. *Pound/Zukofsky: Selected Letters.* Edited by Barry Ahearn. London: Faber, 1987.

Puttenham, George. *The Arte of English Poesie.* Edited by Gladys Doidge Willcock and Alice Walker. Reprint, Cambridge: Cambridge UP, 1970.

Quartermain, Peter. *Basil Bunting: Poet of the North.* Durham: Basil Bunting Poetry Archive, 1990.

Racan, Honorat de Bueil, Seigneur de. *Vie de Monsieur de Malherbe.* Edited by Marie-Françoise Quignard. Paris: Gallimard, 1991.

Rachewiltz, Mary de. *Ezra Pound, Father and Teacher: Discretions.* New York: New Directions, 1975.

Ralegh, Sir Walter. *The Poems.* Edited by Agnes M. C. Latham. London: Routledge & Kegan Paul, 1951.

Reagan, Dale. "An Interview with Basil Bunting." *Montemora* 3 (Spring 1977): 66–80.

Rowe, John G., and William H. Stockdale, eds. *Florilegium Historiale: Essays Presented to Wallace K. Ferguson.* Toronto: U of Toronto P, 1971.

Schuchard, Ronald. "W. B. Yeats and the London Theatre Societies, 1901–1904." *Review of English Studies* 19/116 (1978): 415–46.

Scott, Clive. *French Verse-art: A Study.* Cambridge: Cambridge UP, 1980.

————. *Vers Libre: The Emergence of Free Verse in France, 1886–1914.* Oxford: Clarendon Press, 1990.

Southworth, James G. *The Prosody of Chaucer and His Followers: Supplementary Chapters to "Verses of Cadence."* Oxford: Blackwell & Mott, 1962.

————. *Verses of Cadence: An Introduction to the Prosody of Chaucer and His Followers.* Oxford: Blackwell, 1954.

Spenser, Edmund. *The Minor Poems.* Vol. 2. Edited by Charles Grosvenor Osgood and Henry Gibbons Lotspeich. Vol. 8 of *The Works of Edmund Spenser.* Baltimore: Johns Hopkins Press, 1943.

————. *The Poetical Works of Edmund Spenser in Three Volumes,* vol. 1, *Spenser's Minor Poems.* Edited by Ernest de Selincourt. Oxford: Clarendon Press, 1910.

Starkey, David, ed. *Henry VIII: Royal Meridian: A European Court in England.* London: Collins & Brown, in association with the National Maritime Museum, 1991.

Stevens, John. *Music and Poetry in the Early Tudor Court.* 1961. Reprint, Cambridge: Cambridge UP, 1979.

Swann, Brian. "Basil Bunting of Northumberland." *St Andrews Review* 4/2 (1977): 33–41.

Terrell, Carroll F., ed. *A Companion to the Cantos of Ezra Pound.* Vol. 1. Berkeley: U of California P, 1980.

———, ed. *Louis Zukofsky: Man and Poet.* Orono, Maine: National Poetry Foundation, 1979.

Thompson, John. *The Founding of English Metre.* Reprint, New York: Columbia UP, 1989.

Thorndike, Ashley, ed. *The Minor Elizabethan Drama,* vol. 1, *Pre-Shakespearean Tragedies.* London: J. M. Dent, 1910.

Tottel's Miscellany (1557–1587). Edited by Hyder Edward Rollins. Rev. ed. Cambridge: Harvard UP, 1965.

van der Werf, Hendrick. *The Chansons of the Troubadours and Trouvères.* Utrecht: Oosthoek, 1972.

Weiner, Seth. "Spenser's Study of English Syllables and Its Completion by Thomas Campion." *Spenser Studies* 3 (1982): 3–56.

West, M. L. *Ancient Greek Music.* Oxford: Clarendon Press, 1992.

———. *Greek Metre.* Oxford: Clarendon Press, 1982.

Whittaker, W. Gillies. "Byrd's Great Service." *Musical Quarterly* 27 (1941): 474–90.

Williams, Jonathan. *Descant on Rawthey's Madrigal: Conversations with Basil Bunting.* Lexington, Ky.: Gnomon Press, 1968.

———. "An Interview with Basil Bunting." *Conjunctions* 5 (1983): 75–87.

———. ed. *Epitaphs for Lorine.* Penland, N.C.: Jargon Society, 1973.

Williams, Jonathan, and Tom Meyer. "A Conversation with Basil Bunting." *Poetry Information* 19 (Autumn 1978): 37–47.

Wordsworth, William. *The Poetical Works.* Edited by Thomas Hutchinson. London: Oxford UP, 1928.

———. *The Salisbury Plain Poems.* Edited by Stephen Gill. Ithaca, N.Y.: Cornell UP, 1975.

Wright, George T. *Shakespeare's Metrical Art.* Berkeley: U of California P, 1988.

Wyatt, Sir Thomas. *Collected Poems.* Edited by Kenneth Muir. London: Routledge & Kegan Paul, 1949.

Yeats, W. B. *The Collected Poems.* London: Macmillan, 1950.

———. *Essays and Introductions.* New York: Macmillan, 1961.

———. *The Letters.* Edited by Allan Wade. London: Rupert Hart-Davis, 1954.

Youmans, Gilbert. "Iambic Pentameter: Statistics or Generative Grammar?" *Language and Style* 19/4 (1986): 388–404.

Zukofsky, Celia. "Year by Year Bibliography of Louis Zukofsky." In *Louis Zukofsky:*

Man and Poet, 385–92, edited by Carroll F. Terrell. Orono, Maine: National Poetry Foundation, 1979.

Zukofsky, Celia, and Louis Zukofsky, trans. *Catullus (Gai Valeri Catulli Veronensis Liber)*. London: Cape Goliard, 1969.

Zukofsky, Louis. *"A" 1–12*. London: Jonathan Cape, 1966.

———. *"A" 13–21*. London: Jonathan Cape, 1969.

———. *ALL the collected short poems 1923–1958*. London: Jonathan Cape, 1966.

———. *ALL the collected short poems 1956–1964*. London: Jonathan Cape, 1967.

———. *Prepositions: The Collected Critical Essays*. London: Rapp & Carroll, 1967.

Index

Page references to figures are shown in italics.

Credits